Dialogues with/and
GREAT BOOKS

"In this outstanding study of literary greatness, David Fishelov adds depth to the existing theories of reception history and intertextuality. Recognizing the essential role of parody, re-writing, and adaptation in canon formation, Fishelov gives novel readings of familiar and less familiar dialogues – ranging from Kierkegaard and the Binding of Isaac to Coetzee's *Foe* and *Robinson Crusoe*, and even including Monty Python's parodic treatment of the New Testament. The theoretical discussions and the close readings are enlightening and clearly written." KEN FRIEDEN, Syracuse University, author of *Genius and Monologue*

"This is one of those books that may change the perspective from which you view the literary endeavour. It explores how do literary works of art become canonical, or even acquire the status of a masterpiece. Dissatisfied with the prevalent conceptions that trace the text's reputation either to its inherent aesthetic qualities or to extra-textual socio-cultural forces, Fishelov regards the process as far more complex. The two approaches not only offer merely a partial solution each, but also need to be viewed in the perspective of a 'dialogic' model, where the magnitude and variety of interpretative interactions between a text and its readership hold the key for explaining canonical status. A systematic presentation of types of 'dialogic' interactions in the form of allusions, adaptations, and parodies, among others, is complemented by detailed discussions of a few interesting dialogues with some well-established canonical texts." REUVEN TSUR, Tel Aviv University, Winner of the Israeli Prize in Literary Theory

"Against contemporary theories, that emphasize the hegemonic role of critics in the process of canon formation, Fishelov's original book reminds us that inner literary and artistic 'dialogues' (in the form of allusion, translation, adaptation) are vital in transmitting certain texts and in promoting their status as 'classic'. Fishelov shows the intricate 'dance' performed perpetually by the literary tradition and illustrates it by presenting 'dance partners' like the Biblical Samson and DeMille's Hollywood production; the Pygmalion story in Ovid, in Shaw's play and in *My Fair Lady*; More's *Utopia* and Swift's satirical portrayal of human ideals in *Gulliver's Travels*. Fishelov's astutely selected landmarks of the Western Canon and his nuanced and elegant discussions deepen our understanding of the enduring impact of these texts on modern culture. Professors and students of 'Great Books Courses' will find his approach and the critical tools and distinctions he offers not only stimulating but also quite useful. In fact, his book could serve as a textbook for such courses." NILI GOLD, University of Pennsylvania

Dialogues with/and GREAT BOOKS

THE DYNAMICS *of* CANON FORMATION

DAVID FISHELOV

sussex
ACADEMIC
PRESS
Brighton • Portland • Toronto

Copyright © David Fishelov, 2010.

The right of David Fishelov to be identified as Author of this work has been asserted in accordance with the Copyright, Designs and Patents Act 1988.

2 4 6 8 10 9 7 5 3

First published in 2010 by
SUSSEX ACADEMIC PRESS
PO Box 139
Eastbourne BN24 9BP

and in the United States of America by
SUSSEX ACADEMIC PRESS
920 NE 58th Ave   Suite 300
Portland, Oregon 97213-3786

and in Canada by
SUSSEX ACADEMIC PRESS (CANADA)
90 Arnold Avenue, Thornhill, Ontario L4J 1B5

All rights reserved. Except for the quotation of short passages for the purposes of criticism and review, no part of this publication may be reproduced, stored in a retrieval system or transmitted in any form or by any means, electronic, mechanical, photocopying, recording or otherwise, without the prior permission of the publisher.

British Library Cataloguing in Publication Data
A CIP catalogue record for this book is available from the British Library.

Library of Congress Cataloging-in-Publication Data
Fishelov, David.
Dialogues with/and great books : the dynamics of canon formation / David Fishelov.
p. cm.
Includes bibliographical references and index.
ISBN 978-1-84519-368-3 (acid-free paper)
 1. Canon (Literature) 2. Intertextuality. 3. Influence (Literary, artistic, etc.) 4. Dialogue. I. Title.
PN81.F575 2010
809—dc22
                                                                2009031751

Papers used by Sussex Academic Press are natural, renewable and recyclable products from well-managed forests and certified in accordance with the rules of the Forest Stewardship Council.

Typeset and designed by Sussex Academic Press, Brighton & Eastbourne.
Printed by TJ International, Padstow, Cornwall.
This book is printed on acid-free paper.

Contents

Preface   ix

Part I What Is a Dialogue? What Is a Great Book?

1 Real Life Dialogues   3
   Different Factors and Two Basic Levels   4
   Types of Dialogue (and Monologue Too)   6
   Dialogues: The Passive/Active Scale   9
   Two Words of Caution   12

2 Literary Dialogues   14
   Genuine Literary Dialogues   15
   Echo Literary Dialogues: Reading   18
   Echo Literary Dialogues: Translation, Adaptation   19
   Literary Dialogues-of-the-Deaf   25
   One Table, Two Clarifications   27

3 The Battle of the (Great) Books   30
   The Beauty Party   30
   The Power Party   35
   The Two Parties: Another Angle   43
   Deciding between the Two Parties   44

4 The Dialogic Approach to Great Books   46
   Many and Diverse Dialogues   46
   The Dialogic Approach: Some Facts, for a Change   49
   The Booker Prize and the Limitations of Institutional Power   56
   The Race for Fame: *Candide*, *Rasselas* and QWERTY   62
   Objections to the Dialogic Approach   66
   Models for Literary Dialogues: Ladder, Tree, Ponytail   69
   Dissemination: The Pyramid Model   72

Part II Some Genuine Dialogues with Great Books

5 The Sacrifice Scene – Kierkegaard and Levin — 77
  Kierkegaard's Abraham: Imaginary Poetic Variations — 80
  The Satirical Version of Hanoch Levin — 84

6 Samson – Jabotinsky, DeMille and Milton — 90
  Jabotinsky's Samson: A Secular National Hero — 91
  DeMille's Samson: A Christian, Forgiving Lover — 96
  Ponytail, Genuine Dialogues and Milton's *Samson Agonistes* — 100

7 Jesus Christ – Monty Python and Saramago — 104
  Monty Python's Hilarious Parody — 105
  Saramago's Serious Re-telling — 108
  Parody and Re-writing — 114

8 Horace in Pushkin, Owen and Diderot — 116
  Horace's Glorious Monument in Pushkin — 118
  The Glory of Dying for One's Country: Owen vs. Horace — 119
  The Epigraph for *Le Neveu de Rameau* as an Association Generator — 121
  Anger and Excitement in Horace's *Satire 2.7* — 123
  Excitement and Self-Acceleration in *Le Neveu de Rameau* — 127
  Quotations: Form, Function and Genuine Dialogue — 132

9 Juvenal's *Satire 10* – Johnson and Swift — 134
  Juvenal's Self-Propelling Explosion in *Satire 10* — 136
  Johnson's Taming of Juvenal's Explosiveness — 138
  Swift's Narrative Variation on a Theme — 141
  Johnson and Swift – Form and Spirit — 144

10 Ovid's Pygmalion in Shaw & *My Fair Lady* via Molière — 146
  A Non-Declared Dialogue: Molière's *School of Wives* — 148
  Shaw: Pygmalion as a Sculptor of Speech — 150
  My Fair Lady: Back to Ovid's Pygmalion — 154
  The Complex Chain of DTs (Dialoguing Texts) — 156

11 More's *Utopia* and Some Variations — 159
  Bacon's Scientific Utopia — 160
  Swift contra Utopia, or Sat-opia — 163
  Voltaire's Short Comical Version — 168
  Different Stances and Structural Variations — 169

12 *Robinson Crusoe* – The Variety Principle Revisited	**172**
Robinson Crusoe and the Dialogic Approach	173
Some Versions of Pseudo-Dialogues	175
Versions of Genuine Dialogues	178
A Concluding Image	181
Concluding Remarks	183
Notes	189
Bibliography	203
Index	213

For Omri and Avigal
my favorite partners in dialogue
with Love

Preface

The major argument of this book is that the source of a literary work's perceived greatness lies in the dialogues it generates with readers, authors, translators, adaptors, artists and critics. One can easily agree that there is a high correlation between a book's reputation as a great book and the fact that it has generated many kinds of such dialogues throughout the ages. To explain this high correlation is, however, a more complicated matter. Against prevalent opinion that takes these dialogues to be a by-product of the book's canonical status, this study argues that a work's reputation is an institutionalized result of these accumulating dialogues. In other words, a work's diverse propagation is the source of its reputation much more than the other way around. To disentangle the seeming Gordian knot between diverse propagation and established reputation and to corroborate the dialogic approach to great books, the first part of the study develops some general arguments and distinctions, examines a few test cases and presents the search results of traces of books in a few databases, representing different layers of culture. The second part of the book focuses on some interesting specific dialogues conducted with consensually assumed great books. The respective chapters illustrate different kinds of literary and artistic dialogues and provide an opportunity to examine different aspects of the process by which dialogues contribute to a work's reputation.

Readers interested in literary theory could perhaps be satisfied with the first part alone, whereas readers primarily interested in specific dialogues inspired by several great books might want to focus only on the second part, but the reading of both parts could undoubtedly be beneficial to both kinds of readers. The theoretical arguments of the first part gain full meaning through the specific cases discussed in the second part, and the textually-oriented discussions of the second part rely on concepts developed in the first part and suggest additional theoretical distinctions.

The initial drive for writing the book was my dissatisfaction with the prevailing approach that portrays literary reputation as created by social hegemonies and my wish to vindicate the important role of aesthetic values. Whereas my initial impulse did not abate, I learned during my research that a naïve defense of aesthetic values as the sole explanation of a work's reputation is also inadequate. The dialogic approach to great books advocated here attempts to shed new light on external, cultural factors as well as the relevant intrinsic qualities of a text involved in the dynamics of canon formation. It also offers conceptual and empirical tools for examining the actual dynamics involved in the making of a classic. This approach shows that intertextuality and canon formation, reception theory and close readings are not competing, but rather complementary perspectives on the artistic text, more connected than hitherto assumed.

The dialogical approach to great books grew out of some real-life dialogues conducted with students and colleagues during the past few years. These dialogues played an indispensable role in making the book possible. The questions of students in my course "Dialogues with Great Books," taught at the Hebrew University of Jerusalem, pushed me to elaborate on the different meanings of the two terms of the course's title. I benefited from the comments and responses of participants in conferences and seminars where I presented the dialogic approach to great books: The International Conference of Empirical Studies of the Arts held in Lisbon (September 2004); a conference on Intertextuality in Literature and Culture held at Tel Aviv University (May 2006); the conference of the International Association for Empirical Studies of Literature/IGEL in Munich (August 2006); the departmental seminar of the Department of Comparative Literature at the Hebrew University of Jerusalem (February 2009).

Some principles presented in the first part of the book and in the chapter on *Robinson Crusoe* were recently published in two essays: "Dialogues with/and Great Books: with some Serious Reflections on Robinson Crusoe" appeared in *New Literary History* (Fishelov 2008a), and "What is, Empirically, a Great Book? Or: Literary Dialogues and Canon Formation" in *New Beginnings in Literary Studies*, edited by Willie Van-Peer and Jan Auracher (Fishelov 2008b). I am deeply grateful to Ralph Cohen, editor of *NLH*, and to Willie Van-Peer, the co-editor of *New Beginnings* for their encouragement, criticism and generosity. And Menakhem Perry, general editor of Sifrei Siman-Kri'a/Hakkibutz Hameuchad Publishers, granted me permission to translate Hanoch Levin's skit from *The Queen of the Bathtub* (Levin 1987 [1970]).

I am greatly indebted to Mira Frankel Reich whose stylistic sensitivity, critical mind and wide reading helped to bring my manuscript to a publishable form, and to Anthony Grahame, Editorial Director at Sussex Academic Press, who oversaw the entire process of bringing the book to print, constantly offering invaluable professional advice. I wish also to thank specifically a few colleagues from the Hebrew University of Jerusalem: Debby Gera, whose challenge to my concept of literary dialogue encouraged me to better explain it; Shimon Sandbank, whose insightful comments on my argument about the role of textual dialogues in canon formation compelled me to clarify a few points, especially those related to the archetypal dimension of dialogue-generating works; Tzachi Zamir, whose astute questions about the exact relationship between literary dialogues, aesthetic qualities and canon formation brought me to reformulate several arguments; David Satran, whose friendly but unforgiving eye caught some infelicities in the final version of the manuscript; and the Reader of Sussex Academic Press, who offered highly useful comments and encouraged me to address, in the Concluding Remarks, the issue of dialogues in cultural fields other than literature. Last but not least, special thanks to Yeshayahu Shen of Tel Aviv University, a long-time friend and colleague, with whom I shared ideas when they were still at an embryonic stage. His perceptive critical remarks spurred me to re-think and re-formulate a few important arguments in the first half of the book.

❋ ❋ ❋

Let me add finally that some ideas and methods presented in this study have met resistance from certain conservative literary scholars, especially in regard to my use of results obtained from Google searches on the Internet. Whereas the results of the Google searches play only a small role in my overall arguments, I nevertheless believe such searches may teach us something important about the general dissemination of literary works in culture. Searches in Google databases, like any other research tools, have their power and their limitations, but to dismiss them a priori is to ignore a potentially powerful tool available to literary scholars today. Needless to say, some people who object to the use of Google in a literary study use Google regularly to retrieve information on the Internet (including Googling themselves).

PART

I

What Is a Dialogue?
What Is a Great Book?

Man becomes an I through a You. What confronts us becomes and vanishes, relational events take shape and scatter, and through these changes crystallizes, more and more each time, the consciousness of the constant partner, the I-consciousness.

(Buber 1970: 80)

A language is revealed in all its distinctiveness only when it is brought into relationship with other languages, entering with them into one single heteroglot unity of societal becoming.

(Bakhtin 1981: 411)

CHAPTER

1

Real Life Dialogues

A few years ago, I was preparing a course titled "Dialogues with Great Books" in which we were going to read a series of works inspired by some "Great Books." The planned reading list included pairs like Genesis 22 and Kierkegaard's *Fear and Trembling*, More's *Utopia* and the fourth book of Swift's *Gulliver's Travels*, Shakespeare's *Hamlet* and Stoppard's *Rosencrantz and Guildenstern Are Dead*, among others.

The first meeting was devoted to a presentation of the two key terms of the title: dialogues and great books. First, I explained why I use dialogues in preference to intertextuality, a term that has gained prominence in critical discourse during the past few decades. The word intertextuality is notoriously vague, since it embraces every conceivable relation between semiotic objects. One can despair of attaining one clear definition of this chameleon-like notion, introduced by Kristeva (Kristeva 1980), but still, by tracing its historical emergence and various critical uses, one can argue for its productivity in present and future critical discourse (Worton and Still 1990, Allen 2000, Orr 2003). Apart from the problem of hyper-elasticity, the term is usually employed in theoretical frameworks that reject certain presuppositions associated with the idea of a great book: the existence of hierarchy between literary works, the central role played by the master who produces the literary *master*piece (the term masterpiece originates in art history and was later applied to literature; Cahn 1979) and the uniqueness of a great work (these contrasts are implied in Clayton and Rothstein 1991: 3–36).[1] One does not, however, have to assume that there is a necessary conflict between the concepts of intertextuality and great books; the writings of Genette on intertext, meta-text and hyper-text (Genette 1997 [1982]) and Ben-Porat's study of rhetorical intertextuality (Ben-Porat 1985) illustrate how aspects of intertextuality can be discussed without denying the fact that certain works stand out in literary history.[2]

The advantage of using the term dialogue lies not only in bypassing some undesired connotations associated with intertextuality but also in calling attention to the close affinities between dialogues in ordinary, social interactions (real-life dialogues) and literary and artistic dialogues. My assumption is that by illuminating certain characteristics underlying everyday dialogues we can gain useful insights into the complex dynamics of literary dialogues.

Different Factors and Two Basic Levels

A closer look at any seemingly simple, ordinary everyday dialogue uncovers a complex and multilayered phenomenon. For a social contact to be called a dialogue we need two participants and some kind of verbal exchange between them ("conversation between two or more persons" – *Random House College Dictionary*).[3] But this general formulation in fact covers heterogeneous verbal exchanges. A brief dialogue conducted between strangers to obtain some specific information ("excuse me, how can we get to Highway 101?") does not sound like a dialogue between two intimate friends ("What's up man, you look depressed today?"); a dialogue between a boss and his employee ("Did you send the memo?") differs in many respects from one between two peers ("Tell your secretary to talk to my secretary to set an appointment"); and the dialogue in an Internet Chat ("LOL"), differs from a conversation over a cup of coffee ("well this is funny") not only in form (written vs. spoken) and the expressions used (the set of shortcuts in on-line chats), but also in the very fact that the former provides a whole range of opportunities for playful invention of identities (e.g., "sexy Angela" is in fact middle-aged, bored John) which is significantly limited in the case of two persons meeting in a real coffee shop.

Thus, dialogues can vary due to a variety of factors: the overall goal of the verbal exchange (practical vs. social), the relationship between the two participants (hierarchical vs. equal footing), the diction used in the verbal interaction (formal vs. informal), the technical means of communication (face to face vs. electronically mediated).[4] Some of these factors can be described as constraints imposed on the parties involved, but these constraints are by no means insurmountable: if the dialogue is conducted over the telephone one cannot see the expression on the face of one's interlocutor, but in this case the missing information can be supplemented by words and tone of voice ("I don't know if you can hear me smiling, but I want you to know that you're very amusing") and when one is engaged in an Internet chat, there is always a "smiley" that can be added.

In addition to the above factors, dialogues differ in the degree of actual interaction between the two participants: whereas some dialogues seem superficial, others might appear deeper, more genuine and meaningful. Theoretically, we could restrict our attention to what we consider to be genuine dialogues but if what we want is a better understanding of the dynamics of dialogical exchange, we should keep an open mind and adopt an approach that does not deny the great variety of forms and functions characterizing real-life dialogues – including those that do not rank high on the scale of meaningful dialogues. Further, the above mentioned factors involved in specific dialogues – the technical channel of communication, the social relations of the participants, the variety of goals involved – are merely secondary to the dynamics of different degrees of actual give-and-take characteristic of dialogue qua dialogue.

Thus, the *actual interaction* among the two participants, rather than external factors, should be our base for a typology of dialogues. Let me briefly illustrate this aspect by three examples. In the first case, there is a very minimal, if not superficial level of communication; in the second, the interaction is also relatively small but of a different sort; only in the third is there a high and deep level of involvement and interaction of both parties:

1. A person responds to what the other is saying without really taking into account what she/he is being told, because she/he is too absorbed in her/his own line of thinking ("yah yah, we can eat at home tonight, but there is a great new restaurant around the corner and I've already called and made a reservation").
2. A person who listens attentively to her/his interlocutor and finds her/himself accepting the other person's point of view, and then simply nods to express consent or repeats what the first was saying, either verbatim or with slight changes ("I cannot agree more to what you've just said, it is a great show"). Sometimes the basic, deep agreement between the interlocutors may even be expressed in terms that seem at first to indicate differences ("It is not, as you have just said, an excellent show, it is an amazing, awesome, remarkable show").
3. Two persons advocating different points of view or sentiments or ideologies, trying to listen to each other and to take the other's point of view into account. They might maintain their differences ("I see your point, and I have a counter-argument") or, after a series of give-and-take, reach a happy solution ("you have convinced me on that point" or "good, you've answered my question").

In all such real-life situations, and many more like them, we can discern two important levels: the *outer* (or formal) dimension and the *inner* (or content) one, a distinction roughly corresponding to the basic linguistic distinction between form and content or in more general terms the double articulation or duality of structure of language.[5] The outer dimension contains simply the exchange of words between the two participants. To describe this level, we answer questions such as: How long does the dialogue go on? Which of the two is more talkative? With what intonation are the words uttered? But, as the above examples illustrate, to understand the dynamics of any dialogue we need also to take into account the inner or semantic level. To describe that dimension, we address questions like Do the two participants share a common ground? Do they truly listen to one another? Do they actually respond to each other? Are they involved in any real give-and-take?

Types of Dialogue (and Monologue Too)

Using the suggested distinction between the inner and outer dimensions of the dialogue and crisscrossing the possible combinations, a scheme of some basic types of dialogue emerges. This scheme not only provides basic coordinates for describing and understanding the dynamics of many actual dialogues, it also brings into the picture dialogue's (lonely) counterpart – the monologue. The basic parameters for such a scheme may be formulated in terms of voices: a term that can refer to the outer, audible (and by extension also readable), concrete level, but can also refer metaphorically to a person's point of view, ideology, sentiments etc. ("in what you're saying now, John. I can hear the voice of your wife"). The following table represents the different possible combinations between voices and "voices":

TABLE 1.1
Types of Dialogues (and Monologues)

		Inner Level		
Outer Level		One "Voice"	Two "Voices"	
	One Voice	Genuine Monologue	Pseudo-Monologue	
	Two Voices	Echo-Dialogue (Pseudo-Dialogue I)	Dialogue-of-the-deaf (Pseudo-Dialogue II)	Genuine Dialogue

Let me briefly describe the emerging categories, first the top line (from left to right) and then the second line (from right to left) – which will provide the focus of this study:

Genuine Monologue represents a situation where only one person is heard, and her/his voice gives expression to one consistent point of view or sentiment or ideology. Under normal circumstances, it is relatively easy for us to recognize the (outer) voice of a specific person,[6] but it is more complicated to decide whether we are hearing one "voice" in the sense of one specific, consistent point of view. This decision always depends on our interpretation of the utterance, involving not only our linguistic knowledge but also our knowledge of the world and our acquaintance with the speaker. To determine that a specific utterance expresses one consistent point of view presupposes a certain notion of what constitutes a consistent point of view: logical contradictions are of course excluded, but beyond such clear-cut cases, there is a whole range of semantic relationships that one person could describe as complex but still consistent and another person could exclude from the domain of consistency.

Pseudo-Monologue – or dialogical monologue – represents a situation where only one person is heard, but her/his voice expresses *different* points of view or sentiments or ideologies. Hamlet's famous "To be or not to be" speech can be invoked here as a prototypical example for such pseudo-monologue. And, as in the case of genuine-monologue, to describe an utterance as a pseudo-monologue depends on what we decide to be a relevant, significant difference within a speech. To determine whether we are in the presence of a (complex) genuine-monologue or a pseudo-monologue, we should detect what seem to us to be two or more conflicting points of view.

Genuine Dialogue represents what we usually associate with serious, commendable forms of social dialogue, where the two interlocutors express different "voices" and at the same time are attentive to each other and ready to be engaged in a meaningful exchange of ideas or sentiments. In such genuine dialogues, the interlocutors can maintain their initial, sometimes even antagonistic positions, or be drawn towards the other's point of view (without losing their own) or follow a Hegelian dialectical model and reach synthesis (such cases are illustrated in example [3] above).[7] No matter what the specific outcome, genuine dialogues are characterized by the attentiveness of the participants and their willingness to get involved in some level of give-and-take.

But only too often there are dialogues that do not follow the dynamics and requirements of genuine dialogues. These can be labeled **Pseudo-Dialogue**. My distinction between genuine and pseudo dialogue is partly based on Martin Buber's distinction between I–Thou and I–It relationships (Buber 1970), but without the metaphysical implications of that philosophical discussion. Pseudo-dialogues have two major variations:

Dialogue-of-the-deaf occurs when the two interlocutors represent two distinct points of view or sentiment or ideology, but they seem to fail to engage in any form of give-and-take associated with genuine dialogue (illustration in Example [1] above). In its pure version this category can be described as two *parallel* genuine-monologues. The category is not that rare in social interaction; all too often we find ourselves involved in a "dialogue" where our interlocutor is unable or unwilling to listen and respond to what we are saying, sometimes trying to win the case by raising her/his voice or exerting social power ("you should listen to what I'm saying, I'm your father").[8] Whereas for the actual participants in a dialogue-of-the-deaf the experience is usually a source of frustration, for an outside observer, dialogue-of-the-deaf can be a sober reminder of human disconnectedness. But it can also be the source of a comic effect; in fact, many comic scenes are based on the principle of dialogue-of-the-deaf pushed to an extreme. A classical example of this is a scene between Harpagon and Valère in Molière's *L'Avare*. Harpagon is distraught by the theft of his money and believes that Valère is responsible. Valère is convinced that Harpagon is talking about the "theft" of his daughter, to whom he, Valère, is secretly engaged, and thus they continue for a while with their dialogue-of-the-deaf, before realizing that they are talking about two distinct notions while using similar terms to address them (something dear; something one is dearly attached to). Only in the last line in the following quotation Harpagon finally refers to what he was talking about during their exchange of words:

> Valère: We are promised to each other and have sworn never to be parted.
> Harpagon: Promised? How wonderful! And this commitment to each other is very amusing!
> Valère: We are committed to each other for ever!
> Harpagon: I'll put a stop to it, believe me.
> Valère: Only death can separate us!
> Harpagon: That's taking love of my money a bit far!
>
> (Molière *L'Avare* 5.3)[9]

Echo-dialogue is another way of missing genuine dialogue. Here we hear two (outer) voices but when we listen carefully to what they are saying, we realize that they are in fact expressing the same point of view or sentiment or ideology. The term echo implies not only repetition but also a-symmetry between the two interlocutors: usually one of them is perceived as primary, original, leader and the other plays only "a second fiddle" – repeating either verbatim or in different words what was said; the two can of course change roles during the conversation, but the principle of a-symmetry characterizing echo will be maintained (see example [2] above). An exchange of words between Rosencrantz and Guildenstern in *Hamlet* can illustrate echo-dialogues where we hear two outer voices, but with no significant difference on the deep semantic level. Thus when Hamlet hears the two echoing men address him, he seems to be confusing them:

> Guildenstern: My honoured lord!
> Rosencrantz: My most dear lord!
> Hamlet: My excellent good friends! How dost thou, Guildenstern? Ah, Rosencrantz! Good lads, how do you both?
>
> (2.2.225–29)[10]

The distinction between the two major types of pseudo-dialogue – echo-dialogue and dialogue-of-the-deaf – can also be described as a function of the question to what extent the interlocutors share a common "language": the higher the degree of overlap (of ideological stand, way of experiencing things, sentiments etc.), the closer we get to the realm of echo-dialogue; when the two interlocutors come from two extremely different, almost incommensurable worlds, where they represent for each other a radical "other," the result will most probably be dialogue-of-the-deaf. Only when the interlocutors share some common ground but also differ in certain respects, is there a good chance that they will be engaged in a meaningful, genuine dialogue.

Needless to say, the constructed types of genuine and pseudo-dialogues are not meant to be understood as exclusive classificatory categories: real-life dialogues can illustrate characteristics of more than one type and can evolve from one type to another ("OK, now I'm willing to take seriously what you were saying"). Still, the above table may offer a useful tool for understanding the nature and dynamics of many real-life dialogues and describing their dominant characteristics.

Another way to shed light on the dynamics of real-life dialogues, including cases of echo-dialogue, is by reference to the concept of illocutionary act introduced by J. L. Austin (Austin 1971 [1955]) and elaborated in Searle's theory of speech acts in the philosophy of language (Searle 1969). Applying these concepts to the analysis of dialogue, we can argue that the minimal requirement for a dialogue to take place is a series of related illocutionary or speech acts performed between two interlocutors.[11] While the successive illocutionary or speech acts should be related, not every performed act necessarily fulfills the desired response to the preceding act: in dialogues-of-the-deaf the response is typically *not* the expected one and it is related to it only on a superficial level. In this context, we can recall that the concept of illocutionary act is distinguished, according to Austin, from perlocutionary act: a successful performance of an illocutionary act does not necessarily entail that the expected or hoped-for response is achieved. A successful asking of a question (=illocutionary act) does not guarantee that the question will be answered (=perlocutionary act). Thus, whereas in genuine dialogues we can expect a question to be answered, in pseudo-dialogues this expectation is frustrated: in echo-dialogues, a question can simply be repeated and in dialogue-of-the-deaf a question might be ignored or the interlocutor would come up with an answer – but not to the question that he was asked (alas, how often we encounter such cases). Thus, by using the pair illocutionary act/perlocutionary act and by positing a series of related illocutionary acts as a necessary requirement for a dialogue, we can better analyze real-life dialogues where not every question is actually answered, not every argument is rebutted with a counter-argument and not every expression of sentiment is responded to with an expression of empathy (or resentment).

Dialogues: The Passive/Active Scale

To better understand the complex dynamics of dialogues and the methodological issues involved in describing different kinds, let us look more closely at a case mentioned above: a person listens attentively, nods in consent but without verbal response. Such a situation was labeled as a version of echo-dialogue. Theoretically, we could describe it as a case of monologue; after all, only one person is actually pronouncing words. Still, it is more useful to consider such cases as a (relatively) *passive* version of echo-dialogue, for at least two reasons. First, real-life conversations are performed not only through explicit utterances; extra-verbal means are constantly used, notably a whole range of gestures that are part of non-verbal communication (Knapp and Hall 2006). Non-verbal gesticulation like nodding, hand waving, winking and the like may not only enhance or modify the words uttered but may sometimes alter their meaning altogether (e.g., changing a straightforward statement into an ironic comment). Secondly, the moment we accept that the concept of dialogue includes not only the outer, observable or audible dimension but also the inner nature of the ongoing exchange and the participants' states of mind (attentiveness, willingness to be involved in give-and-take), it becomes clear that there is no reason to exclude such cases. In passive echo-dialogue the two participants are in fact involved in an actual exchange of ideas and sentiments. The only differentiating mark of this case is that one participant does not express her/his contribution to the dialogic exchange by explicit verbal means. A nod, however, conveys as much information – cognitive and emotional – as an explicit equivalent utterance ("Yes" or "OK"), indicating that the participant has heard the words spoken to her/him, has internalized the message of the leading (or prime) speaker, accepts that message and wants to convey that acceptance.

Thus, there are good reasons to describe cases of the sequence speech → nodding as a version of echo-dialogue. We should note, however, that this methodological decision has immediate consequences for the way we understand and delineate the concept of monologue. If the sequence of speech → nodding is described as a (passive) case of echo-dialogue, then the category of genuine monologue automatically and dramatically shrinks. The moment such cases are appropriated by the category of echo-dialogue, they are deducted from the category of monologue which now includes only cases where a speaker expresses her/his ideas or sentiments without taking into account the effect of her/his words on a possible interlocutor. This semi-autistic attitude can be due either to the speaker's not being interested in a reaction or because there is no actual audience for the monologue. Perhaps such pure cases of monologue are hard to find in real life, but then pure cases of any category are always hard to find. Still, we can imagine cases where a speaker wants to get certain things off her/his chest without paying any real attention to a listener's state of mind and without any expectation of reciprocity. Using Jakobson's scheme for describing the functions present in communicative situations (Jakobson 1960), we can think of pure monologues as cases where the emotive function is fully dominant.

In dialogic situations, on the other hand, we can detect the co-existence of at least two functions described by Jakobson: the emotive, whereby the speaker wants to express her/his emotions and point of view and the connative, whereby she/he aims at affecting the listener's attitude and state of mind (persuading, soliciting an answer etc.). Note that the speaker's intentions in and of themselves are not a sufficient condition to create a dialogue; if the listener is totally detached, either because of a technical reason ("I can't hear you; there is no reception on my cell phone") or mentally ("sorry, I was daydreaming; what did you say?"), there is no dialogue. It takes two not only to tango but also to conduct a dialogue. Even in cases of dialogue-of-the-deaf, where there is no real give-and-take, the participants still share a willingness to maintain the superficial dialogue; perhaps this is not much, but at least it signals that the participants do not want to break the minimal communicative cooperation among themselves, sometimes because they know that breaking this appearance of a dialogue could lead to a confrontation (some "Middle East peace talks" throughout the years could illustrate such a situation).

After calling attention to the methodological considerations involved in describing the sequence of speech → nodding as a case of echo-dialogue (and its consequences on the category of monologue), we can note that nodding marks a very minimal, almost passive kind of response – compared, say, to a verbal retort. And, among verbal reactions, there is a whole range, moving from the laconic "OK" to a verbose, enthusiastic speech of acceptance (in cases where the interlocutor wants to express consent). Note, however, that there is no automatic correlation between the nature of the reaction, namely its semantic content (consent, rejection) and the degree of our activity: both consent and negation can be expressed in a short retort or at length. There is, however, one fairly steady correlation between content and form: when an interlocutor wants to express a complex reaction to what was said, she/he would usually go beyond a laconic response. Apart from this tendency, we can draw a scale on the axis of minimal-maximal or passive-active regardless of the specific semantic content of the reaction. Furthermore, the very utterance of verbal response does not guarantee that we have a meaningful reaction, part of a genuine dialogue; it only marks a relatively high degree of involvement on the part of the participant – compared, for example, to simply nodding.

When an interlocutor decides to speak, she/he signals her/himself as an active participant in the dialogue. In terms of content, however, the response might directly address the conversational demand – in what would become part of a genuine dialogue – but can also swerve from it into different, unexpected directions. This swerving occurs either because the interlocutor was not really paying attention to what she/he was told (thus, dialogue-of-the-deaf) or because it is part of a deliberate move to convey an indirect but nevertheless effective contribution to the conversation in what Paul Grice calls conventional implicature (Grice 1975). Thus, to adapt Grice's famous example to today's terms, if a professor decides to discuss in a letter of recommendation a Ph.D. student's agility in using a computer program (instead of discussing her/his intellectual abilities and scholarly potential), the conventional implicature would be that we are dealing with an incompetent candidate. According to the distinction between pseudo and genuine dialogues, such cases are not necessarily dialogue-of-the-deaf because the conversational demand (to evaluate the student's ability) is actually answered, albeit in an indirect (or even tortuous) way.[12] We can also describe such situations as pseudo-pseudo-dialogues: they have the appearance of a dialogue-of-the-deaf (the professor was asked to evaluate the student's intellectual abilities and instead she/he comes up with a comment on the student's technical skills). But when we take into account the many rich ways of communication, including conventional implicatures, we realize that they in fact maintain the "ping-pong" of conversational demand-answer. Hence we have here a case of (non-typical) genuine dialogue.

Jakobson's multi-functional description of the communicative situation, Austin's concepts of illocutionary and perlocutionary acts, Searle's concept of speech acts and Grice's concepts of conversational demand and implicature have been brought into the discussion to show the complexity of levels involved in any dialogue: outer and inner, form and content, intentions and expectation, conventions and personal inventions, reciprocity and pseudo-reciprocity and the fact that not every dialogue requires an active verbal participation of the two interlocutors, let alone the same degree of activity.

To conclude this section: the decision to describe nodding as a minimal, almost passive case of echo-dialogue is important not only because it complies with the multi-dimensional model of dialogue proposed here and not only because it is compatible with our day-to-day experience where in almost every dialogue one person is more verbally active, but also because it will allow us later – when we move to the literary field (see next chapter) – to describe reading as a passive form of echo-dialogue, thus as the equivalent of nodding in real-life conversation.

Two Words of Caution

First, to point out the dual layers involved in any verbal interaction (outer and inner; form and content), and proposing the distinction between different types of dialogue (genuine and pseudo – with the two sub-types of the latter) and different degrees of activity on the part of the two participants (passive and active), does not mean to resolve the philosophical question whether human speech is fundamentally based on dialogue or monologue. Although Bakhtin makes a strong case in insisting on dialogue's central role in human language,[13] this study does not intend to pursue philosophical arguments, only to call attention to the multilayered, complex nature of dialogues. Secondly, although we can agree that genuine dialogue should be practiced more often in social communicative situations and that pseudo-dialogue is not a commendable social practice – especially some dialogue-of-the-deaf – it is not my purpose here to preach certain social modes of behavior and to censure others, only to promote our understanding of patterns of communicative activities.

Finally, the terms retort, response and reaction used throughout the discussion of the dynamics of dialogue might create the impression of a behaviorist model for dialogues. This of course is not the case: not only because reactions in dialogues are mediated through complex psychological processes but mainly because the dynamics of a dialogue is not dictated by causality. One *chooses* to participate (or not) in a dialogue and one chooses the specific type of response. We can describe an answer as a response to the "stimulus" of a question, but we have to acknowledge that answering the question directly is but *one* option chosen by the person: she/he could ignore the question or respond to a different question altogether or answer the question but indirectly – depending on her/his emotional needs and intentions. The logic governing dialogues is not causal but rather teleological, directed by the participants' rhetorical goals. The fact that the same utterance can produce different reactions in different (genuine and pseudo-) dialogues defies the causal logic according to which one stimulus brings about one reaction.

CHAPTER

2

Literary Dialogues

The previous chapter elaborated on different types of real-life dialogues, because literary dialogues, which form the main subject of this study, seem closely related in structure and function to real-life dialogues. Further, by considering the different levels and factors involved in real-life dialogues we can gain some insights and conceptual instruments for approaching the dynamics of literary dialogues. These close affinities should not of course obscure the obvious differences. First, typical cases of real-life dialogues are based on oral communication while most of modern literary activity is done in the written form. Note, however, that some literary communication was (and still is) conducted orally: not only when we move back in history or to folklore literature performed orally, but also in some corners of contemporary literary life (e.g., poetry readings). Besides, there are many and quickly growing channels of real-life, everyday dialogues performed in the written form: E-mails, Internet chats, text-messages on mobile phones. In this context we may recall Barbara Herrnstein Smith's concept of natural discourse which is not restricted to oral communication but rather includes written forms like personal letters, diaries, etc. (Smith 1978). The dividing line between what Smith calls natural discourse and fictive or literary discourse does not necessarily overlap the distinction between oral and written communication. What distinguishes natural from literary texts lies in different strategies of perception and comprehension. Whereas the understanding of natural utterances is inseparably linked to its context, the understanding of literary or fictive works is "severed" from the context of its composition and is conducted, because of cultural conventions, according to mimetic or representational principles. Even if we do not accept Smith's distinctions en bloc, her discussion makes a good point in arguing that the oral–written division is not necessarily the most important distinction in understanding everyday and literary communicative situations. The technological developments in communicative means since she wrote her pivotal essay (cell phones, Internet chats, etc.) seem to corroborate her ideas.

   Secondly, real-life dialogues (even in the broad sense introduced here) are characterized by an immediacy that is absent from most typical cases of literary dialogues. This difference has some practical consequences: a listener is bound to listen when the speaker utters her/his words; a reader or a reader who becomes a respondent, on the other hand, can take or leave the book at will, not necessarily when it was sent to her/him by the author/publisher; she/he can stop and resume reading according to a personal whim that has nothing to do with the author/publisher's act of initiating the book. And, if such a reader decides to write a literary reaction, it can be done years (even hundreds of years!) after the book was published.

Finally, another important and conspicuous difference between real-life and literary dialogue is that everyday dialogues are usually a continuous, ongoing series of exchanges of words between the discussants, and concludes either because of technical constraints ("sorry, I have to go, we'll continue some other time") or because the dialogical dynamics lead to a happy closure ("thank you, you've answered my question," "fine, you've convinced me on that point"). Literary dialogues, on the other hand, take the form of only two "répliques" (or retorts)[1]: the activating, source text and the activated, responding text. In that sense, they are more closed and finite, at least on the technical, outer level, than their real-life counterparts. Needless to say, literary dialogues may still be open and indeterminate on the interpretative level – like any other literary phenomenon.

Still, despite some practical and technical differences, the fundamental situation of real-life dialogues can be found in literary dialogues: an addressor (speaker/author) initiates the dialogue by uttering some words, expecting someone to absorb and respond, and an addressee (listener/reader-interpreter) who attentively absorbs the words/text, which contain certain ideas and sentiments, and signals willingness to be engaged in some kind of communicative exchange.[2]

Genuine Literary Dialogues

Let us move now to the basic distinction introduced in the last chapter between genuine and pseudo-dialogues. It seems easy to apply the concept of real-life genuine, dialectical dialogue to the literary arena. In fact, most cases that will be discussed in the second part of this study belong to that category: an author (or painter, sculptor, etc.), after reading a literary work attentively, responds to it in a dialectical way by writing (or producing in other media) a work that takes issue with some aesthetic or ideological dimensions of the first work. An author may write a parody of the text or develop it in a new direction or subvert it. Let us take a relatively simple case of dialectical literary dialogue: parody. To call a literary (or other artistic) work a parody implies: (a) that the maker of the parody is familiar with the parodied work, (b) that she/he finds certain aspects of that work open to criticism and (c) has decided to express this criticism by using the comic mechanism of partial imitation and distortion (or deviation or substitution) characteristic of parody. Shakespeare's Sonnet 130 may illustrate the dialectic literary dialogue present in the dual levels characteristics of every parody:

> My mistress' eyes are nothing like the Sun;
> Coral is far more red than her lips' red;
> If snow be white, why then her breasts are dun;
> If hairs be wires, black wires grow on her head.
> I have seen roses damasked, red and white,
> But no such roses see I in her cheeks,
> And in some perfumes is there more delight
> Than in the breath that from my mistress reeks.
> I love to hear her speak, yet well I know
> That music hath a far more pleasing sound.
> I grant I never saw a goddess go;
> My mistress when she walks treads on the ground.
>   And yet, by heaven, I think my love as rare
>   As any she belied with false compare.

Shakespeare's parodic treatment of Petrarchan-like love poetry is based on juxtaposing a series of prevalent Petrarchan metaphors to an opened-eye description of the beloved's looks.[3] The systematic manner in which the poem progresses, evokes a long tradition of love poems, starting with the Song of Songs. At the same time, it establishes the speaker as an objective, unbiased observer and builds up his credibility. The effect of the naturalistic observations is to denigrate the image of the beloved woman and to drag her from the heights of a conventional pedestal to what may seem a rather repellent earthy base ("And in some perfumes is there more delight / Than in the breath that from my mistress reeks"). But this rhetorical move is reversed in the concluding couplet: suddenly we learn that the naturalistic description was part of a larger and deeper way of treating a beloved woman. One can look with open eyes at women of flesh and blood, including their inevitable human imperfections, and at the same time love them. Further, by arguing that conventional, hyperbolical metaphors are founded on lies ("false compare"), the poem suggests that the sentiments expressed by such imagery are fake or at least hollow. Thus, Shakespeare responded to conventional Petrarchan poetry with an effective parody that not only exposes the fallacies of the original but also outlines a positive alternative. In a very important sense, Sonnet 130 is a prototypical parody, but by virtue of the concluding couplet it goes beyond the boundaries of simple parody.[4]

Authors can express non-acceptance of a work in non-parodic ways. They can evoke the original text, argue with some of its formulations, poetics or ideas and offer an alternative without necessarily using the playful, comic mechanism of parody. When Mayakovsky wrote his long poem titled "To Sergei Esenin," he was trying to pay tribute and to deal with the legacy of the well-known poet who had committed suicide a few years earlier. Mayakovsky also wanted to dispute the nihilistic implications of Esenin's last poem, written on the eve of his suicide in 1925. Esenin's lines read:

> Goodbye, my friend, goodbye.
> My sweet one, you are in my heart.
> Predestined separation
> Holds the promise of future reunion.
>
> Goodbye, my friend, without a touch of the hand, without a word,
> Do not be sad, do not knit your brow in sorrow, –
> In this life, dying is nothing new,
> Though, of course, living is no newer.[5]

To which Mayakovsky, poet of the Russian revolution, responds in the concluding lines of his own poem with the bold, life-affirming words:

> In this life,
>   It is not hard
>   To die.
>   To make a life
>   That is much harder.[6]

Unlike Shakespeare in Sonnet 130, Mayakovsky does not adopt playful parody in order to reject Esenin's stand, but rather presents an alternative to what he conceives to be a Romantic attitude, tainted with decadence and resignation. True heroism lies, says Mayakovsky, not in willingness to give up one's life, but in a stubborn resolution to endure life with all its hardship. This high rhetoric exercised here against Esenin's tragic decision did not prevent Mayakovsky from taking his own life only a few years later.

Shakespeare's and Mayakovsky's examples differ on many levels. Thematically they tackle different issues: Shakespeare focuses on the nature of love and the right way to express it; Mayakovsky copes with the existential question of taking one's life in face of life's difficulties. They also differ in the place the originating text holds in their own text: in Shakespeare, the greatest part of the poem is devoted to a critical exposé of the source, while in Mayakovsky only the concluding section directly evokes Esenin's swan song. They are also miles apart when it comes to tone: Shakespeare uses playful parody to convey his critical attitude, and Mayakovsky opts for a declaratory tone verging on pathos, without any comic, parodic effect. Still, despite all these differences (and there are more), both Shakespeare and Mayakovsky can be described as engaged in a genuine literary dialogue: they know the source texts well, they have internalized what these source texts have to say, to a certain extent they have embedded these texts in their own poems – and they argue against them. In other words, they are engaged in typical dialectical relationships with these texts. From a reader's point of view, these dialectical relationships constitute a vital part of the process of grasping the poems' meanings and effects. Note, however, that to describe these texts as genuine dialogues is not necessarily to valorize them; to be a genuine dialogue is not a guarantor, in and of itself, against artistic flaws.

Echo Literary Dialogues: Reading

Whereas some texts react to other texts in meaningful, if sometimes unpredictable ways, other texts, while evoking other texts, do not create a truly dialectical relationship with them. And, as in real life, the non-dialectical relationship can take two forms: in the first, there is a high degree of resemblance between the two texts (hence, echo-dialogue) and in the second, the two are only superficially related (thus, dialogue-of-the-deaf). Let us look first at echo-dialogues. Structurally, the main characteristic of an echo-dialogue lies in the fact that although there are two participants in the interaction, only the "voice" (i.e., ideas, sentiments, point of view) of one of the two is expressed (or dominates).

In the previous chapter (the section "Real-life Dialogue: the Passive/Active Scale") the sequence of speech followed by nodding was described as a minimal, passive version of echo-dialogue (compared to an openly verbal reaction). What would be the equivalent of such a real-life sequence in the literary field? Assuming that the role of the leading, initiating participant in a real-life dialogue corresponds to the author of the original text, it becomes clear that the corresponding literary situation of this passive, minimal version of echo-dialogue can be found in every act of reading; in other words, a minimal, passive literary echo-dialogue can be found in the sequence of publishing a literary text followed by reading it. Reader-response criticism has shown us that the act of reading involves highly complicated cognitive processes, outlined, for example, in the exemplary studies of Wolfgang Iser (Iser 1978). But, as Pierre Bayard has recently reminded us (Bayard 2007), in reality reading is an umbrella term covering a wide spectrum of phenomena moving from attentive close-reading to superficial skimming (not to mention reading and then, alas, forgetting). When a person buys a book or borrows it from a library (or downloads an electronic book onto a computer), it is like signaling a willingness to listen to someone in real-life conversation. To actually read the book – following its words, images, plot, characters, sentiments, ideology – is like a continuous nodding in response to the words of the leading interlocutor in real life. Note, we do not have to actually agree to everything we read nor to transform our ideology or way of life, but during the act of reading we do absorb, to a certain extent, albeit temporarily, the author's perspective on things. The reader could easily have put the book aside but rather chose to be absorbed in the author's world and words (hence "nodding").

If reading can be described as representing the most passive form of engagement in a literary dialogue, on the opposite side of the passive/active scale we would find works that actively react to the original text in different forms of genuine dialogue (discussed in the previous section), echo-dialogue and dialogue-of-the-deaf (to be discussed shortly): a reader becomes an author, re-writes the work, or alludes to it or writes a book review on it or paints a portrait of the book's main character, etc. In fact, we can draw a scale that moves from passivity to a response of a more active, productive kind. A reader can "passively" enjoy the reading of a book, absorbing and appreciating its form and content, satisfied with this private aesthetic experience, without sharing it with others.[7] The reader can go beyond the private sphere, may recommend the book to a friend and while doing so, provide a brief summary of the plot. The reader may introduce the book in a book club meeting, this time adding to plot summary also some thoughts, impressions and evaluation. Now imagine another reader, an amateur painter who starts idly sketching the main character of the book; this same reader-painter can throw away the sketch and forget about it, but she/he can also take the sketch to the studio, add vivid details, background and color and then try to get the picture into an exhibition. These relatively simple examples may illustrate the move from the passive form of echo-dialogue towards more active forms of reaction.

Echo Literary Dialogues: Translation, Adaptation

Perhaps it is methodologically debatable whether we should describe the act of reading as a literary echo-dialogue (as it is debatable whether to describe the sequence of speech → nodding as echo-dialogue in real life). But there are other important manifestations of echo-dialogues in literature, characterized by more active modes of treating a text. A prototypical example of a situation where an originating text is re-heard can be found in a ubiquitous phenomenon of literary life – translation.[8] Translations of literary works may vary in many respects, but when one thinks of the common, basic meaning of the term – "A version in a different language" (*Random House Dictionary*) – it becomes clear that every translation illustrates to some degree the idea of an echo-dialogue: a reader of a literary work decides to re-write or "repeat" the text, trying to preserve and repeat its important characteristics in the new language. We know however that the specific characteristics that are preserved may vary greatly from one translation to another, depending on the period, the school and the individual talent of the translator. In a sense, the term translation can be seen as an umbrella concept, covering heterogeneous phenomena in different cultures and periods (see, for example, Brower 1974, Lefevere 1992, Robinson 1991 and Toury 1995).

A useful way to describe this heterogeneous field is by highlighting two ideal states that every translator strives to attain. On the one hand, a translation should resemble the original as much as possible; this tacit demand requires an attempt to replicate as many layers and characteristics of the source-text as possible: its meanings, tone, imagery, form, sounds, etc (the ideal of replication). On the other hand, a translation should read and be read as an independent text in the target language, as if originally written in that language (the ideal of domestication). These two aims always stand in a tense relationship. An attempt to entirely fulfill the demands imposed by the first would produce an awkward, almost unreadable text in the target language;

an attempt to totally accomplish the second would compromise some important characteristics of the source-text. When Alexander Pope translated Homer into iambic pentameter, he was trying to domesticate the Greek epic in English poetry of his time, which lacked a tradition of dactylic hexameters, and paid the price of distancing his translation from the ideal of replication. Had Pope opted for preserving the original epic meter, he would have paid a different price, namely that the poem's rhythm would sound rather artificial to English ears. Thus, every translation can be described as a necessary compromise between the two competing ideal states and every inclination towards only one of them has a price tag (and every compromise between the two has a price as well).[9]

It is crucial to emphasize that not every translation automatically belongs to the category of literary echo-dialogue but rather only simple, relatively predictable translations. The more a translation is unpredictable, the more we find ourselves in the realm of genuine dialogue. True, most translations can be crudely described as literary echo-dialogue: the translator's aim is first and foremost to reproduce the source text in a different language; but if a translator wishes to add something to the outcome, and that something is unpredictable and is not related to the linguistic rules of the two languages involved, then she/he has performed an act of genuine dialogue. Note that echo and genuine dialogues (as well as dialogue-of-the-deaf) are not exclusive categories but rather point to a dominant characteristic: thus, when we decide to describe a specific translation as primarily or dominantly an echo-dialogue this does not mean that it lacks any dimension of genuine dialogue. Furthermore, when translators give some prominence to their own ideas, style and sensitivities they may be described as conducting a genuine dialogue with the source text. Needless to say, the decision whether to describe a specific translation as an echo or a genuine dialogue depends on the relative weight we assign to its new, unpredictable dimensions (compared with other relevant translations), thus, it is an interpretative act, not a mechanical cataloging.

In addition to simple translations, there are other kinds of texts that can be described as pertaining to the underlying principle or category of literary echo-dialogues. One such type can be found in what was known as imitation in the England of the eighteenth century: an attempt to tailor the source-text to contemporary literature, culture, knowledge and sensibilities. Samuel Johnson's opening lines to his translation of Juvenal's Satire 10, titled "On the Vanity of Human Wishes," may provide a representative illustration. Juvenal opens his satire with: "In all the lands that stretch from Gades to the Ganges" (Juvenal 1940: 193). Johnson substitutes totally new geographical pointers – "Let Observation, with extensive view, / Survey Mankind, from *China* to *Peru*," (Johnson 1974: 115) – that would not have been recognized by the Romans. By introducing these changes in locations Johnson was trying to preserve for contemporary readers the overall effect of Juvenal's opening lines (the source's function): an invitation to an all-embracing outlook over the known globe. Eighteenth-century imitations in England opted for maintaining the function while sacrificing the specific details or material, or, in the terms introduced earlier, choosing the domesticating ideal over the ideal of replication. The two oppositions – of abstract function vs. concrete linguistic material and of domestication vs. replication – are by no means synonymous. Still, there is a great overlap between the two pairs: opting for preserving the concrete material of the source text usually means that a translator has adopted the ideal of replication; and when a translator thinks more of the abstract-functional level, most chances are that she/he will incline to the ideal of domestication. When a translator takes seriously the goal of finding equivalents for the concrete units composing the source-text (words, sentences, paragraphs, stanzas and metrics), there is a greater risk of losing sight of the text as a conveyer of overall effects (i.e., abstract function). And when an attempt is made to find an equivalent for the overall intended effect or function of the source-text, there is a greater temptation to ignore some of its concrete units.

An interesting example of the historical variability of the meanings of the term translation through history can be found in Plautus' postponed prologue to *The Braggart Soldier* (*Miles Gloriosus*), presented in the second act of the play by Palaestrio, the trickster. Palaestrio declares there that "the Greek name of this comedy is Alazon, a word which we translate as Braggart" (Plautus 1995: 133) thus implying that the present text is but a Latin version or translation of a Greek play. While the play to which Plautus refers did not survive, it is reasonable to assume that *Milies Gloriosus* was not only a simple translation of the Greek original but rather "a mixture of close translation and free adaptation" (Hunter 1985: 18). Most Roman playwrights paid tribute to Greek theater and when they presented their work as merely a Roman version of a Greek play, their audience did not consider this an artistic defect or lack of originality (admiration of originality came only with the Romantic movement), but rather as a marker that the author was working within a highly regarded literary tradition. But to declare that he was only presenting a Latin version of a Greek play does not mean that all Plautus did was in fact a simple word-for-word translation; free adaptation would probably be a more accurate way to describe the process that the Greek *Alazon* underwent before it became *Miles Gloriosus*.

As the above examples show, the specific nature of literary translations can vary greatly. When discussing translation we should not only pay attention to the specific nature of any concrete text but also be aware of the different terms used in the field: translation, version, rendition, imitation, interpretation.[10] Sometimes the same term can designate different phenomena; sometimes different terms indicate the same practice or outcome. From our perspective here, translations can be situated at different points on the imaginary line moving from echo to genuine dialogue. To help us decide where exactly we should situate a specific translation the leading question is: To what extent is the target-text predictable? In other words, if the target-text looks like a product of a translating machine, we are dealing with a simple, echo-dialogue.

If on the other hand there are significant levels of the target-text that could not have been predicted based on knowledge of the two pertinent languages, we move towards a genuine-dialogue.

Before going on to discuss other forms of literary echo-dialogue, it is important to note that despite the structural similarity between translations and real-life echo-dialogues, they differ in two important respects. First, linguistic variations that are usually considered insignificant in real-life conversations – e.g., the specific choice of words, register, formal patterns – may acquire great significance in literary translations. When an interlocutor repeats what she/he has heard with some minor changes in wording, we tend to dismiss the specific variations and explain them by various contextual factors ("she used a different word because she comes from a different educational background"). In literary translations, on the other hand, we tend to see such variations as significant, intentional decisions aiming at achieving certain effects ("the word of a higher register was chosen to highlight the elevated tone of the poem").

Secondly, and most importantly, an echo-dialogue in a real-life situation is usually regarded as dull and unsatisfactory, especially in situations where we expect the two interlocutors to engage in genuine dialogue ("he is only repeating what he heard, without adding anything new to the conversation"). Literary translations, on the other hand, even simple, relatively predictable ones, can fulfill a significantly innovative role in the target literary and cultural system. The very decision to translate certain works into a given language can have far reaching consequences for the target literature and culture, broadening their horizons by introducing new modes of expression, literary forms, ideas, sensibilities and ideologies. Even the most superficial comparative analysis of cultures will show that those fostering literary translations are usually richer and more productive than those blocking them because of xenophobia or ideological rigidity.

In addition to translations, there are other literary phenomena that can be described as repeating the original, source-text, albeit differently, and thus can illustrate the basic principle of echo-dialogue. If the raison d'être of literary abridgments and adaptations is to bring to readers (or spectators) an original text, while changing only the length, the wording or the medium, we have prototypical cases of echo-dialogue.

The multi-faceted relations between literary works and movie productions, as well as the post-modern situation where the lines between the original work and its various disseminations have become blurred, have set off a growing interest in adaptations and related phenomena (see, for example, Hutcheon 2006 and Sanders 2006). Sanders proposes an interesting distinction, reflected in the title of her book, between adaptation and appropriation: "An adaptation signals a relationship with an informing sourcetext or original; a cinematic version of Shakespeare's *Hamlet* ... remains ostensibly *Hamlet*, a specific version, albeit achieved in alternative temporal and generic modes, of that seminal cultural text. On the other hand, appropriation frequently affects a more decisive journey away from the informing source into a wholly new cultural product and domain" (Sanders 2006: 26). For some purposes this is a useful distinction, but it will not help us in understanding the significant differences between genuine dialogues and dialogues-of-the-deaf; since neither is a straightforward case of adaptation, we will lump them together here as appropriations, thus ignoring the different motivations and effects of genuine dialogues and dialogues-of-the-deaf.

As in translations, so in adaptations we can distinguish between cases that render texts according to certain preconceived principles or rules and those that operate in a less obvious, predictable manner. Adapting a story to be read by children, for example, usually implies abridgments, simplification, avoidance of sensitive issues (e.g., sex) and adhering to certain registers of language. But not all abridgments-adaptations necessarily comply with a preconceived set of rules and some of them may produce unexpected effects, closer to the realm of genuine dialogue. This is the case with the hilarious show put on by the Reduced Shakespeare Company (http://www.reduced-shakespeare.com): while formally obeying the rules of abridging a source text, it takes these principles ad absurdum, to comic effect. The concept that helps us to distinguish between echo-adaptations and adaptations of genuine dialogue is – as in the case of translations – rooted in expectations and predictability: the more an adaptation was made according to a known set of rules and hence is of predictable outcome, the more it can be described as echo-dialogue.

Since the term echo-dialogue might imply something disrespectful, let me add a clarification. Compared to texts illustrating genuine-dialogues, echo-dialogues are usually rated low on the scale of originality. Still, contrary to Romantic notions, originality is not the only asset a literary or artistic work can possess. Echo-dialogues can be successful and significant literary and artistic phenomena. Perhaps they will not become part of the great books club, but they are nevertheless a valuable part of literary life. Literature with no rich echo-dialogue activity in the form of translations and adaptations is bound to become rigid and dull.

When many and diverse translations are introduced into a literature, this may demonstrate its openness to new sensibilities, and ensure a dynamic growth of horizons and repertoire. True, there is a significant difference between developed and under-developed (young, weak or dependent) literary systems: the former have a rich repertoire and models that the latter lack (Even-Zohar 1978: 54–59). Hence the role of translations, for instance, in young, under-developed literary systems is much more important than in fully developed ones: the initial stages of creating Roman literature, for example, were closely linked to many translations from Greek. When Quintilian said that "*Satura ... tota nostra est* [Satire ... is all our own]" (Elliott 1960: 100) he was admitting that all other Roman literary genres were based on Greek models. Still, even in fully developed literary systems, translations may play an important role in re-vitalizing their models and repertoires: when Garcia

Marquez' novels were translated into English, his fantastic realism opened new imaginative paths for contemporary English novelists.

As for adaptations of literary works (another example of echo-dialogue), they too play an important role in the distribution and circulation of literature among different audiences. Adaptations targeting children broaden the horizons of young readers; cinematic adaptations introduce literary works to audiences that are not habitual readers of literary texts. As scholars, rather than adopt a lofty attitude toward simplifying, echo-dialogue adaptations, we should ask ourselves what would happen if such adaptations would not exist at all? No one would like to be left with only a limited set of adaptations that have conformed to certain high standards and have been sanctioned or authorized. Let a hundred flowers bloom – even when some of them are not to our individual taste. As will be argued later, the flourishing of a variety of literary dialogues – including simple, echo-like translations and adaptations – is not only a sign of the vitality of a literary system, but when a specific book evokes such blooming or procreation it is the hallmark of its greatness.

Before going on to the next dialogical type or principle, it would be instructive to remember the story of Echo as it is told by Ovid (*Metamorphoses* 3. 339–510). Ovid's version of the myth of Echo and Narcissus is a tragic story, culminating in the death of these two characters, incapable of conducting a genuine dialogue:

> He no longer retains his colour, the white mingled with red, no longer has life and strength, and that form so pleasing to look at, nor has he that body which Echo loved. Still, when she saw this, though angered and remembering, she pitied him, and as often as the poor boy said 'Alas!' she repeated with her echoing voice '*Alas!*' and when his hands strike at his shoulders, she returns the same sounds of pain. His last words as he looked into the familiar pool were 'Alas, in vain, beloved boy!' and the place echoed every word, and when he said 'Goodbye!' Echo also said '*Goodbye!*' [11]

A reminder: the nymph Echo was punished by Juno for using her eloquence in helping Jupiter get away with his love affairs with other nymphs; the punishment makes Echo only capable of repeating the last words she has heard; hence, when she wants to express her love for Narcissus, she can only echo his last words; Narcissus, being a beautiful arrogant young man, rudely rejects Echo's advances. Echo, deeply distressed by Narcissus' rejection, is absorbed into her obsession and her existence diminishes until "Only her bones and the sound of her voice are left. Her voice remains, her bones, they say, were changed to shapes of stone." Narcissus himself is punished for rejecting Echo and dies adoring his own reflection, without realizing at first it is himself he is so desperately desires. Unable to leave his beloved, he finally perishes from hunger. Narcissus's death is thus a symmetrical "echo" to Echo's death, repeating the principle of no response from the beloved.

Aside from the similarities between the stories of Echo and Narcissus, there are also interesting differences: Echo acts on behalf of love (both in protecting

Jupiter and in pursuing Narcissus), whereas Narcissus rejects the possibility of real love, thus making him the more culpable; his drama takes place on the visual, not the auditory plane and his mistake is not only moral but also cognitive (most of the time he does not realize what he is seeing).

The Echo and Narcissus myths were brought here not for their own sake but rather in order to note some fundamental difference between the mythical story as told by Ovid and the way echo-dialogues function in literary life. For Ovid, Echo and Narcissus are two variations of a basically tragic story, stemming from a person's inability or unwillingness to combine love with genuine dialogue. The outcome is death: Echo's inability to express something of her own is portrayed as the source of her agony and death; and Narcissus's unwillingness to relate to something other than himself is the cause of his end. Thus, both "inspiring-text" (= Narcissus) and "inspired-text" (= Echo) perish because they cannot create genuine dialogue between I and Thou. The myths can be seen as a powerful warning against such psychological tendencies and their cost.

Looking at literary life, however, reveals a much less grim picture and echo-dialogues seem to be related to the principle of life and love. To produce a literary echo-dialogue is surely an act of love on the part of the writer, translator or artist involved. This act of love is usually accepted as such and encouraged by the author of the inspiring, "Narcissistic" text (at least when she or he is still around). Furthermore, the echo-like act of love is closely related to a principle of life: in fact, we can see a mutually dialectic process whereby the lives of both texts, inspiring and inspired, are enhanced. The more a text gives rise to echo-dialogues, the more it grows, its presence is stronger and, in a complementary manner, the stronger the status of a text in literary life, the greater the chances that its translations, adaptations and other forms of echo-dialogue will become visible and have better chances to gain their own status and assure their own survival. The story of echo-dialogues in literary life thus seems to demonstrate almost the opposite of what the myth tells us: not an inability to communicate that culminates in death but rather an ability to combine love, life and procreation.

Literary Dialogues-of-the-Deaf

After looking at various forms of literary echo-dialogue, we can move to the next category and ask what could be considered a literary counterpart of everyday dialogue-of-the-deaf. In such cases we see how an author indeed evokes a text but does so only on an outer level, using it as a superficial springboard for her/his purposes, without paying too much attention to its specificity and without instituting a true dialectical relationship with it. To a certain extent one can argue that such cases are in fact ubiquitous in textual relationship: after all, in every allusion or quotation or evocation of a text, an author is using that text for her/his own purposes. While there is a certain grain of truth in that statement, it is still useful to distinguish between cases where an author is attentive to a text and those where a text is evoked only on a superficial level. Sometimes we come across an epigraph that shows the writer's erudition but has little semantic significance. Or we may encounter an expression in a poem borrowed from a famous canonical text, but without any meaningful impact; it is merely part of the poet's poetics, demonstrating familiarity with the canonical text and bestowing an elevated aura on the new text.[12] It is clear that describing a specific allusion or epigraph as dialogue-of-the-deaf depends on interpretation: we may recognize the allusion, examine the relationships between alluding and alluded and then determine that this relationship is not truly dialectical.

Let us take a brief look at a relatively complicated case of literary dialogue-of-the-deaf: Dryden's *Absalom and Achitophel* (1681). In this long satirical poem, Dryden evokes the biblical story of King David (II Samuel xiii–xviii), rebelled against by his son Absalom, abetted by Achitophel, a former counselor of the King. Dryden was not interested in the biblical story for its own sake; he was using it to address contemporary issues, supporting Charles II (= King David) and denouncing his opponents, who were striving to exclude Charles' legal successor, James, Duke of York (hated for his known Catholicism) and to promote the Duke of Monmouth in his stead (= Absalom). A central figure in this attempt was Lord Shaftesbury, represented in Dryden's allegorical satire by Achitophel. Based on the initial resemblance between the two situations – an attempt to replace the legal heir to a ruling king by another candidate – Dryden re-tells the biblical story, conjuring up many more real and alleged similarities that serve his fundamental purpose: to support and even glorify Charles II and to denounce those who were trying to challenge the legal successor by promoting their candidate.

Dryden's poem may serve his moral convictions and political goals. It may also demonstrate his great literary talent and inventive imagination. But this literary tour de force does not lead to a genuine literary dialogue – despite its impressive achievements and magnitude. The argument here is not necessarily based on the fact that Dryden, keen to thicken the network of similarities between the two situations, falls into some bending of historical facts and anachronisms, confusing the ancient Hebrews with post-biblical Jews; referring to institutions like the Sanhedrin, (line 390), established long after the time of King David, among many others. These factual lapses, in and of themselves, are not major difficulties. Literary art should not be measured according to historical accuracy and an author may bend historical facts or linguistic details to serve an artistic aim. The lapses are, however, symptomatic of Dryden's lack of interest in the original biblical story for its own sake. This last statement may sound strange at first, especially if we take into account Dryden's deep acquaintance with the Bible and the fact that his long poem (1031 lines) is presented as a re-telling. Still, it is quite clear that Dryden's work does not represent a dialectical relationship with the originating text. Rather, there is a unidirectional flow of meanings: what serves his purposes is taken from the biblical story and other things are simply repressed. Even more importantly, the reader is not expected to ponder the intricate network of similarities and dissimilarities between the two texts – the hallmark of genuine dialogues.

Note that by describing a specific literary text as a dialogue-of-the-deaf, I do not wish to bury it or to praise it. When we are present at a dialogue-of-the-deaf *in real life*, we usually feel discomfort and make a critical comment: either when we actively participate in such a dialogic exchange ("hey, you're not listening to me!") or when we witness it as listeners ("this politician does not respond to the questions of the anchorman; he keeps evading them, uttering clichés"). In other words, we do have some tacit expectation that a dialogue in real life should, at least occasionally, be a genuine dialogue. When it comes to the literary field, we are willing to set such expectations aside. In other words, we are ready to suspend a moral stand ("it's not fair to use this text") and to give an author more leeway in her/his judgment of what is a legitimate artistic response. Earlier, we saw that there is a difference between the way we evaluate echo-dialogue in a real situation and literary echo-dialogue (simple translations, adaptations etc.): the former are considered flawed, the latter play a constructive role in literary life. A similar distinction holds for everyday and literary dialogues-of-the-deaf. An author might not be attentive to the evoked text, but the outcome may be a valuable work, promoting the author's imaginative world and in such cases the inattentiveness is not only forgiven but also welcome.

In fact, part of what Bloom describes as the stamp of literary strength (based on "misreading" of "strong poets"), may be described as a kind of dialogue-of-the-deaf.[13] The problem with Bloom's model, however, is that the emphasis he puts on dialectical strife does not leave room for the more congenial dialectical relationship that characterizes many literary genuine dialogues. Not every dialectical coping with a text or poet has to be described as expressing an urge to annihilate the parent figure. Strife, negation, combat, is but one side of the dialectical coin; listening, internalizing, containing, is the other. And there is no reason to restrict the model to literary relationships that can be described in terms of Freudian "Family Romance" and patricide; literary dialogues are richer and more heterogeneous, as suggested by Clayton and Rothstein (1991: 10–11).[14]

One Table, Two Clarifications

The following table sums up the basic principles underlying some types of literary dialogue discussed in this chapter.

Two comments should be added to this table. First, unlike TABLE 1.1, which presented different types of real-life dialogues *and* monologues TABLE 2.1 focuses only on literary dialogues. Note that the title of TABLE 2.1 refers to literary dialogues on the level of the literary communicative situation (rela-

TABLE 2.1
Types of Literary Dialogues

	Inner Level		
	One "Voice"	Two "Voices"	
Inner Level — Two Voice (= Texts)	Echo-Dialogue (Pseudo-Dialogue I) Reading (minimal, passive); Simple, predictable Translations, Adaptations	Dialogue-of-the-deaf (Pseudo-Dialogue II) Superficial Allusions and Epigraphs; Inattentive, non-dialectical Evocations of texts	Genuine Dialogue Meaningful Allusions and Rewritings (and also non-predictable Translations, Adaptations and Parodies)

tionship of texts and authors to texts and authors), not to dialogues *represented* in literary works (i.e., two characters talking to each other in a play or a novel). Represented literary dialogues can be described (with slight modification) according to categories presented in TABLE 1.1. When we focus, however, on types of literary dialogues between an inspiring and an inspired text, the category of monologue becomes irrelevant. Monologues can of course be represented in literary works, especially drama. But one should not confuse a monologue as part of a *represented* communicative situation in the fictive world of a literary work with the literary communicative situation itself. In the latter, we assume that there are always two "players": author and reader (or playwright and audience), hence, every literary communicative situation is dialogic by definition. True, unlike real-life communicative situations, the literary communicative situation is very often *mediated* in various degrees: in drama and fiction by dramatis personae, the fictive world and a narrator, and in poetry by the poem's speaker, although it is assumed that lyric poetry provides a framework for a more direct expression of sentiments, and a direct addressing of the reader.[15] The crucial point is that regardless of the degree of mediation involved, we assume that an author, by writing and publishing a literary work, wishes to convey something (ideas, emotions, sensibilities, images, world-view – and usually all of this) to a reader. An author can invent a narrator who does not show any interest in a listener (e.g., in some of Beckett's novels), thus presenting a (genuine) monologist, but the author who invents a solipsistic narrator is not solipsistic but rather is engaged in a literary dialogue with the reader.

Secondly, TABLE 2.1 uses the same labels in different places on the chart (e.g., translation in both echo and genuine dialogues). The reason for this should be clear by now: some literary forms and activities that illustrate different categories of genuine and pseudo dialogues are actually not made of one piece. Translations and adaptations, for example, primarily belong to the category of echo-dialogue; but there are unpredictable translations and adaptations that could be better described as genuine dialogues. This is also true of other literary phenomena which may be formally defined as allusion, epigraph, re-writing and even parody. Whether to describe a specific case of these literary phenomena as a genuine or pseudo-dialogue (and in case of the pseudo – whether echo or dialogue-of-the-deaf) depends on the actual semantic relationship existing between the source text and the present text. And to understand these relationships we have to provide an interpretation (however heuristic) of the two pertinent works.

CHAPTER

3

The Battle of the (Great) Books

After illustrating the multifaceted nature of dialogue in real life and the complex nature of literary dialogues, my next undertaking in the introductory meeting of the "Dialogues with Great Books" course was to expound the highly controversial concept of "great books". The questions "What is a great book, what is a literary masterpiece, how is the canon formed?" have haunted literary studies for many years, and have become more pressing during the past few decades with the challenges presented to the Western Canon.

Three centuries ago, literary critics were waging "The Battle of the Books," arguing about criteria for determining literary eminence. The focus of the debate was whether the list of great books should be restricted to the ancients or be open to the moderns. Today, literary critics are again arguing the question of literary greatness, but with two important differences. First, since the time of the old debate, the boundaries of the canon have been dramatically changed and challenged: then, the radicals tried to introduce some modern authors into the canon, thus undermining the first attribute in the notorious trio of dead, white and male.[1] Today, conservatives and radicals disagree on the proportion and the pace by which the canon should embrace marginalized voices, but nobody, not even the most rigid of the old guard, defends the outdated, racist and chauvinistic triad. Furthermore, in addition to arguments concerning the sanctioning of specific works or set of aesthetic values, some contemporary radicals try to undermine the very assumption that a book's greatness depends on its intrinsic aesthetic qualities.

Among the many concrete answers given to the question "What is a great book?" we can detect some shared assumptions, and the diverse schools can be grouped into two major "parties": the beauty party and the power party.[2]

The Beauty Party

The beauty party, which dominated literary criticism for centuries, assumes that the status of a great book is a function of certain aesthetic qualities inherent in the work. There may of course be significant disagreements among members of the beauty party. First, some of them do not even use the term "aesthetic quality." The term acquired its modern, contemporary meaning relatively late, during the nineteenth century.[3] Before that, discussions about aesthetic qualities used terms like "art," "beauty," "poetic," "taste" and the like. Secondly, different thinkers and schools who share the belief in the role of aesthetic qualities (whether they are called such or not) in determining a book's fate in the hall of fame, still disagree about the specific nature of these qualities.

Aristotle, the first great thinker assigning to art – and to theory of art – an autonomous status ("I propose to treat of Poetry in itself": Aristotle 1895: 7 [1447a]) of course did not use the term "aesthetic qualities." Still, when in the seventh chapter of the *Poetics* Aristotle discusses the magnitude or length of the plot, he suggests a dual principle that can easily be formulated as two aesthetic principles or requirements that a successful artistic work should manifest: "a certain length is necessary, and that length one that may be easily embraced by the memory ... the limit as fixed by the nature of the drama itself is this: the greater the length, the more beautiful will the piece be in respect of such magnitude, provided that the whole be perspicuous" (Aristotle 1895: 31 [1451a]). The artist should strive to maximize the plot's magnitude but this magnitude is constrained by the necessity of perceiving it as one unit. Thus, there is a latent tension between the two requirements: the more an artist attempts to enrich the work, to put more "stuff" into it (events, characters), she or he endangers its perception as a meaningful whole. Likewise, if the artist cares only about securing a tight, perceptible, small structure – the principle of striving to include more, and more varied material suffers.

This dual aesthetic criterion arises out of Aristotle's famous prerequisite of any artistic work, namely that it be mimetic (i.e. the plot's structure as an imitation of action). Artistic works may differ in medium, genre, style or subject matter, but they all exemplify the mimetic principle: "Epic poetry and tragedy, Comedy and also dithyrambic poetry, and the greater part of the music of the flute and of the lyre, are all in their general conception modes of imitation" (Aristotle 1895: 7 [1447a]) and imitation is the basic, natural source of the enjoyment we get from art: "every one feels a natural pleasure in things imitated" (Aristotle 1895: 15 [1448b]). There is no reason that we should limit our attention to mimetic art in the way Aristotle postulated it; were we to do that some important artistic phenomena would be excluded from the field (e.g. abstract painting). The interesting thing is that if we set aside Aristotle's mimetic theory of art, we can still consider the dual aesthetic principle he suggests in chapter seven – at least in its broad meaning of variety within unity – as a useful aesthetic criterion.

Note that an issue commonly recurring in the history of Western thinking about art and aesthetics is concealed within the dual criteria: the tension between the descriptive and the prescriptive. Was Aristotle simply describing the structural principles underlying artistic works or was he prescribing certain ideals the artist should strive to follow? Was he doing the latter thinking that he was doing the former? No matter how we decide in the specific case of Aristotle, there can be no doubt that discussions of aesthetic qualities are always charged – explicitly or implicitly – with value judgments.

Assuming we agree that a specific text possesses certain aesthetic qualities, making the descriptive statement "text A has aesthetic qualities X, Y, Z," it is almost impossible to escape the laudatory overtones of such a statement.

This underlying tension between the descriptive and the prescriptive, between *presenting* what we can find in (good!) artistic texts and *recommending* what we find there – is evident also in modern discussions of aesthetics and literary theory. Here too there are still some important disagreements. A brief look at some modern pronouncements of what constitutes (laudable) aesthetic quality in a literary work can reveal these disagreements – but also some common motifs.

Even within the relatively homogeneous school of New Critics, which focuses attention on the work's semantic complexities, one can find different emphases. William Empson, in an influential book published as early as 1930 (Empson 1947), proposed ambiguity as the true sign of good poetic work. As the title of his book suggests, there can be different – according to Empson seven – types of ambiguity. In fact here ambiguity becomes an all-embracing term, covering a wide array of phenomena – from linguistic puns to what can be best described as a schism in the psyche of the author.

Another influential New Critic, Cleanth Brooks, suggests that the language of poetry (and, by implication, of literature) is the language of paradox. It might seem that the term 'paradox' belongs to the realm of sophistry, but, Brooks counter-argues: "there is a sense in which paradox is the language appropriate and inevitable to poetry. It is the scientist whose truth requires a language purged of every trace of paradox; apparently the truth which the poet utters can be approached only in terms of paradox" (Brooks 1949: 66). Expressing oneself through paradox is not exclusive to poetry: "most of the language of lovers is such... so is most of the language of religion – 'He who would save his life must lose it'; 'The last shall be first'" (Brooks 1949: 75). In poetry, however, paradoxes are not necessarily expressed in such an open, straightforward way but through a constant re-inventing of language itself and by making the "connotations play as great a part as the denotation" (Brooks 1949: 69). What Brooks describes and illustrates in his readings of some poems are deep metaphors underlying the composition: the calm, sleepy city as a powerful giant in Wordsworth's "Composed upon Westminster Bridge"; and the mundane lovers as saints in Donne's "The Canonization."

A focus on semantic tensions, paradoxes and complexities also characterizes an essay by Allen Tate, "Tension in Poetry." Tate assigns the term a specific meaning: "I am using the term not as a general metaphor, but as a special one, derived from lopping the prefixes off the logical terms *ex*tension and *in*tension. What I am saying, of course, is that the meaning of poetry is its 'tension,' the full organized body of all the extension and intension that we can find in it" (Tate 1949: 60). And, as in the case of Brooks, supportive examples for this principle can be found in metaphors (broadly understood), where we have a concrete image on the one hand and an abstract meaning on the other. There is always some level of incompatibility and even contradiction between the two levels. Tate analyses, for example, Donne's comparison of the two souls of the lovers (in "Valediction: Forbidding Mourning") to a thin piece of gold beaten by a jeweler, and he comments: "Now the interesting feature here is the logical contradiction of embodying the unitary, non-spatial soul in a spatial image ... The finite image of the gold, in extension, logically contradicts the intensive meaning (infinity) which it conveys; but it does not invalidate that meaning" (Tate 1949: 61). In Tate's case it becomes clear that such poetic tensions not only characterize poems but are the hallmark of good poetry. If poets do not succeed in creating the constant move from image to abstract meaning – replete with contradictions but also fraught with meanings – they will find themselves developing only one pole (extension or intension) and either producing "analytic" poetry or, even worse, contributing to "mass language" which appeals to existing affective states. In fact, Tate devotes about half of his essay to expose the shortcomings and the dangers of these two types of poetic "fallacies."

Another influential aesthetic principle was introduced by Monroe Beardsley who, in a discussion on the logic of the explication of metaphor, proposes a general dual principle of interpretation, a principle that seems to imply the desirable aesthetic characteristics of a literary text: "First, there is the principle of Congruence ... in assembling, or fitting out, the admissible connotations of words in a poem, we are guided by logical and physical possibilities. But second, there is the Principle of Plenitude. All the connotations that can be found to fit are to be attributed to the poem: it means all it *can* mean, so to speak" (Beardsley 1958: 144). It is clear that in certain respects Beardsley here continues the line of thinking of the New Critics – the central role played by metaphor as the locus of poetic and aesthetic qualities, the focus on connotations – and in another sense he seems to resort to Aristotle's requirements of an artistic text – that it be long and hence heterogeneous but at the same time perceptible and hence structured.

Leaving the Anglo-Saxon critical tradition and moving to another influential twentieth-century school of criticism, the Russian Formalists, we can cite Shklovsky's notion of "making strange." Shklovsky tries to describe the raison d'être of literary works and of art in general: "And art exists that one may recover the sensation of life; it exists to make one feel things, to make the stone *stony*. The purpose of art is to impart the sensation of things as they are perceived and not as they are known. The technique of art is to make objects 'unfamiliar,' to make forms difficult, to increase the difficulty and length of perception because the process of perception is an aesthetic end in itself and must be prolonged. *Art is a way of experiencing the artfulness of an object; the object is not important*" (Shklovsky 1965: 12). One can detect in this much quoted passage a tension between the idea that art's mission is to reconnect us with the world ("to make the stone *stony*"), because habitualization and conventional modes of presentation have "devoured" the perceptible world, and the idea that art's mission is to highlight art itself. This tension, however, is not a real contradiction: when art departs from conventional, habitual modes of presenting the world (modes in which both the objects and the modes of presentation are "invisible"), the prolonged, complicated process of presentation and interpretation foregrounds both the new artistic means – and the represented objects or the world at large.

As Victor Erlich suggested, the Russian Formalists' notion of art as a way for re-discovering the world resembles the Romantic concept of "the sense of novelty and freshness" (Erlich 1955: 179) associated with a "natural," "innocent" child-like perceptions of the world, before it is "devoured" by adult, socialized, conventional modes of perceptions. The Russian Formalists' emphasis on art's "technique" and on the way a poet handles subject matter can suggest close affinities (though not direct influences) with some New Critics' pronouncements (Erlich 1955: 272–75).

The Formalists' attention to manipulations of conventional modes of representation was developed by Jan Mukarovsky, a member of the Prague Structuralist Circle, who gave Shklovksy's ideas a linguistic and historical dimension: First, he argued that the aesthetic qualities of a literary work should not be identified with any specific linguistic or stylistic feature. Rather, the aesthetic or poetic quality is a function: "Poetic language is permanently characterized only by its function; however, function is not a property but a *mode of utilizing* the properties of a given phenomenon. Poetic language belongs among the numerous other functional languages, each of which is an adaptation of a linguistic system to a certain goal of expression. Aesthetic effect is the goal of poetic expression ... the aesthetic function ... concentrates attention on the linguistic sign itself – hence it is exactly the opposite of a real orientation toward a goal which in language is the message" (Mukarovsky 1976: 9). One can see in this formulation an interesting combination of Russian Formalist concepts with the Kantian idea of art as an activity with no real, practical orientation.

What is even more interesting: since language is a dynamic system and linguistic norms evolve, and since the aesthetic or poetic effect is produced by deviating from established linguistic norms, it follows that the aesthetic effect is not stable and secure for all readers in all times: "What was intended by the poet to be aesthetically effective can lose this effect, while, on the contrary, components which originally remained untouched by the poet's artistic intention can acquire aesthetic effectiveness" (Mukarovsky 1976: 14). Thus, for example, a neologism, an intentional deviation from an existing norm – thus producing an aesthetic effect today – can become common usage tomorrow and thus lose its aesthetic effect. In a complementary way, what was part of a linguistic norm at one point – thus carrying no aesthetic import – reintroduced in a text after some centuries suddenly gains aesthetic value because it deviates from the contemporary norm and is felt as an "archaism." Thus, Mukarovsky's concept of an aesthetic quality adopts the perspective of a dynamic linguistic system as the bedrock from which the aesthetic effect can emerge. It is no longer the specific artistic text and its concrete set of aesthetic qualities or "devices" but rather the complex, multi-layered relationship between linguistic and literary norms and the concrete manipulations of these norms by specific use and texts.

The last decade of the twentieth century saw an important contribution to the beauty party in the form of Harold Bloom's defense of the Western Canon (Bloom 1994).[4] Bloom's contribution is significant on two fronts. First, his sweeping polemic tone against what he terms "schools of resentment" – driven, he says, by moral and political agendas or an "odd blend of Foucault and Marx" (Bloom 1994: 38) – has re-vitalized the debate around the questions of why, how and of what the canon is formed.[5] Secondly, his insistence on poetic *strength* ("All strong literary originality becomes canonical" – Bloom 1994: 24) broadens the perspective offered by the beauty party, enabling its supporters to talk about qualities that go beyond traditional aesthetic qualities like beauty and harmony.

Another interesting issue that divides thinkers of the beauty party is related to the ontological or epistemic status of the relevant aesthetic qualities: are they on the same level as other qualities of a text (e.g., its length) and hence can be discussed and even measured in objective terms or are they subjective, as in the popular saying that beauty is in the eyes of the beholder. In a classic article that has led to many discussions in modern aesthetics, Frank Sibley proposed that aesthetic concepts such as "*unified, balanced, integrated, lifeless, serene, somber, dynamic, powerful, vivid, delicate, moving, trite, sentimental, tragic*" have a special status relative to other qualities of the work of art. No group of structural or observable features of an object "is ever logically sufficient" for an aesthetic concept (Sibley 1987: 64, 69). Non-aesthetic descriptions may provide sufficient conditions for *not* applying an aesthetic quality to an object but they do not entail positive aesthetic assertions. An alternative radical view has been advocated by Eddy Zemach, arguing that aesthetic qualities have the same objective status as other textual qualities: "A detailed nonaesthetic description of a Chinese vase can give a reason not only against thinking that it is crude but also for believing it is elegant" (Zemach 1997: 99).

Thus the beauty party offers a wide gallery of specific aesthetic qualities to choose from and contains many factions with regard to the question whether aesthetic qualities have objective, subjective or inter-subjective status. Despite these differences, most partisans of the beauty party share the basic belief that the status of a great book (or other work of art) is a function of its (relevant) aesthetic qualities, discerned by readers or spectators or listeners: the more these qualities can be found in a specific work, the better its chances to be included in the great books club.

The Power Party

During the past few decades, followers of the beauty party are in decline and on the defensive. The contemporary dominant tone belongs to what can be labeled the power party, challenging certain presuppositions of centuries-long critical discourse. Aspects portrayed by followers of the beauty party as *objective* or *inter-subjective* aesthetic qualities,[6] are regarded by followers of the power party as qualities agreed upon by a specific cultural elite; what were advocated as *universal* qualities are exposed as representing the concrete interests of specific historical hegemonies; what was presented as a quality – or qualities – *inherent* to the literary work, is unmasked as an outcome of institutionalized modes of interpretation.

The latter point was forcefully argued by Stanley Fish. He conducted an exercise in which students of a poetry class, told that an assignment list of authors left on the board from a previous class "is" a religious poem of the seventeenth century, came up with some insightful readings of the "poetic text," bringing into play strategies operative in interpretation of poetry (e.g. seeing every detail as significant; assigning symbolic meanings to names etc.). This exercise was intended not only to demonstrate the students' competence (or virtuosity) in producing poetic interpretation, but to challenge certain deep oppositions assumed by most of us when dealing with texts, like the opposition between "objective" text "out there" and a "subjective" reading of it:

> The conclusion, therefore, is that all objects are made and not found, and that they are made by the interpretative strategies we set in motion. This does not, however, commit me to subjectivity because the means by which they are made are social and conventional ... we do *not* have free-standing readers in a relationship of perceptual adequacy or inadequacy to an equally free-standing text. Rather, we have readers whose consciousnesses are constituted by a set of conventional motions which when put into operation constitute in turn a conventional, and conventionally seen, object. My students could do what they did, and do it in unison, because as members of a literary community they knew what a poem was ... and that knowledge led them to look in such a way as to populate the landscape with what they knew to be poems. (Fish 1980: 331–32)

As with partisans of the beauty party, advocates of the power party differ on many specific issues. Marxist thinkers, for example, emphasize the role of social and economic infra-structure in explaining the production of literary works. The decision as to whether a literary work is included in the great books club reflects the interests of the prevailing ideology, which reflect the interests of the ruling class, which reflect the production structure in a society. Thus, for example, if a contemporary English critic recommended Defoe's *Robinson Crusoe*, he was in fact reflecting – knowingly or unknowingly – the ethos of individualism and capitalism that was developing in eighteenth-century England, embodying the interests of the growing bourgeoisie and reflecting the accelerated industrialization the country was going through at the time.

Leo Trotsky, one of the leaders of the Soviet revolution and an opponent of Stalin (assassinated, in exile, by an agent of Stalin), also wrote some essays on art and literature. One of his most interesting pieces, written in 1923, is devoted to an acerbic polemic against the Formalists in general and Shklovsky in particular. The essay not only gives a glimpse into the intellectual atmosphere and debates of the Twenties in Russia but also provides some lucid formulations of the relationship between literature and historical reality. The Marxist approach to literature, Trotsky assures the reader, does not mean that literature is created by economics nor does it entail dictating the content and topics of artistic creation:

> It is unquestionably true that the need for art is not created by economic conditions. But neither is the need for food created by economics. On the contrary, the need for food and warmth creates economics. It is very true that one cannot always go by the principles of Marxism in deciding whether to reject or to accept a work of art. A work of art should, in the first place, be judged by its own law, that is, by the law of art. But Marxism alone can explain why and how a given tendency in art has originated in a given period of history; in other words, who it was who made a demand for such an artistic form and not for another, and why. (Trotsky 1996 [1923]: 56)

Against the formalist description of art, focusing on language and form as (according to Trotsky) isolated, independent and dominant entities, Trotsky stresses the interconnectedness of language, literature, culture and social reality. True, literature has its autonomy and its laws, but in order to *explain* the "why and how" of literary phenomena, one has to resort to the social base. The Formalists' attribution to language of an independent, privileged status is a clear indication of their "idealism" – the ultimate insult a Marxist can hurl at an opponent:

> The Formalist school represents an abortive idealism applied to the questions of art. The Formalists show a fast ripening religiousness. They are followers of St. John. They believe that 'In the beginning was the Word'. But we believe that in the beginning was the deed. The word followed, as its phonetic shadow. (Trotsky 1996 [1923]: 59)

Some Neo-Marxist thinkers suggest more sophisticated versions of the relations between infra socio-economic 'base' and literature as part of society's 'superstructures'. While accepting the idea that the structure of production is at the base of human history, they acknowledge the autonomy of superstructure systems (ideology, art, law) and the dialectical relationship between the two levels.[7] Concepts like 'reflection', 'ideology', 'language', 'structure', 'form' (and even 'determine') receive different meanings in the conceptual frameworks developed by Lukács, Williams, Balibar and Machery, Jameson and Eagleton.[8]

An interesting version of Neo-Marxism can be found in Lucien Goldmann, who proposed the concept of *homology* as a mediator between literary form and factors operative on the level of the 'base.' He first developed and applied the idea of homology to an analysis of Pascal and Racine in France of the seventeenth century and then also to the modern novel:

> The novel form seems to me, in effect, to be the transposition on the literary plane of everyday life in the individualistic society created by market production. There is a rigorous homology between the literary form of the novel, as I have defined it with the help of Lukács and Girard, and the everyday relation between man and commodities in general, and by extension between men and other men, in a market society. (Goldmann 1996 [1963]: 210)

Later in the essay, Goldmann outlines a few points that characterize a Marxist position within the sociology of literature. One of these points makes reference to great achievements in literature:

> The relation between the collective ideology and great individual literary, philosophical, theological, etc. creations resides not in an identity of content, but in a more advanced coherence and in a homology of structures, which can be expressed in imaginary contents very different from the real content of the collective consciousness. (Goldmann 1996 [1963]: 212)

Thus the concept of homology of structure emerges in the discussion of literary forms and genres as well as that of specific works. A great literary achievement is strongly connected to the "collective consciousness" in which it was produced, but the affinities are not necessarily found in particular themes or content. Thus, a great work is not necessarily a direct product of social reality and collective consciousness, but it manifests the contemporary structure of both.

The second half of the twentieth century in France was a fertile ground for intellectual controversies in the humanities, especially in sociology, philosophy and history. One important figure that emerged from the debates between Marxists, Existentialists and Structuralists was Michel Foucault, who can be seen as an honorary member of the power party. For it was he who gave such an important place to the concept of power in understanding social interactions. For Foucault, the concept of power is quite broad; it is not understood in a negative and narrow meaning, as a repressive element, nor is it confined to its use by the state:

> What makes power hold good, what makes it accepted, is simply the fact that it doesn't only weigh on us as a force that says no, but that it traverses and produces things, it induces pleasure, forms knowledge, produces discourse. It needs to be considered as a productive network which runs through the whole social body, much more than as a negative instance whose function is repression. (Foucault 1984: 61)

Thus, power should be looked for, and found, not only in traditional, official sites; in a sense, structures of power, manipulations of power are everywhere in the social fabric. In addition to focusing attention on ubiquitous mechanisms of power, coercions and enticements, Foucault is also famous for challenging the concept of the author:

> The author does not precede the work; he is a certain functional principle by which, in our culture, one limits, excludes, and chooses; in short, by which one impedes the free circulation, the free manipulation, the free composition, decomposition, and recomposition of fiction. In fact, if we are accustomed to presenting the author as a genius, as a perpetual surging of invention, it is because, in reality, we make him function in exactly the opposite fashion. One can say that the author is an ideological product, since we represent him as the opposite of his historically real function. (Foucault 1984: 118–119)

Any talk about "this author, who wrote a universally accepted masterpiece, is a genius" can be doubly unmasked as a statement representing in fact a power structure. Not only is "a universally accepted masterpiece" a product of a specific mechanism of power and hegemony, assigning high cultural values to some chosen artifacts, but also the very concept of "this author" and "genius" are part of the manipulation – exclusion, limitations, coercion, enticement – exercised by the mechanism of power.

Whereas advocates of the beauty party focus on a-historical concepts such as masterpieces, canon and genius (Clark 1979; Bloom 1994, 2002), partisans of the power party emphasize the historical circumstances in which the literary work is produced and received. Contrary to T. S. Eliot and Harold Bloom, thinkers suspect of essentialism, Hans Robert Jauss's *Towards an Aesthetic of Reception* offers, according to Paul de Man, a new perspective "no longer directed toward the definition of an actual canon but toward the dynamic and dialectical process of canon formation," and Jauss's concept of horizon of expectation "is never available in objective or even objectifiable form, neither to its author nor to its contemporaries or later recipients" (Jauss 1982: xi–xii).

Another influential contribution to the power party can be found in the thinking of Pierre Bourdieu and his concept of the literary field. Bourdieu draws (in his Figure 1) three rectangles contained in each other, and gives the following explanation:

> In figure 1, the literary and artistic field (3) is contained within the field of power (2), while possessing a relative autonomy with respect to it, especially as regards its economic and political principles of hierarchization. It occupies a *dominated position* (at the negative pole) in this field, which is itself situated at the dominant pole of the field of class relations (1). It is thus the site of a double hierarchy: the *heteronomous* principle of hierarchization, which would reign unchallenged if, losing all autonomy, the literary and artistic field were to disappear as such (so that writers and artists became subject to the ordinary laws prevailing in the field of power, and more generally in the economic field), is *success*, as measured by indices such as book sales, number of theatrical performances, etc. or honours, appointments, etc. The *autonomous* principle of hierarchization, which would reign unchallenged if the field of production were to achieve total autonomy with respect to the laws of the market, is degree specific consecration (literary or artistic prestige), i.e. the degree of recognition accorded by those who recognize

no other criterion of legitimacy than recognition by those whom they recognize. In other words, the specificity of the literary and artistic field is defined by the fact that the more autonomous it is, i.e. the more completely it fulfils its own logic as a field, the more it tends to suspend or reverse the dominant principle of hierarchization; but also that, whatever its degree of independence, it continues to be affected by the laws of the field which encompasses it, those of economic and political profit. The more autonomous the field becomes, the more favourable the symbolic power balance is to the most autonomous producers and the more clear-cut is the division between the field of restricted production, in which the producers produce for other producers, and the field of large-scale production [*la grande production*], which is symbolically excluded and discredited (this symbolically dominant definition is the one that the historians of art and literature unconsciously adopt when they exclude from their object of study writers and artists who produced for the market and have often fallen into oblivion) (Bourdieu 1993: 37–38).

Bourdieu was quoted at some length because his conceptual and terminological framework, while influenced by Marx and Foucault, insists on the autonomy of the literary field. According to Bourdieu, the symbolic power assigned within the literary field is autonomous not only in the sense that it is not a direct function of general social and economic factors; at times, this symbolic power (recognition, status, honor) can be a *reversed* function of social and economic powers: the fact that a book is a best seller can become a disadvantage in the eyes of those who assign symbolic power within the literary field (e.g. academic critics). And, in a more general perspective, historiographers can be biased against works which have gained economic success, and thus contribute to their falling into oblivion.

Bourdieu's concept of cultural and literary field was applied by C. J. Van Rees to the question of a literary masterpiece (Van Rees 1983). Van Rees proposes a systematic account of the mechanisms of criticism as the major factor for assigning the status of a masterpiece to a literary work, distinguishing between three levels of criticism: journalistic reviewers, essayists and academic critics, arguing that "the contributions made by the three distinct types of critics *complement* each other" (Van Rees 1983: 400). His approach directly challenges an assumption made by advocates of the beauty party: "what is decisive in text's valorization and in its being awarded more or less quality is the number of critical discourse written on this text and not, as is currently assumed, its allegedly intrinsic properties" (398). While assigning a decisive role to institutionalized criticism and especially to reputed academic critics, Van Rees does not believe that the critics' rankings are based on any privileged insights into intrinsic textual qualities (409). A critic applies certain implied normative concepts of what is literature and her/his reputation reflects only her/his position within the hierarchical system of the institution of criticism (and "an academic critic's reputation is made if he succeeds in coining certain terms," 408). As long as one is interested in investigating certain aspects of the institution of literary criticism, one can be satisfied with Van Rees's perspective. But there is a long way between adopting this basically sociological perspective on criticism and offering a satisfactory account of how a literary work becomes a masterpiece. Institutional *arbiter elegantiae*, ancient and modern alike, has usually less power to dictate enduring canonicity than he/she would like to think. Van Rees admits, for instance, that a critic's credence is partly based on the fact that her/his assessment "is believed to be compatible with the reputation already enjoyed by an author" (413). But from where such an independent reputation can emerge if all that we have according to Van Rees is an autonomous institution of criticism perpetuating its own hierarchies.

Richard Ohmann also proposes a hierarchical model for describing and explaining canon formation according to which after the "sifting" made by reviews in literary journals, come the decisive step performed by the academia: "the college classroom and its counterpart, the academic journal, have become in our society the final arbiters of literary merit, and even of survival" (Ohmann 1983: 206). Ohmann's perspective, however, also pays tribute to "bottom-up" processes of attaining large readership: "novels moved toward a canonical position only if they attained both large sales (usually, but not always, concentrated enough to place them among the best-sellers for a while) and the right kind of critical attention" (ibid.). As a Neo-Marxist, Ohmann relates both "top-down" value-endowing activities of the academia, and "bottom-up" processes of reaching large readership to class interests. This class is the "Professional-Managerial," characterized as sharing "one relation to the bourgeoisie and another to the working class" (Ohmann 1983: 209). The attempt to characterize the specific interests of this class and, more importantly, what are its values and how they are translated into the realm of preferring certain literary works over others, yields some complicated arguments leading to the assertion that this class promotes a dominant ideology that has at its root, for example, "the premise of individualism" (219). Ohmann is also aware of the fact that the promotion of certain ideals by an ideological hegemony does not exclude a critical attitude of authors towards these ideals (Ibid). At this point one may wonder whether individualism is unique to the "Professional-Managerial" class and, if not, and if authors may also treat some ideals critically, what explanatory power do the notions of class and hegemony have. Ohmann's emphasis on both "top-down" and "bottom-up" processes seems valid. But if we call attention to readership, critics and the academia, why should we exclude other kinds of dialogues generated by texts (e.g. adaptations)? Another crucial question left unanswered by Ohmann's argument is: How exactly do the interests of the "Professional-Managerial" class affect the shaping of the already established canon, including figures such as Homer and Shakespeare.

Another offshoot of Bourdieu can be found in the book-length study of John Guillory (1993). The author develops the concept of 'cultural capital' as distinguishable from money or material goods but still part of social structure and power. Guillory is quite convincing when he argues that contemporary attacks on the Western Canon by marginalized groups (women, blacks) miss the point in their demand to be more represented, because the way the canon is "representative" differs from representing constituencies in the legislative and governmental institution. He argues that instead of focusing attention on the specific composition of university reading lists, syllabus and curricula, critical attention should be given to the school system, responsible for preserving and transmitting the 'canon' which is part of a person's acquired cultural capital: "Canonicity is not the property of the work itself but of its transmission, its relation to other works in the collocation of works – the syllabus in its institutional locus, the school" (Guillory 1993: 55). Guillory's comprehensive study seems symptomatic of a specific version of Neo-Marxism: while presenting itself in the introduction as "sociologically informed" (x), the study focuses almost entirely on detailed, highly complicated analyses of *texts* (e.g., Cleanth Brook's reading of the Metaphysical poets), intended primarily to expose their ideological presuppositions and their tacit assumptions about what is, and should be, the canon. Whereas one can find a few thoughtful observations in these lengthy analyses, they cite almost no actual facts of social reality.

These quotations, mainly taken from Marxist and Neo-Marxists thinkers of the power party, can show there is a wide range of positions as to the specific relationship between literature and social reality and social power structures: positions that see literature as another product of the base, arguing that the ultimate explanation of literary phenomena is to be found within social reality (Trotsky); an approach that rejects the model of causal relations and develops the idea of homological relations between social reality and literature (Goldmann); a theory which uncovers the power structure and hegemonic interests motivating every cultural act and every discursive act (Foucault); a position stressing the autonomy of the literary field vis-à-vis social and economic structures (Bourdieu); elaborating on the concept of cultural capital as an autonomous structure and on its relation to canon formation (Guillory). Despite all these interesting and significant differences, advocates of the power party share the argument that supporters of the beauty party who assign to some books the status of greatness serve (either innocently or in *mauvaise foi*) the interests of ruling hegemonies.[9]

Certain statements coming from advocates of the power party have generated criticism from scholars and critics fearing that adopting its perspective would lead to reducing the literary work to a social document and thus impoverishing our experience of it. Criticism of the power party does not come only, as expected, from advocates of aesthetic values. When Charles Altieri, for example, argues "that it is a mistake to read cultural history only as a tawdry melodrama of interests pursued and ideologies produced" (Altieri 1983: 37), he rejects historicist reductive readings of literary texts, insisting on "partially reading against historical specificity, so as to highlight those qualities of the work that transcend the genetic situation" adding that "We need the specificity of a work, need it to maintain an otherness with something different to say to us" (57). Whereas Altieri points out that "Models of dialogue like Hans-Georg Gadamer's tend to deny this difference," the notion of a genuine dialogue proposed in this study allows, even encourages this difference as a vital part of the dynamics of reading a literary work which does not necessarily conform to our set of beliefs.

The Two Parties: Another Angle

The distinction between the beauty and the power parties partly overlaps another distinction: between certain value-charged approaches to the question "What is a great book?" and some factual and institutional aspects of canon formation. In other words, the question "What is a great book?" can camouflage two different questions: (1) "What are the institutional aspects of canon formation?" which is a *factual* question and (2) "What constitutes literary greatness?" begetting many answers that depend on the critic's viewpoints (aesthetic, ideological or what have you).[10] Indeed, we should be cautious not to confuse factual or sociological observations and statements deriving from a personal set of criteria about the desired nature of great books. A statement like "the Ministry of Education has a great role in determining curricula in high schools and hence in establishing the literary canon" and a statement like "a great work of art has to express the depth of human nature" do not address the same question.

Thus we can discern two different focuses and two different sets of questions, two different logics (empirical vs. personal) that do not interfere with each other. Theoretically, people holding a specific set of aesthetic criteria can accept the results of empirically oriented sociological research but still adhere to their personal predilections and tastes (e.g., "I grant that *Hamlet* holds a central place in the Western Canon, but I still think it to be a verbose and pretentious work hence not a truly great book."). And a study focusing on the institutional aspects of status-gaining can ignore the value-charged aspects of the field ("I don't care about the aesthetic value of this work, the only thing that matters to me is whether it was included or excluded from the curriculum of a Great Books course"). Despite that separation, these issues are not totally unrelated. What happens, for example, when people want to promote their views and values about what constitutes a great work? The moment we try to go beyond merely pronouncing our value-charged beliefs and pointing to specific works ("I believe a truly great work is and should be short; look at Sappho's lyric poetry"), when we try to corroborate this personal belief, we will inevitably step into the realm of facts and institutional reality ("Look how the short poems of Sappho have won the admiration of generations of readers," where the second half of the sentence already reaches into supposed facts). In a complementary way, during a factual study of institutional aspects of canon formation some methodological decisions are inevitably "tainted" with value-charged presuppositions. Should we consider Oprah Winfrey's book club an important factor, side by side with college Great Books courses, as representing the contemporary literary canon? There are dozens of methodological decisions that any sociologically oriented research has to take when dealing with the question of the literary canon – and none of them is value-free and all of them possess certain aesthetic and ideological implications about what is right and wrong, good and bad, in good or bad taste.

Thus, while acknowledging the different agenda that can be camouflaged behind the big question of "What is a great book?" we should also be aware that they belong to one and the same broad field. In that respect, the two sets of questions – factual-institutional and personal-criteria-charged – roughly correspond to the two parties outlined before: the power party is closely related to factual-institutional questions and the beauty party (especially if we widen our understanding of aesthetic terms) is related to the personal-criteria-charged perspective. And while partisans of the two parties can pursue parallel lines of investigation, it is also not surprising that they often step on each other's toes, precisely because they ultimately relate to the same broad field.

Deciding between the Two Parties

Each of the prevailing parties has some appealing arguments and it is difficult to dismiss either of them. The beauty party sheds light on a deep reason that makes us read literary works – the pleasure of the aesthetic experience they provide. It can also explain many cases where a book that has gained eminent status demonstrates a conspicuous set of aesthetic qualities. The power party, on the other hand, uncovers some important mechanisms which confer on a book the status of a great book. Status and status-gaining are, after all, sociological concepts, and institutions like schools, colleges, critics, literary historians, endowments for the arts, literary prizes (among others) do play a crucial role in a book's way to fame and glory as well as its retention of them.

So if each party has its strong points and they differ on some basic assumptions, perhaps all we can do is choose sides according to personal predilections and individual sympathies. If we try to put purely personal preferences aside and if forced to choose, the beauty party seems a preferable option.[11] First, because some arguments of the power party are patently circular: they explain the high prestige of a work by pointing to prestige-granting factors; explanation and explicandum are taken from the same domain. Secondly, because theories of the power party tend to deny the special experience of pleasure and awe that we have when reading a great book. Furthermore, some of these theories, by putting an emphasis on the role of "authorized communities" to determine a work's greatness undermine art's autonomy and the role of the individual reader in shaping her/his reaction to a specific work (Fishelov 1993b). True, advocates of the power party can come up with counter-arguments to these objections. They can suggest, for instance, that such objections stem from a "bourgeois ideology" assigning a special, fetishistic status to the literary work. Thus, we have to admit that these objections do not offer conclusive arguments that could tilt the scale once and for all in favor of the beauty party.

While we can see how the concepts of the two parties shed light on the complex question of "How and why does a literary work become a great book?" we also have to admit that they have their limitations – regardless of our personal sympathies or the arguments hitherto presented. First, both parties are too much entangled in ideological and political agenda.[12] Representatives of the beauty party are usually associated with a conservative approach, supposedly committed to protect the accepted Canon. Those of the power party, on the other hand, advocate a critical, radical outlook, in an attempt to reshape the existing canon, either through introducing silenced, marginalized voices or by exposing it as dependent on relativistic grounds.

Even when we try to neutralize the ideological motivations or commitments of the two parties (an impossible task, of course, according to the power party), they both have built-in shortcomings, limiting our understanding of the complex process by which a literary work achieves, and maintains, the status of a great book. The beauty party fails to explain the *dynamic* nature of the literary canon. If the aesthetic qualities of literary works are inherent, universal and objective (or inter-subjective), it is reasonable to assume that the list of great books would remain unchanged throughout the ages. But literary history shows us that this is not the case and that there are shifts, especially in the relative status of certain works within the canon. The power party, on the other hand, fails to explain the *stable* elements of the canon. If the status of a great book is a function of changing social and ideological hegemonies, we would expect the list to change dramatically with the permutations of economic, social and ideological hegemonies. But despite such influences, many literary works (Homer, Shakespeare and many others) keep their reputation as great books throughout the ages.

So if the two parties have strong points but also weaknesses, perhaps all we can do is choose one of them (because we like it; because we have some ideological convictions), and try to ignore its weak points, reiterating arguments against the other party in a typical dialogue-of-the-deaf. Or, perhaps, there is another way out of this conceptual circle.

CHAPTER

4

The Dialogic Approach to Great Books

To avoid the conceptual flaws of the two parties and their burden of ideological commitment a new approach is needed. But how can we formulate a new approach that will not look like another version of one of the two prevailing parties?[1] While thinking of ways to break the conceptual deadlock, the answer emerged from the very title of the "Dialogues with Great Books" course and in the realization that the link between the two key terms of the course's title was stronger than anticipated.[2]

Many and Diverse Dialogues

Even a superficial look at the list of great books chosen for the course showed that they have inspired many and diverse literary, artistic and critical echoes and (genuine and pseudo-) dialogues throughout the ages. This phenomenon, which led me to offer the course in the first place, seemed on second thought to be non-accidental. And if the chosen list can show us something general about the fate of great books, perhaps the two terms of the title are related on a deeper level. Thus, the leading hypothesis of this study: *a consensually perceived great book is one that evokes many and diverse types of literary, artistic and critical dialogues* (in the form of local allusions, epigraphs, parodies, translations, adaptations, pictorial, theatrical and cinematic representations, scholarly interpretations, etc.).

The different types of literary dialogues were discussed at some length in a previous chapter. Here we should explain two key terms added to the proposed definition of a great book. First, the quantitative adjective "many" should be understood as a relative term. It is obviously relative, first, to the size of the respective cultural community. To say that a literary work has inspired or generated one thousand echoes or dialogues is almost meaningless if one does not specify the size of the relevant literary community (or communities). When these thousand echoes are found in a community of one million people, something significant is being said about its impact; in a literary community of a hundred million – very little. Note also that when one speaks of numbers one has to take into account also the period, medium and means of communication. The base-line numbers of recorded echoes in a culture where reading and writing are limited to the social elite differ from the numbers detected in a culture based on mass media and modern communication systems.

Further, "many" is relative to neighboring literary works. It would be misleading to compare the sheer number of echoes left by a complex lyrical poem to that of a novel: the latter addresses, as a rule, a wider readership than the former and it is reasonable to assume that the number of its echoes, at least those of the passive kind, are going to be much higher. Thus, different genres, for example, may have different "coefficients" in comparing the numbers of 'echoes', and we can assign the adjective many only with these factors in mind.

Moreover, the various references to a literary work do not have a uniform weight or significance. Everyone who has conducted even a superficial search on the Internet has discovered the magnitude of irrelevant "junk" occurrences as well as the tendency of some of them to re-occur under somewhat different titles (e.g., a new edition of a book will show up in the publisher's site but also in many sites related to the publishing industry). Consequently, in conducting an Internet search we have to be cautious and use some pertinent "filters" eliminating redundancy and irrelevant results. In searching for echoes left by Homer's *Odyssey*, for example, we have to use both "Homer" and "Odyssey" because if we search for "Odyssey" alone, we may get many superfluous results related to travel agencies who like the term "Odyssey."

After taking into account the complex factors involved in determining whether a specific work has generated "many" dialogues, it became clear that relying on sheer quantitative criteria was partial and unsatisfactory. Moreover, the above definition introduces the principle of *diversity*. This factor is a crucial criterion, so crucial that it can sometimes outweigh the quantitative factor. The reasons for introducing this criterion are twofold. First, a look at the list of works chosen for my "Dialogues with Great Books" course showed that all of them have not only generated many typical literary echoes (e.g., translations, adaptations, allusions etc) but also other kinds of dialogues: paintings, movies, stage productions, critical discussions etc. Secondly, following a more theoretical consideration, the likelihood that a specific work will keep on inspiring readers (and authors) lies in the fact that its 'echoes' are heterogeneously distributed. If a work evokes many reactions but only of one kind – it is embraced by many critics but of one school of criticism or it sells many copies but only to a specified readership – its chance to join the "great books club" is significantly smaller than that of a work that evokes diverse reactions – embraced by critics of different schools of thought or read by diversified readerships.[3] In that respect, cultural phenomena may resemble a principle that can be found in biology: a species' chances of survival depend, ceteris paribus, on the *diversity* of its gene pool (Fishelov 1993a: 19–52). Literary and cultural phenomena, of course, have their specific characteristics, but they may also comply with some general principles of survival, dissemination and adaptation.[4]

Before presenting some data that came out of the leading hypothesis of this study, I offer two brief comments on thinkers who paved the way to the dialogical perspective.[5] Hans Robert Jauss, whose studies were mentioned earlier in presenting different thinkers of the power party, rightly points out that an artistic work of the past needs "the productive work of understanding in order to be taken out of the imaginary museum and appropriated by the interpretive eye of the present" (Jauss 1982: 75).[6] Jauss's position is closely related to the dialogic perspective and at one point he even makes use of the term dialogue when he proposes that history of art should be regarded "as a process of production and reception, in which not identical functions but *dialogical* structures of question and answer mediate between past and present" (74; my emphasis). The dialogical perspective, however, differs from Jauss's perspective on two fronts. First, by limiting the dialogical structures to that of "question and answer" Jauss seems to ignore a whole range of attitudes that present readers, writers, artists and critics can adopt towards works of the past. They can "answer" its "question" but they can also elaborate, argue against, misplace, parody, pay homage to it (among other things). Furthermore, the dialogical structures of re-interpretation, reception and production take part, according to Jauss, in "the intellectual and emancipatory function of art" (74). Whereas one can hail this elevated social function, there is no reason to postulate such emancipatory or liberating function in the historiography of art and literature. As with forms of dialogues, so with functions of art: they are more diverse than the one favored by us.[7]

Barbara Herrnstein Smith, in her description of literary and cultural endurance, rightly calls attention to the close relationships between the assignment of value to certain literary works and their continuing cultural reproduction. A work that has fulfilled certain functions for a community at a specific time and place has a better chance not only to be physically preserved but will also be "more frequently read or recited, copied or reprinted, translated, imitated, cited, commented upon, and so forth – in short, culturally re-produced" (Smith 1988: 48). Smith's insightful description – to which the present study owes much – lacks, however, two things. First, her emphasis on texts as fulfilling given social functions plays down the power of certain texts to resist social demands and sometimes even to re-shape them. Secondly, while Smith's description of the dynamics of cultural and literary endurance seems convincing, her generalizations are not accompanied by any specific models or facts to corroborate them. The dialogic approach acknowledges the potential of certain qualities in texts to generate many and diverse cultural "re-productions" and, most importantly, attempts to develop certain models, methods and research tools that would enable us not only to identify patterns of text-procreation but also to empirically test a few hypotheses about the correlations between a canonical status assigned to a work and the generation of echoes and dialogues.

The Dialogic Approach: Some Facts, for a Change

The dissatisfaction with ongoing futile ideological debates about the canon has spurred some researchers to look for quantitative aspects of the issue. Let me briefly mention here three such attempts. Charles Murray has accomplished in his *Human Accomplishment* (Murray 2003) the task of compiling lists of scientists, philosophers and artists representing the highest achievements in their respective fields. The only problem with Murray's highly impressive work is its restriction to historiographies, encyclopedias, and dictionaries, thus ignoring other, equally important, dialogic dimensions involved in the process by which a literary and artistic work acquires greatness. Another pertinent work in this context is David Damrosch's study of the changes in the canonical status of some British Romantics as reflected in MLA International Bibliography entries (Damrosch 2006). The author proposes a useful, three levels system operative within the canon: a *hypercanon* (or consensual "major" authors), a *countercanon* (or "contestatory" voices of "newcomers") and a *shadow canon* (or "minor" canonical authors). Using MLA data, Damrosch shows how the third level of *shadow canon* is mostly affected by the changing attention of critics and scholars. As with Murray's book, however, Damrosch's illuminating discussion gives too much weight to the role of scholarly works in canon formation. Marc Verboord (Verboord 2003) represents another interesting attempt to apply quantitative methods to the issue of canon formation. First, the author persuasively presents certain conceptual and methodological shortcomings associated with the use of the term 'canon' (e.g. its quasi-descriptive quasi-laudatory use), thus choosing to examine different indicators of what he prefers to call *literary prestige* within the literary field (a perspective especially indebted to Bourdieu and Van Rees). Verboord launches a systematic and comprehensive analysis of different critical institutions or players on the literary field: literary prizes, academic studies (scholarly journals, monographs), literary encyclopedias, prizes for popular literature, encyclopedias of popular literature and publishing houses. Analysis of the separate databases may indeed tell us something interesting about an author's literary prestige, but Verboord's attempt to integrate all indicators into one comprehensive list of ranking yields some counterintuitive, disappointing results. In the concluding table of the study (Table 9, Verboord 2003: 278), summing up the ranking of authors by their institutional literary prestige, we find, for example, that Philip Roth is fourth from top whereas Leo Tolstoy has to settle for the twenty fourth position (and Thomas Mann for twenty fifth). Verboord's study can remind us that in addition to rigorous statistical methods one should also use common sense when integrating statistical results from different sources.

The remaining part of this chapter is devoted to a presentation of a few results obtained in some searches, following the hypothesis that connects the assumed greatness of a book with the quantity and diversity of echoes and dialogues it evokes. Technically, the Internet was used for all my searches.

Note, however, that some of the searches focused on traditional databases (e.g., a library catalogue), and the Internet provided only a convenient means of communication.

Rather than conduct random searches, my point of departure was three existing, independent lists of "great books" from three "traditional" sources: *Norton Anthology of World Masterpieces* edited by Maynard Mack et al. (1997), David Denby's *Great Books* (1996), tracing the curriculum of a Great Books course taught at Columbia University during the nineties, and the entries in *Masterpieces of World Literature* by Frank N. Magill (1952). This point of departure has at least one obvious methodological advantage: it safeguards the searches from becoming totally circular. If I had focused on works I thought to be (famous) great books, the chances are that the searches would only corroborate my initial (intuitive) belief in their fame. True, the fact that my point of departure consisted of lists of books that have already gained greatness in the view of the editors or (in the case of Denby) professors did not make my search "innocent." But by relying on these lists the searches were by no means tailored to my personal taste or educational background. Even more importantly, these lists are independent not only of my personal favorites but also provide a valuable *independent* reference point for the searches. To examine the *correlation* between works which have gained a consensual canonical status and the number and diversity of generated echoes and dialogues is not to define the one by means of the other.

Since my leading hypothesis was that great books leave traces on different levels of culture, the number and diversity of echoes and dialogues generated by the books on the three lists were checked by using four different search engines:

1. Google; this popular, all inclusive search engine was deliberately chosen to provide a rough approximation of the work's general distribution in Western, English speaking culture. As already mentioned, the greatest problem with Google was to avoid as much as possible retrieving "junk" results.[8]
2. Google-Image; this search engine shows images related to a work: paintings of the major characters, book jackets, etc. To use this search engine might lead to something valuable not only because literary works serve as a source for many visual artists, but also because sometimes images related to a work become an important association or even focal point related to that work (e.g., Hamlet with Yorick's skull).
3. The Clio search engine of Columbia University; as opposed to the first two searches, this database represents a more "elitist" domain. There is a relatively serious and meticulous process of selection, done by experts and scholars, before an item (usually but not exclusively a book) is purchased and shelved in a university library.[9]
4. Finally, International Movie Database (IMDb). This search engine

traces all movie adaptations and productions based on specified literary works.

These four engines can provide a heuristic picture of "traces" left by literary works in different layers of culture: different media, genres (literary as well as scholarly) and social strata (popular and elitist). As expected, the results obtained in the Google searches yielded the largest numbers and those of IMDb the smallest. This of course is not surprising, because to produce a movie is a relatively costly business. We should note, however, that the production of movies involves a variety of artists (screenwriters, camera men, director, actors, etc.) and reaches a wide audience.

First, the four searches were conducted for works listed in my three source books. Then a separate table was constructed for the search results of seventeen works that appear in all three sources. This group, representing a relatively high consensus on merit and status, may be labeled "the hard core" of the series. TABLE 4.1 presents the results obtained for the seventeen works included in all three sources. It should be emphasized that this list of titles is very partial: most works in Denby's *Great Books*, for example, belong to the pre-modern world and thus some novelists of the nineteenth and twentieth centuries who are consensually perceived as authors of great books (e.g. Tolstoy, Joyce among others) are not represented. Thus, the list should not be taken as representing THE hard core of THE canon but only "the hard core" *of the three sources*, serving to examine the correlation between patterns of dissemination and the consensual status of a work. While some of these correlations are indicative of the way works gain and maintain their status as great books, my purpose in focusing on this list (alphabetically ordered by the works' title) is by no means to offer an authoritative list of great books.

The results in TABLE 4.1 represent searches done during March 2009. Needless to say, some of these results keep changing, especially in Google and Google-Image, indicating the extremely rapid growth of the Internet.

To get a bird's-eye-view of the results, we can reduce the specific numbers to numbers of digits, and get the following TABLE 4.2.

The search results of the "hard core" works showed a relatively high degree of consistency. They were characterized by high numbers of occurrences in the specific searches as well as a wide range of distribution among different genres and media. Further, as TABLE 4.2 demonstrates, these results formed a distinct pattern: when the search results of Google were an X digit number, the results of the Google-Image were an X minus one or (more rarely) two digit numbers, the Clio searches were an X minus three or four digit numbers and the results of the IMDb search were an X minus four, five or six digit number (e.g., in searches for *Tartuffe*, the Google result is a six-digit number, Google-Image a five-digit number, Clio a three-digit number and IMDb a two-digit number).[10]

Of course, this formula is based on partial and to a certain degree arbitrary decisions (the choice of the specific search engines etc.), but still it is symptomatic and not insignificant.[11] To illustrate why it is significant, let us look at

52 | *What Is a Dialogue? What Is a Great Book?*

TABLE 4.1
Results of Searches of the Canon's "Hard Core"

Work	Google	Google, Image	Clio, Columbia	IMDb
Aeneid – Virgil	479,000	22,500	409	7[12]
Antigone – Sophocles	303,000	13,500	340	19
Candide – Voltaire	579,000	45,100	170	5
Divine Comedy – Dante	602,000	54,200	233	1
Don Quixote – Cervantes	796,000	51,600	956	50[13]
Faust – Goethe	1,540,000	113,000	952	7
Gargantua and Pantagruel – Rabelais[14]	238,000	16,900	139	0
Gulliver's Travels – Swift[15]	579,000	54,200	196	15
Hamlet – Shakespeare	4,500,000	424,000	1,125	58
Iliad – Homer	1,430,000	59,000	998	5
Medea – Euripides	276,000	12,800	223	8
Odyssey – Homer	3,250,000	146,000	785	15
Oedipus Rex – Sophocles[16]	384,000	16,600	248	12
Paradise Lost – Milton	1,140,000	54,500	868	3
Prometheus Bound – Aeschylus[17]	128,000	5,190	183	0
Tartuffe – Molière	292,000	28,300	157	13

TABLE 4.2
The Number of Digits of Results for the "Hard Core"

Work	Google	Google, Image	Clio, Columbia	IMDb
Aeneid – Virgil	6	5	3	1
Antigone – Sophocles	6	5	3	2
Candide – Voltaire	6	5	3	1
Divine Comedy – Dante	6	5	3	1
Don Quixote – Cervantes	6	5	3	2
Faust – Goethe	7	6	3	1
Gargantua and Pantagruel – Rabelais	6	5	3	0
Gulliver's Travels – Swift	6	5	3	2
Hamlet – Shakespeare	7	6	4	2
Iliad – Homer	7	5	3	1
Medea – Euripides	6	5	3	1
Odyssey – Homer	7	6	3	2
Oedipus Rex – Sophocles	6	5	3	2
Paradise Lost – Milton	7	5	3	1
Prometheus Bound – Aeschylus	6	4	3	0
Tartuffe – Molière	6	5	3	2

some results of works that were not part of the "hard core." TABLE 4.3 contains the search results obtained for four works mentioned only in Magill's *Masterpieces of World Literature*:

TABLE 4.3
Results of Searches of Works with Ephemeral Success

Work	Google	Google, Image	Clio, Columbia	IMDb
"Abe Lincoln in Illinois" – Rohert E. Sherwood	32,500	3[18]	11	4
Dear Brutus – J. M. Barrie	898	23	6	0
Nocturne – Frank Arthur Swinnerton	1,400	0	4	0
Wreck of the Grosvenor – William Clark Russell	403	6	0	0

Note that these results are characterized, first, by dramatically smaller overall numbers and secondly they show uneven distribution in different genres and media. Among other things, they corroborated my initial impression that Magill's list was based on biased selection criteria, favoring English and American works of the first half of the twentieth century. They may also tell us something about the fate of works that enjoy ephemeral critical acclaim.

To further corroborate the leading hypothesis that the number and diversity of echoes and dialogues a work generates affect its canonical status, I checked (during May 2009) two works, Sophocles' *Ajax* and *Philoctetes*, which were part of the Literature Humanities list at Columbia in 1961–62 but were dropped at some point and were not included in the 1991 list (Denby 1996: 466).

TABLE 4.4
Results of Searches of Two Works Dropped from Literature Humanities

Work	Google	Google, Image	Clio, Columbia	IMDb
Sophocles, *Ajax*	115,000	3,770	126	0
Sophocles, *Philoctetes*	70,500	3,120	129	0

The results clearly indicate that general dissemination has an effect on a work's canonical status, as reflected in university reading lists:[19] compared to Sophocles' *Oedipus Rex*, which was continuously part of the reading lists, the search results of the two plays are significantly lower in all search engines (notably in film adaptations: 12 of *Oedipus Rex* compared to none). A similar pattern can be detected with works that were once included in *Norton Anthology of World Masterpieces* but were taken out of its 3rd edition (Mack 1997). Focusing again on Sophocles, we can see how *Oedipus at Colonus* shows significantly lower numbers: 113,000 in Google, 5,630 in Google-Image, 116 in Clio and only 1 in IMDb. These numbers seem to tell the same story: academic, status-giving reading lists and anthologies are adjusting to represent works that have gained wide and diverse presence in culture.[20]

It is an interesting question whether the (relatively) large number of dialogues and echoes a book evokes during the first period of its publication guarantees even larger numbers later on, in what S. K. Merton called "the Matthew effect," referring to Matthew 25:29: "Unto every one that hath shall be given, and he shall have abundance; but from him that hath not shall be taken away even that which he hath." Charles Murray calls this "the accumulative advantage" (Murray 2003: 93–94).[21] Unfortunately, the results obtained were not analyzed according to the original generation date of each reference (which is virtually impossible when it comes to all-inclusive results from Google, for instance). Thus we cannot determine whether the formula would work here. My guess is that it might work in most cases, but not in all, and it would largely depend on the type of dialogue involved (for further discussion of this issue, see the section on *Candide* and *Rasselas* in this chapter). This is one of the questions that the dialogic perspective on the issue of great books opens for further investigation and makes the whole project worth pursuing, adducing various pertinent factors that affect the outcome of the process of generating echoes and dialogues: genre, period, culture.

Not every genre generates the same kinds of dialogue: a major way for a dramatic work to become a great book is to go on generating stage productions;[22] a lyric poem may acquire its reputation when it is anthologized and re-anthologized, and gets diversified critical readings. As for period: in the pre-Gutenberg era, a major factor in the survival and distribution of a literary work depended on its being manually copied (usually by monks) and consequently the number of manuscripts would be considered an important factor. In print culture, however, counting individual copies of a book may still matter, but one should add another important factor – the number of editions. And as for the cultural factor: certain cultures (e.g., the Russian) have a strong tradition of poetry reciting, and such live performances serve as a major way of transmitting and interpreting poetry, whereas in other traditions, the reading of poetry is mainly private and individual, in one's home.

To illustrate the special attention that we need to give to stage productions when discussing dialogues with dramatic works, let us look at some statistics of productions of the greatest author of plays: Shakespeare. A stage production is perhaps the most important dialogue a play could generate, because plays are mainly written to be put on stage: this is their *raison d'être* and their primary mode of living. Furthermore, a stage production is an efficient way to bring the text to a large audience and an opportunity for various artists (directors, actors, stage designers etc.) to show their talent and to offer their interpretation of the text. These interpretations vary greatly. Philip Edwards, for example, in his survey of recent stage productions of *Hamlet*, notes that "there have been many estimable Hamlets lately, but few outstanding

Hamlets" (Edwards 2003: 74) thus suggesting that the level of an actor's performance does not always agree with the level of the production as a whole. From our dialogic perspective, we can note different degrees of predictability, generating a whole range of dialogues that move from echo to genuine (and sometimes even a dialogue-of-the-deaf when a director uses the text to promote a personal agenda). TABLE 4.5 is taken from the database of The Designing Shakespeare Collections, which is part of AHDS (Arts and

TABLE 4.5
Number of Productions of Shakespeare's Plays

List of Plays (Alphabetically arranged)[23]	AHDS *(Arts and Humanities Data Services)*
A Midsummer Night's Dream	77
All's Well That Ends Well	11
Antony and Cleopatra	29
As You Like It	47
Comedy of Errors	24
Coriolanus	18
Cymbeline	15
Hamlet	82
Henry IV, parts 1 and 2	29
Henry V	28
Henry VI, parts 1, 2 and 3	14
Henry VIII	6
Julius Caesar	31
King John	7
King Lear	45
Love's Labour's Lost	20
Macbeth	82
Measure for Measure	33
Merchant of Venice, The	40
Merry Wives of Windsor, The	22
Much Ado About Nothing	33
Othello	35
Pericles	14
Richard II	25
Richard III	40
Romeo and Juliet	55
Taming Of The Shrew, The	33
Tempest, The	46
Timon of Athens	9
Titus Andronicus	10
Troilus and Cressida	20
Twelfth Night	67
Two Gentlemen of Verona	20
Winter's Tale, The	33

Humanities Data Services), available on the Internet.[24] This database has a very particular focus – the performance history of Shakespeare in Britain over the forty-year period 1960–2000. The database is thus limited to forty years in Britain, but within its limits it gives a good idea of the attractiveness of a play for theatre managers and directors. The five plays gaining most productions have been highlighted (in bold).

In the following TABLE 4.6 the performance results found in AHDS are added to the results of the four searches used earlier to trace references, echoes and dialogues with literary works. The top five in each of the respective searches are marked.

Note the relatively high correlation between all search results when it comes to the top of the list: in three of the top five of TABLE 4.5 there is a consistent agreement between all databases (i.e. *Hamlet*, *Macbeth* and *Romeo and Juliet*[25]). Thus, it seems that the same logic that we followed when trying to examine correlation between pattern of dissemination and consensual status of works with a claim to fame operates also when we focus our attention on one particular author (Shakespeare) and one particular genre (dramatic works): some writings of this greatest of dramatic poets stand out as generating more, and more kinds, of dialogues than others, and there is a conspicuous correlation between different layers of dissemination. Theoretically, there is no reason why one work would not gain many productions but only little scholarly attention (or the other way around). But when we check the actual figures of the greatest of the greatest, we find that only a small group of works consistently gain many stage productions, and movie adaptations, and editions, and scholarly discussions, and pictorial representations and many other general references in culture.[26]

Results are not always as clear as with Shakespeare's plays. In most cases, awareness of factors such as genre, period and culture would make our search for textual dialogues more complex, nuanced and multilayered and fill us with caution when we come to draw conclusions from the results obtained in technical searches.

The Booker Prize and the Limitations of Institutional Power

To further investigate the impact institutional, top-down factors have on the reputations of literary works, let us briefly examine the fate of novels that win the Man Booker Prize for Fiction. The prize, commonly known as the Booker, aims to reward the best novel of the year written by a citizen of the Commonwealth or the Republic of Ireland. Whereas there have been times when the prize was associated with literary scandals and its own reputation oscillated between the subversive and the respectful (English 2002; 2005: 203–5), about a decade after its inception it became the most influential British literary prize, capable of giving an enormous boost "in publicity, renown and book sales for its winner" (English 2002: 114) or in the language

The Dialogic Approach to Great Books | 57

TABLE 4.6
Shakespeare: Four Searches and Number of Productions

List of Plays (Alphabetically arranged)	Google[27] Image	Google-	Clio	IMDb[28]	AHDS
A Midsummer Night's Dream	911,000	59,400	277	34	77
All's Well That Ends Well	208,000	12,300	145	3	11
Antony and Cleopatra	305,000	16,700	235	12	29
As You Like It	736,000	51,000	274	12	47
Comedy of Errors	331,000	26,600	147	14	24
Coriolanus	270,000	13,200	205	4	18
Cymbeline	342,000	12,900	209	5	15
Hamlet	5,250,000	255,000	1,116	84	82
Henry IV, parts 1 and 2	545,000	27,300	323	5	29
Henry V	699,000	44,500	275	15	28
Henry VI, parts 1, 2 and 3	315,000	16,900	200	5	14
Henry VIII	479,000	53,700	152	4	6
Julius Caesar	945,000	69,700	306	18	31
King John	316,000	21,800	178	2	7
King Lear	1,030,000	72,800	549	25	45
Love's Labour's Lost	25,800	3,160	137	3	20
Macbeth	2,850,000	119,000	608	51	82
Measure for Measure	385,000	20,500	248	4	33
Merchant of Venice, The	625,000	40,300	286	24	40
Merry Wives of Windsor, The	167,000	14,200	141	13	22
Much Ado About Nothing	646,000	46,400	195	14	33
Othello	2,280,000	81,600	559	49	35
Pericles	436,000	15,000	145	2	14
Richard II	461,000	19,500	220	9	25
Richard III	691,000	45,100	275	21	40
Romeo and Juliet	1,930,000	107,000	436	121	55
Taming of the Shrew, The	378,000	30,700	176	27	33
Tempest, The	635,000	64,800	432	19	46
Timon of Athens	226,000	8,300	166	1	9
Titus Andronicus	263,000	17,800	171	5	10
Troilus and Cressida	195,000	10,200	187	4	20
Twelfth Night	816,000	61,600	248	23	67
Two Gentlemen of Verona	251,000	12,300	102	2	20
Winter's Tale, The	137,000	13,800	220	5	33

of the prize's official web site, it " has the power to transform the fortunes of authors and even publishers . . ." (http://www.themanbookerprize.com)

Thus, we can examine the Booker prize as a miniature test case for the overall dynamics of canon formation. The prize, alongside other prizes and awarded honors, is both a part (a synecdoche) of top-down factors responsible for advancing a literary work's reputation or prestige (English 2002; Verboord 2003) and perhaps also analogous to (hence a metaphor or parable of) the elusive dynamics of the canon. To assemble a committee (a "synod") composed of persons renowned in the literary field, to ask them to draw up a shortlist out of dozens of candidates (submitted by publishers) and then to select one book (and, by way of exception, two books) that will be elevated on a pedestal: this process can be seen as a mini-version of the complex, top-down processes of canon formation in general. Hence, to learn something about the fate of works that have won the Booker is also to have an indirect lesson about the power and limitations of top-down factors in the dynamics of canon formation.

An important indication of a work's canonical status is the number of scholarly articles written about it. Thus, my first search was for references in the MLA International Database to books that had won the Booker. The search focused on references during the ten years following the winning of the prize since its inception in 1969 to 1998.[29] Then I checked if there were references to the authors *before* they won the prize.[30] TABLE 4.7 presents the results of these two searches, enabling us to compare the impact of the prize on an author's fame, as far as it is represented in scholarly journals.

Even a superficial look shows at once that the list of Booker Prize winners is quite heterogeneous: out of thirty two authors of the chosen years, eleven were quite new faces on the literary scene with no prior scholarly references, a few others were very well established authors (e.g. Iris Murdoch, William Golding) and still others (e.g. Graham Swift, Ian McEwan) already enjoyed some reputation when they won the prize. As for the image of the Booker Prize as a sure guarantor for securing an author's place in the hall of fame, the MLA results might raise some questions about that popular (but unexamined) image. We can see that even after winning the prize, eight works did not stimulate the writing of any scholarly article (at least in the journals covered by the MLA Bibliography) and another five produced only a single article in the relevant period. Thus, about a third of the winning books evoked almost no echo on the level of scholarly discourse during the period that one expects to be most ripe for such a critical activity. There are, however, a few cases where winning the Booker seem to have played an important role in promoting critical and scholarly dialogues: six winning works initiated two-digit figures of scholarly response. The most impressive cases in that respect are those of Arundhati Roy and Salman Rushdie: the former moved from zero references before winning the prize to fifty-six devoted to *The God of Small Things* and the latter went, again from none, to twenty-four articles discussing *Midnight's Children*. Such impressive impact, however, is the exception, characterizing only a small minority of the winners. It is by no means the norm. The average number of scholarly articles devoted to winners of the Booker (6.625) might be higher than the average of a randomly chosen list of other literary prizes, but if we take into account the fact that winners who were already established authors (e.g. Iris Murdoch) would have had articles written about their work regardless of the prize, it seems that the impact the prize has on encouraging the writing of scholarly articles is not that impressive. In other words, if one

TABLE 4.7
The Impact of Winning the Booker in MLA

Year / Author, Title	MLA: Before the prize	MLA: During the decade after the winning
1969 / P. H. Newby, *Something to Answer For*	6	0
1970 / Bernice Rubens, *The Elected Member*	0	0
1971 / V. S. Naipaul, *In a Free State*	6	4
1972 / John Berger, *G.*	0	1
1973 / J. G. Farrell, *The Siege of Krishnapur*	0	1
1974 / Nadine Gordimer, *The Conservationist*	4	5
1974[31] / Stanley Middleton, *Holiday*	0	0
1975 / Ruth Prawer Jhabvala, *Heat and Dust*	4	5
1976 / David Storey, *Saville*	8	2
1977 / Paul Scott, *Staying On*	6	1
1978 / Iris Murdoch, *The Sea, the Sea*	131	3
1979 / Penelope Fitzgerald, *Offshore*	0	0
1980 / William Golding, *Rites of Passage*	212	5
1981 / Salman Rushdie, *Midnight's Children*[32]	0	24
1982 / Thomas Keneally, *Schindler's Ark*	34	1
1983 / J. M. Coetzee, *Life & Times of Michael K*	6	2
1984 / Anita Brookner, *Hotel du Lac*	0	0
1985 / Keri Hulme, *The Bone People*	0	14
1986 / Kingsley Amis, *The Old Devils*	71	0
1987 / Penelope Lively, *Moon Tiger*	2	4
1988 / Peter Carey, *Oscar and Lucinda*	10	4
1989 / Kazuo Ishiguro, *The Remains of the Day*	4	16
1990 / A. S. Byatt, *Possession: A Romance*	10	2
1991 / Ben Okri, *The Famished Road*	2	16
1992 / Michael Ondaatje, *The English Patient*	53	32
1992 / Barry Unsworth, *Sacred Hunger*	0	0
1993 / Roddy Doyle, *Paddy Clarke Ha Ha Ha*	0	3
1994 / James Kelman, *How Late It Was, How Late*	4	0
1995 / Pat Barker, *The Ghost Road*	7	1
1996 / Graham Swift, *Last Orders*	36	7
1997 / Arundhati Roy, *The God of Small Things*	0	56
1998 / Ian McEwan, *Amsterdam*	45	4

assumes that an author's lasting fame or reputation or prestige is secured by winning the Booker, one is bound to be disappointed.

It could be instructive to take a closer look at the two years where there were two winners: Nadine Gordimer's *The Conservationist* and Stanley Middleton's *Holiday* won together in 1974 and in 1992 Michael Ondaatje's *The English Patient* won together with Barry Unsworth's *Sacred Hunger*. But whereas the prize helped to promote the literary prestige of the two authors who already enjoyed varying degrees of literary fame (Gordimer and

Ondaatje), it left no marked effect whatsoever on the reputation of the other two winners (Middleton and Unsworth). This may lead us to believe that there are factors affecting the building of an author's reputation that are stronger than the mere winning of a literary prize, no matter how intensive its public relations.

To further examine the role played by the Booker within the overall context of an author's dissemination and reputation, searches were also conducted in four databases introduced earlier: Google, Google-Image, Clio and IMDb. TABLE 4.8 presents results of these four, together with the MLA search results (of the decade following the prize-winning), showing the number of references to the works.

These results seem to corroborate our reservation concerning the popular

TABLE 4.8
Winning the Booker: In Four Searches and MLA

Year / Author, Title	Google[33]	Google-Image	Clio	IMDb	MLA
1969 / P. H. Newby, *Something to Answer For*	2,810	334	3	0	0
1970 / Bernice Rubens, *The Elected Member*	711	277	3	0	0
1971 / V. S. Naipaul, *In a Free State*	15,900	3,800	7	0	4
1972 / John Berger, *G.*	210,000[34]	16,400	4	0	1
1973 / J. G. Farrell, *The Siege of Krishnapur*	22,300	2,250	4	0	1
1974 / Nadine Gordimer, *The Conservationist*	27,100	1,760	7	0	5
1974 / Stanley Middleton, *Holiday*	2,970	324	2	0	0
1975 / Ruth Prawer Jhabvala, *Heat and Dust*	13,800	1,870	9	1	5
1976 / David Storey, *Saville*	4,900	307	3	0	2
1977 / Paul Scott, *Staying On*	5,480	531	5	1	1
1978 / Iris Murdoch, *The Sea, the Sea*	57,300	2,410	6	0	3
1979 / Penelope Fitzgerald, *Offshore*	8,930	586	3	0	0
1980 / William Golding, *Rites of Passage*	13,400	1,770	3	0	5
1981 / Salman Rushdie, *Midnight's Children*	365,000	8,230	19	0	24
1982 / Thomas Keneally, *Schindler's Ark*	10,400	1,980	1	1	1
1983 / J. M. Coetzee, *Life & Times of Michael K*	16,800	550	9	0	2

Year / Author, Title					
1984 / Anita Brookner, *Hotel du Lac*	16,100	1,940	4	1	0
1985 / Keri Hulme, *The Bone People*	12,500	2,900	2	0	14
1986 / Kingsley Amis, *The Old Devils*	8,540	689	4	1	0
1987 / Penelope Lively, *Moon Tiger*	11,400	702	3	0	4
1988 / Peter Carey, *Oscar and Lucinda*	64,000	3,360	7	1	4
1989 / Kazuo Ishiguro, *The Remains of the Day*	**635,000**	**6,460**	**15**	**1**	**16**
1990 / A. S. Byatt, *Possession: A Romance*	64,000[35]	8,930	2	1	2
1991 / Ben Okri, *The Famished Road*	18,100	2,510	8	0	16
1992 / Michael Ondaatje, *The English Patient*	**72,900**	**7,560**	**13**	**1**	**32**
1992 / Barry Unsworth, *Sacred Hunger*	12,400	728	3	0	0
1993 / Roddy Doyle, *Paddy Clarke Ha Ha Ha*	27,400	2,430	5	0	3
1994 / James Kelman, *How Late It Was, How Late*	19,800	764	2	0	0
1995 / Pat Barker, *The Ghost Road*	41,400	2,740	2	0	1
1996 / Graham Swift, *Last Orders*	20,400	2,380	5	1	7
1997 / Arundhati Roy, *The God of Small Things*	**105,000**	**9,130**	**9**	**0**	**56**
1998 / Ian McEwan, *Amsterdam*	107,000	14,200	6	0	4

image of the Booker as a guarantor of literary fame. The Prize did not help some works to reach the wide, deep and varied dissemination which marks truly great books. Perhaps the Booker gave these writings a boost that went beyond "fifteen minutes of fame" – but not much beyond. Still, some works seem to have left a marked impression beyond timed-out, fleeting fame. To trace possible correlations between the different search results, the top five results are marked (in bold) in each search (in IMDb ten works are marked, because no work stimulated more than one movie adaptation; in Clio, two works that came up with nine references were marked). Of the thirty-two, four emerged as sharing at least four of the highest results in the different databases. As with the plays of Shakespeare discussed in the previous section, it seems that there is a recurring principle: the more we approach the top, the more we have *convergence* between different pertinent levels of dissemination and reputation.[36] In other words, by distinguishing itself on only one level (e.g. winning a prestigious literary prize) a work does not ensure its way to become a classic. However, if a work distinguishes itself on many different levels of dissemination and reputation, there is a good chance it will hold a place in the hall of fame. Or, to use the formula introduced earlier: a work's procreation enhances its reputation.

Furthermore, when we consider the Booker Prize as reflecting the role that institutional, top-down factors play in the dynamics of canonization, we can infer two important things. First, we will acknowledge the power of such institutions to single out certain works, to bestow monetary and symbolic capital on their authors, to dominate for a certain period the media and the buzz of literary life. Second and more important, we concede that this power is limited: after the flash-lights wane, the PR people have collected their fees and copies of the book have reached the public, other factors come into play. And most of these factors are not dominated by institutional agencies but ultimately have to do with the willingness of a writer, a painter, a translator, a scholar or a film-maker to become engaged in a dialogue with a specific work; true, the winning of a literary prize such as the Booker gives a book high visibility and increases the chances that it will evoke literary, artistic and critical dialogues. For such dialogues to actually occur, however, the work has to possess certain qualities that affect different readers, writers and artists.

The Race for Fame: *Candide*, *Rasselas* and QWERTY

In the year 1759, two works appeared, written by two prominent men of letters: Voltaire published *Candide* and at about the same time Samuel Johnson wrote and published *Rasselas*. If we imagine a race for fame between these two works conducted over the past two hundred and fifty years, there is no doubt that we shall pronounce Voltaire's *Candide* the winner. There are indications of its stronger position in today's republic of letters. When we browse, for example, through anthologies of literary masterpieces, the pattern seems consistent: the more selective the list is, the more likely it is to include Voltaire's work, but not Johnson's. Johnson's *Rasselas* (or selections from it) can of course be found in some respected anthologies devoted to English literature, such as *The Norton Anthology of English Literature* or *The Oxford Anthology of English Literature*, but when we move to an anthology such as *The Norton Anthology of Literary Masterpieces*, where more exclusive selection criteria were applied, or to lists of books comprising Great Books courses in some leading universities (e.g. at Columbia University, presented in Denby's *Great Books* 1996), *Candide* will still be present, but not *Rasselas*. The same applies to volumes offering lists of great books: *Rasselas* appears, for example, in Magill's *Masterpieces of World Literature* (1952), which contains about five hundred works, but disappears from Burt's *The Literary 100*, which undertakes to list the most influential novelists, playwrights, and poets of all time (Burt 2001).[37]

So why has *Candide* won this imaginary, but also quite real race for fame against *Rasselas*? It would be instructive to compare the fate of these two works, not only because they were published at almost the same time but also because they bear a few conspicuous similarities, noted by many readers and critics. Boswell, for example, tries in *The Life of Samuel Johnson* not only to vindicate Johnson of the charge of having been influenced by Voltaire's work, published about two months before *Rasselas*, but also to advocate the superior spiritual qualities of the work of his admired author: "Voltaire, I am afraid, meant only by wanton profaneness to obtain a sportive victory over religion, and to discredit the belief of a superintending Providence: Johnson meant, by shewing the unsatisfactory nature of things temporal, to direct the hopes of man to things eternal" (Boswell 1952: 241–42). When a French translation of *Rasselas* came out in 1760, a French reviewer, after pointing out the similarities between the two works, also stressed the nobler, less sensational nature of Johnson's work: "*Candide*, en un mot, nous rend en horreur à nous-même, & *Rasselas* nous fait les objets de notre proper compassion; il ne nous désespère pas; il nous invite seulement à nous corriger" (Johnson 1990: 255).

In terms of genre, both works are variations on a philosophical tale, inviting readers to reflect on moral issues and the meaning of life; they are both travel stories, taking their main characters to explore new countries and different cultures; both Candide and Rasselas, the characters, are young men who seek to broaden their intellectual horizons and deepen their existential experience and thus can be seen as precursors of the Bildungsroman; and during these travels, they are both accompanied by, at least part of the way, by an elderly, presumably wise person (Martin and Imlac). The two works even share a philosophical drive to rebut a naïve, optimistic view of life. Thus, it seems that both books enjoyed similar conditions at the starting point in the race for fame. To consider why one of them ended up as a clear winner might show us something important about the dynamics and endurance of literary fame.

In seeking an explanation, we can of course opt for some pre-prepared positions of the two prevalent parties presented earlier. To explain *Candide*'s stronger standing as based either on aesthetic qualities or on social hegemonies, however, would be quite unsatisfactory. There is no reason to assume, for example, that parody, burlesque and satire, most evident in *Candide*, are "better" aesthetic qualities than the subtle irony and the serious tone of Johnson in *Rasselas*. And to prove that Voltaire's story has been continuously promoted during the past two and a half centuries by social and ideological hegemonies one would have to adopt a large set of convoluted assumptions.[38] If we choose to stick to either of these ready-made positions, we would commit ourselves to many, too many complicated presuppositions concerning questionable hierarchies of aesthetic values or speculations about the way an assumed zeitgeist dictates the promotion or rejection of literary works.

The dialogic approach suggests a more promising direction: *Candide* has won the race for fame because it has generated a wider and more varied series of echoes and dialogues throughout the ages. Note that both works enjoyed initial success among readers, but whereas *Rasselas* had six English editions during Johnson's lifetime (Tillotson 1969: 1020), *Candide* enjoyed about twenty editions in *the year* of its publication alone (Voltaire 1966: 75) and between 1759 and 1778 we have more than forty documented French editions (Voltaire 1957: lxv–lxxiv). True, Johnson's *Rasselas* generated an impressive number of echo-dialogues: "between 1759 and 1800 *Rasselas* was available to readers in six foreign languages and some fifty editions, English and non-English" (Johnson 1990: 58).[39] This wave, however, looks weak compared to the number and variety of echoes and other kinds of dialogues generated by Voltaire's *Candide*: alongside many (authorized and pirated) editions and translations, we may bear in mind some inauthentic sequels, notably *Candide, ou l'optimism, seconde partie*, and imitations (Voltaire 1958: 679). By 1803 at least ten such continuations and imitations had been published (Thacker 1967).

In addition to the welcome the two books received, we should note that it was *Candide* which also provoked virulent public debate and was denounced and banned by civic and religious authorities alike, notably by the Administrators of Paris, the Great Council of Geneva and the Catholic Church. In other words, it generated a considerable literary scandal. Literary scandal is neither a necessary nor a sufficient condition for securing literary fame: a work can ignite an ephemeral scandal but many works have made their way to greatness without the aid of one. Still, it is reasonable to assume that a literary scandal promotes a book's visibility and can serve as a catalyst for educing additional echoes and dialogues which in turn contribute to advance the work's reputation. Assuming that, as far as intrinsic qualities are concerned, two works have the same potential for gaining fame and assuming further that one of them provokes a scandal, we (together with some public relations people) can see the advantage this might have in promoting a book.

Literary scandals are sometimes related to a work's aesthetic qualities, especially when they challenge established aesthetic norms, but more often such scandals are ignited because a work taps some sensitive ideological, religious, political or moral issues (e.g. Rushdie's *The Satanic Verses*, Nabokov's *Lolita*). Note also that literary scandals and the role they play vis-à-vis a work's reputation are not an exclusively modern phenomenon. They might have an important place in the contemporary market of cultural capital (English 2002, 2005) but they also had a role in earlier periods, as the case of *Candide* can exemplify.[40]

To illustrate the dynamics by which an initial wave of responses (sometimes including negative ones) may contribute to an increasing number of responses, echoes and dialogues that continue to proliferate, let us make a brief digression into a case in the history of economics and technology. The QWERTY case, named after the six upper left-hand letters on the typewriter keyboard, was examined in a ground-breaking essay by Paul David (David 1985), attempting to explain why this specific keyboard layout became the standard of typewriter manufacturers. The conclusion was, contrary to what we would assume, that the QWERTY layout did not necessarily offer the quickest method for using our fingers on the typewriter; in fact, it was designed to slow down typists a bit, to avoid jamming of keys in early mechanical models of typewriters. But after it was adopted by typing schools and major manufacturers, people did not bother to change it, even when the mechanical problems which caused the jams were solved in electronic typewriters (let alone computer keyboards). This tendency to adhere to suboptimal structures is described by Stephen J. Gould as a general principle characterizing biological and cultural evolution alike (Gould 1991: 59–75).[41]

If the best conceivable option does not always prevail in cases where we have a relatively simple and defined structure and function (i.e. typing words quickly on a keyboard) why should we assume that the best conceivable artistic structure (with all its complexities and built-in disagreements about taste and values) would prevail? In other words, there are good reasons to assume that from the moment a work has acquired a certain degree of success and reputation we will witness a self-propelling dynamics, relying on the work's established fame, not necessarily on the superiority of an intrinsic set of (purely aesthetic) qualities. Of course, we do not have to deny the existence of certain such viable and laudable intrinsic qualities, but we should be careful not to mystify them or detach them from the actual responses they generate in different readers, writers, artists and critics. The conclusion is almost unavoidable: the surviving, flourishing literary works are not necessarily the best conceivable ones, but rather those that have already generated a considerable body of varied echoes and dialogues.[42] The QWERTY case from the history of technology can serve as a sobering lesson of how certain phenomena may become canonical without necessarily being "the best"; works that have already generated a significant wave of echoes and dialogues have a better chance to be read, re-read, taught, interpreted, re-written, adapted and consequently be perceived as part of the canon in what Barbara Herrnstein Smith calls "the dynamics of endurance" (Smith 1988: 47–53).

A significant wave of echoes and dialogues, including positive critical reviews, seems to be a necessary condition in a work's way to literary fame. Robert Escarpit was probably right when he argued against the Romantic myth of rescuing a hidden masterpiece from total oblivion in a future generation (Escarpit 1971: 84). The significant wave of echoes and dialogues does not have to follow immediately on the work's publication. Sometimes it does, as the case of *Candide* illustrates, sometimes it is postponed a few decades.[43] But without such a wave, the chances of a work to secure fame, reputation and canonical status are small. Note, however, that this canonical status is not forever secure; the tide of literary taste may change and in order to keep its high place within the canon, won by virtue of a significant wave of echoes and dialogues, the literary work has to keep generating them to maintain its place on Parnassus.

To exemplify this ongoing process in the case of *Candide* and *Rasselas*, let us look at TABLE 4.9, presenting the results of searches (conducted on February 2009) for different kinds of echoes, references and dialogues initiated by the two works, traced in different databases. These searches are similar to those conducted in the previous section, with three additional databases (Google Scholars, the International Database of MLA and Doollee – The Playwrights Database), enabling us to reach a more nuanced picture of the dissemination of the works in different layers of culture: general references and artistic and scholarly works.[44]

TABLE 4.9
Results of Seven Searches of *Candide* and *Rasselas*

	Google	Google-Image	Google-Scholar	Clio	MLA	IMDb	Doollee[45]
Voltaire, *Candide*	168,000	29,600	7,330	170	94	5	7
Johnson, *Rasselas*	94,100	3,920	2,730	113	54	0	0

The conclusion seems clear: *Candide* not only enjoyed a bigger and wider wave of echoes and dialogues following its initial publication, but has continued, until these very days to generate a more significant and varied wave, including some important adaptations (e.g. Leonard Bernstein's operetta) – thus securing its fame and leaving for *Rasselas* the respected second place.

Objections to the Dialogic Approach

Despite my satisfaction with the outcome of these experiments, it is difficult to believe that the results obtained so far would convince ardent proponents of the power and beauty parties, or resolve once and for all their ongoing debate. Furthermore, the proposal to see a great book as a function of textual dialogue may be charged with circularity: of course we can define all works evoking many and diverse textual dialogues as great books (thus goes the argument) but then we can also define a great book in any other way (e.g., a work that won the Booker prize). My answer is, first, that my approach is not tainted with simple, vicious circularity. My definition of a great book relies on the concept of textual dialogues, but my definition of textual dialogues does not rely on what a great book is. Moreover, my searches were conducted on the basis of certain existing lists of great books (the three source books), they were not tailored to conform to some preconceived ideas, but rather they tried to check whether there is any kind of *correlation* between certain works named great books and the pattern of their appearance and distribution in culture.

Another objection that may be raised to the dialogue approach is that the proposal to see a great book as a work evoking many and varied kinds of literary, artistic and critical dialogues, does not provide a *satisfactory explanation*. According to this critique, the dialogic approach only points to a "symptom" of being a great book, not to the "root" of its status. In other words, the proposed formulation merely substitutes the question "Why does a literary work become a great book?" by the question "Why do some books evoke many and diversified kinds of literary, artistic and critical dialogues?" And the ultimate answer would still lie, as representatives of the two prevailing parties might claim, within their theoretical baggage, either in specified aesthetic qualities or in the fostering of the interests of specific hegemonies. And, to a certain degree, this may be the case.

The proposed approach does not presume to offer any ultimate explanation, but rather to deepen our understanding of the dynamics of canon formation. By moving our attention from a search for "an ultimate explanation" to checking specific hypotheses concerning the actual dynamics by which a work evokes different echoes and dialogues in different layers of literature and culture, we take the debate to a more promising territory than that offered by the two parties (whose proposed explanations have deeper problems than that of the dialogic approach). In this new territory we can get some relief from pre-conceived ideological convictions, activate certain empirically oriented methodologies, and achieve a better understanding of how certain literary works have become focal points in literary and cultural history. True, dialogues generated by a work can be described as "symptoms" that need further explanation (preferably by intrinsic aesthetic qualities). Still, these "symptoms" are as close as one can get to "the real thing": they are the direct, observable manifestation of the meeting ground of inherent textual qualities and social and cultural reality.

What is even more significant, by focusing on the generated dialogues we are invited to perceive these works not as static entities, sitting there on the shelves as revered objects, but to observe how they play an active, influential role in the work of writers, artists and critics.[46] Describing great books as static (aesthetic) objects is in fact a common fallacy, shared by both parties. One major advantage of my proposal is the possibility of replacing the question "Is this work a great book or not?" with the understanding that a literary work is in a continual process of *becoming* a great book by virtue of the dialogues it keeps producing or stimulating.

In addition to the conceptual objections, the dialogic approach can be challenged from a different angle which could be termed "the *Harry Potter* effect" after the famous mega-bestseller. If the large number of echoes left by a book is indeed an important criterion for introducing it into the club of great books, the *Harry Potter* series might be considered (after the Bible) the great book of all time. A brief check in the Google search engine reveals that it leaves far behind any work such as the *Odyssey* from the "hard core" of any list of great books.[47]

Furthermore, its echoes are not restricted, as might be expected, to large readerships, movie productions and popular culture (games etc.); it also attracts, surely but not slowly, critical attention: the number of scholarly books and articles devoted to *Harry Potter* is constantly growing.[48] Thus, at least superficially, this series of books also seems to fulfill the requirement of variety of dialogues and echoes.

In face of these overwhelming search results, one can simply inscribe the *Harry Potter* series in the list of great books and try to put aside any elitist scruples. The price we would pay for this position seems, however, quite high: it might go against the intuition and judgment that place Homer's *Odyssey* or Shakespeare's *Hamlet* in a different league than the *Harry Potter* series. But how can we raise such an objection without renouncing the dialogic approach altogether? Two answers may suggest themselves. First, the principle of *variety* applies also to periods, and with the *Harry Potter* series we are dealing with a contemporary work that has not yet been tested on that level. In fact, by reminding ourselves that variety means also variety of periods, we may be evoking the good old principle that a great book has to pass the "test of time." Contemporary success, even huge, may be ephemeral; only the work's ability to transcend its contemporary audience and the boundaries of the immediate cultural circumstances in which it was produced and received is a true mark of its greatness. Consequently, we should be extremely cautious when dealing with contemporary works in our research.

Another response to the challenge of the *Harry Potter* case calls attention to the fact that the books are aimed almost solely at a juvenile readership. Thus, the principle of variety of dialogues is only partly fulfilled not only because we are dealing with a contemporary work (lacking a variety of periods), but also because most of its readers belong to only one, specified group. We should not of course exclude from our research books targeting specified audiences, juvenile or adult (in a sense, every book has a specified target audience, at least in the initial stages of its distribution). But many great books are characterized precisely by their ability to transcend their original target audience: Defoe's *Robinson Crusoe* and Swift's *Gulliver's Travels* were composed as books for adults, but gained much of their reputation as desired reading for children and youngsters (at least in abbreviated form).

At this point, it becomes clear that the search tools offered so far are in some respects not sufficiently sophisticated and nuanced. They do not distinguish, for example, between the mention of a book in a commercial advertisement (very many of those found in the *Harry Potter* searches) and those found, say, in a genuine literary context. At this stage of research, the crude Internet searches probably lack pertinent differentiation. More refined search tools would provide not only gross numbers, but also an algorithm for weighing the numbers obtained: for example, literary allusions – a typical case of genuine literary dialogue – should be assigned more weight and significance than commercial advertisements. Such a suggestion is, of course, not based on ideologically motivated aversion from commercial capitalism, but on the conviction that a literary allusion represents a more important factor in literary life than an advertisement.[49] To put this point differently: when a work stimulates another writer or a painter to evoke that work, it is a clear indication of its high potential as literature, as opposed to its being merely a commodity.

Models for Literary Dialogues: Ladder, Tree, Ponytail

Is there a structural model we can use to describe the relationships produced between a text and the ensuing specific dialogues it evokes? Perhaps we can use a ladder-like structure, where the first rung corresponds to the source text on which all subsequent texts are built. But a ladder-like model can be misleading. It implies an incremental development: as if the second rung is constructed on the first one, the third relies on the second, the fourth on the third etc. We know that this is not how literary dialogues work and evolve. An author may be familiar with the textual tradition associated with a great book, but she/he can also generate a dialogue with that work without knowing that tradition, let alone rely on a preceding literary dialogue (= the rung beneath her/his own on the ladder). Furthermore, an author may be aware of the textual heritage of a great book, but deliberately decide not to evoke that tradition and rather to conduct an unmediated, direct dialogue with the text in attempting a fresh look at it. The ladder-like model has another disadvantage: it implies a hierarchy between the different rungs, as if the more we move in time, the more we have "advanced" in an imaginary evolutionary line. This implication should be rejected, as it was rejected in biological discussions, and for the same reason: because there is no need to assign higher value to phenomena that occur late on the axis of time. Milton's *Paradise Lost* is not a more advanced or valued literary dialogue with Homer's epic than Virgil's *Aeneid* – it is simply a different dialogue, situated at a different historical point.

The ladder-like model was rejected in biological thinking, and has been replaced by a model that can be useful also in discussing literary dialogue: the model of the branching bush or tree. If the originating text is the trunk, we can regard subsequent literary dialogues as branches that flourish from it. This model overcomes the tacit hierarchical assumption associated with the ladder-like model. No branch is superior to another; each has its validity and place and contributes to the overall development of the tree.[50] This development is not unidirectional, like the one assumed by the ladder model, but can branch out in different directions.

The tree model thus overcomes some fundamental shortcomings of the ladder model, but it does not capture two important dimensions of the structure of literary dialogues. For this, I would like to introduce the ponytail model.

The Tree Model

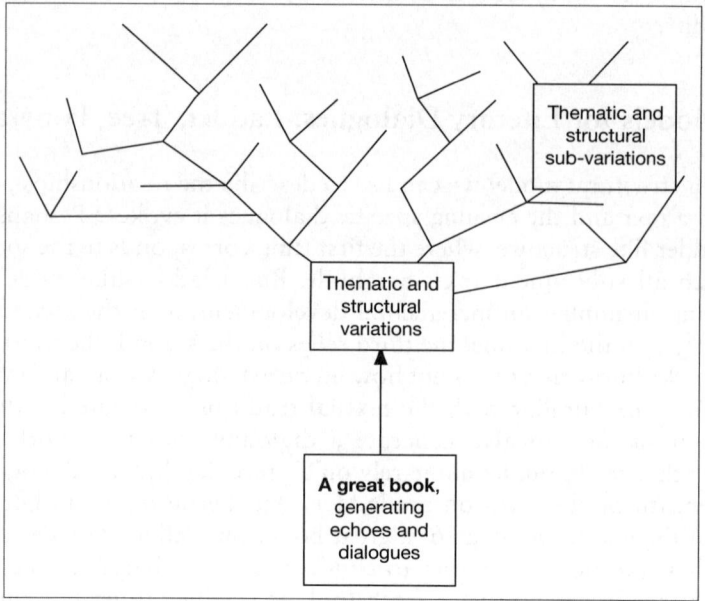

The Ponytail Model

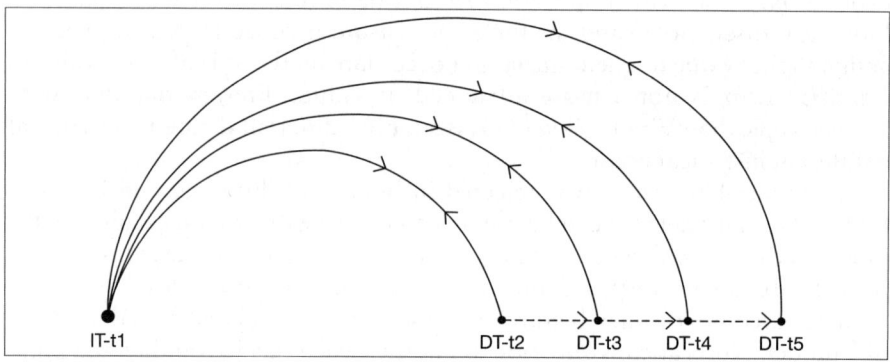

IT = Initiating Text (a great book)
DT = Dialoguing Text
t1, t2, – different points of Time, starting with t1 of IT
Continuous Line = Necessary Relationship
Broken Line = Optional Relationship
Arrow = a flow of meanings

A few words of clarification: all Dialoguing Texts go back to the Initiating Text, hence we have a continuous line, marking a necessary relationship; thus, for example, Fénelon's *Télémaque* (say, it is a DT-t2), written at the very end of the seventeenth century, conducts a dialogue with Homer's *Odyssey* (= IT), composed around the eighth century BC (= t1). And Joyce's *Ulysses has to* evoke Homer's epic if it wants to be considered a text dialoguing with it. If we focus on the line connecting the Dialoging Text with the Initiating Text, we see two arrows, pointing in opposite directions: from the IT to the DT and from the DT to the IT. The former is marking the fact that the flow of meanings from the IT to the DT is a necessary part of understanding a DT. To assume that there is a flow of meaning from IT to DT does not mean that in reading the DT we remember the IT in details or possess a comprehensive interpretation of that text. All it says is that the reader has identified the IT as such and has some ideas about it (i.e. some part of notions circulating about that book) and that the reader considers some of these ideas to be pertinent to understanding the effects of DT (Joyce, like the *Odyssey*, re-tells in *Ulysses* the quest of a son for a father and the father's adventures as they approach each other). The arrow in the other direction (from DT to IT) is perhaps less obvious, but we should assume that the reading of a DT affects at least to some extent the way we understand the IT (we see Homer's *Odyssey* "in different eyes" after reading Joyce's *Ulysses*, discovering in it some further meanings), hence there is also a flow of meanings that goes "backwards."[51] We can of course claim that reading Homer through Joyce's "glasses" is anachronistic and for certain purposes we could attempt to re-construct a reading free from what the DTs tell us about the IT. Such an attempt, however, can sometimes be quite difficult (can we simply forget Freud when we read today Sophocles' *Oedipus Rex*?). And no matter how successful we are in our attempt we should concede that during the reading process of a DT, the bi-directional flow of meanings is almost unavoidable. Thus, a bi-directional flow of meanings, mutually enriching relationship, is a mark not only of a true allusion (see Ben-Porat 1978), but also of dialoguing texts, especially but not exclusively genuine ones.

Whereas the line between IT and each DT is continuous, the line that goes from one DT to the next one is discontinuous, marking the fact that it is optional for an author of a DT to use, evoke or dialogue with a previous DT. Does Joyce's novel dialogue with Fénelon's *Télémaque*, or for that matter with any other text of the rich tradition of dialogues with Homer (for that tradition, see Stanford 1954)? The answer is that it can conduct such a dialogue, but it does not have to; it depends on the author's knowledge, interests and artistic goals.

Were we able to combine the tree and the ponytail model into one graphic representation, we could get closer to seeing the patterns in which a great book echoes, procreates and disseminates through time.

Dissemination: The Pyramid Model

To conclude this section, let me suggest one more graphic model: the accumulated heterogeneous body of dialogues generated by a great book as a graduated pyramid. The base contains the largest, but also most superficial body of echoes circulating in culture. The greater part of this layer consists of phrases or characters' names or images or concepts associated with a work. Perhaps the most frequent type of reference to a literary work or to an author occurs where the name of a character or author has become part of language itself, especially as an adjective: "to fight against this Kafkaesque bureaucracy would be quixotic." It is debatable whether we should treat such occurrences as actual echoes – even the faintest – of a work or dismiss them and accept "quixotic," for example, as directly as "naively unrealistic," without assuming an evocation of Cervantes's work. Whereas such cases may demonstrate an author's ultimate victorious tap on eternity's doors – the name of Cervantes' character, for example, will live as long as languages that use his name as an adjective live – we should keep in mind that such a victory does not guarantee the actual reading of the work from which it emerged.

As to the question whether we should include expressions like "quixotic" in our reckoning of references to a specific work, my answer is that there is no a-priori answer. Rather, the answer depends on the specific context in which the expression is used and more specifically on whether there are additional elements in the text (or utterance) that call to mind Cervantes' work: "tilting at these windmills was quixotic of him" suggests more than simply "it was quixotic of him to fight these impediments" and when we read "tilting at windmills was quixotic of him, especially since he has no Sancho Panza at his side" – we can confidently treat this as an allusion to *Don Quixote*. Perhaps not a genuine literary allusion with a full fledged, simultaneous activation of two texts and contexts, but there is no doubt that such a saying is a clear and loud echo of Cervantes' work.

Other examples of such glancing allusions to works consist in quoting short phrases. Most people who can quote the phrase "to be or not to be" know of course that it is Hamlet's, but only a small number of them know how the speech goes on or are familiar with the play in its entirety; and people who have not read Tolstoy's *Anna Karenina* can nevertheless cite the opening lines about the difference between happy and unhappy families. When it comes to cases like these, we should usually not need supportive evidence to consider them as allusions to the originating works. But they can be tagged shallow echoes.

As part of the wide base of the pyramid, where we find such glancing, local echoes associated with a work – traceable in many results obtained in a Google search – we can include the passive form of echo-dialogue: reading. In cases where the book we are dealing with has been abridged or adapted, there is a good chance that most readers know the work from such a version, especially in the case of adventure stories like Homer's *Odyssey* or Defoe's *Robinson Crusoe*.

After passive forms of echo-dialogue, characteristic of the wide base, we may encounter on the next step of the pyramid many cases of genuine dialogue in the form of developed allusions as well as cases of dialogue-of-the-deaf where writers and painters may evoke a work but appropriate it to their own agenda. Here we will find also active forms of echo-dialogue, in the shape of pictorial representations, review-articles, full-fledged interpretations. On the next step come translations, adaptations and abridgements, and the pyramid's peak consist of comprehensive re-writings and cinematic adaptations.

The pyramid model is designed to represent the distribution of different kinds of dialogues in terms of their quantity. The sides are graduated, not straight (in mathematical terms – a geometric, not arithmetic series), to emphasize that whereas some types of dialogues come in thousands, en masse, others yield only a few instances. The principle of moving upward in the graduated pyramid is simple and stands in reverse proportion to the energy and resources invested: the more energy invested in a dialogue, the smaller number of dialogues produced, and vice versa. Viewed from this perspective, it becomes clear why we find only a few cases of genuine re-writings at the pyramid top, together with cinematic adaptations. The former require originality, the latter demand money and a relatively large crew.

By now it should be evident that there is no simple, direct correlation between the axis of pseudo- and genuine dialogue and the upward movement in the pyramid. True, the pyramid's base is populated almost exclusively by echo-dialogues, whereas at the very top we will most likely find genuine dialogues. Nevertheless, some versions of pseudo-dialogue can be found in a relatively high position in the pyramid, because they require an investment of relatively high energy (e.g. the case of simple movie adaptations), and some cases of genuine dialogues can be found in the middle area of the pyramid – because they are short, local allusions which do not require a high investment such as comprehensive re-writing or even simple translation. If we also compute issues of dialogue length – local allusions as opposed to comprehensive re-writings – perhaps a greater degree of correlation between the axis of genuine–pseudo dialogues and height on the pyramid will emerge, but even then there would be cases of echo-dialogues at a relatively high location because they require a high investment of energy (but not as high as that of genuine dialogue of the same type).

So here is a graphic representation of the pyramid, summing up the quantitative distribution of the different types of dialogues discussed in this chapter.

74 | *What Is a Dialogue? What Is a Great Book?*

A Pyramid of Dialogues

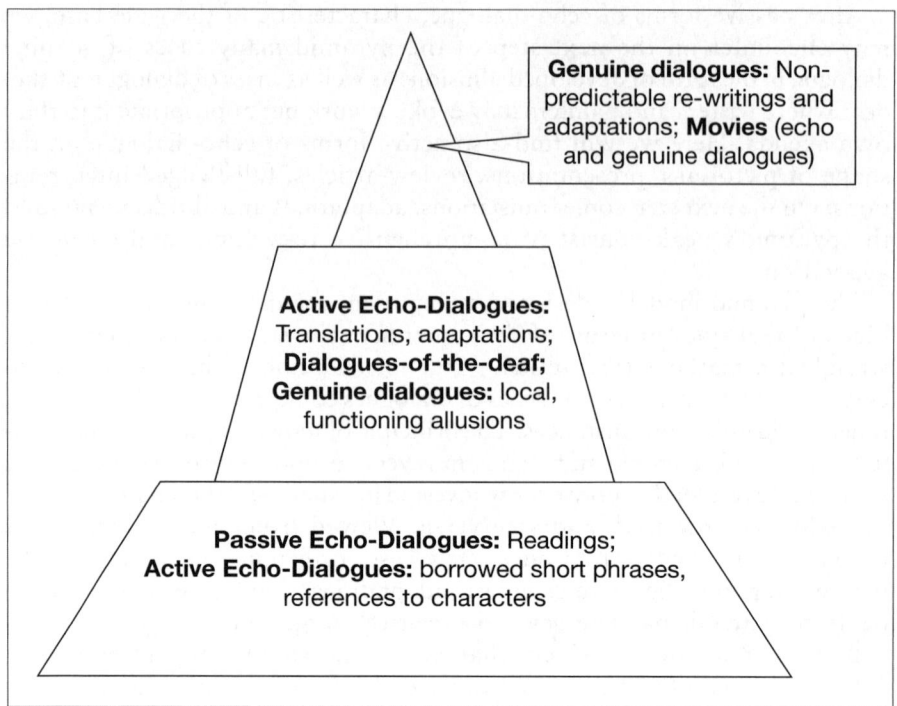

PART II

Some Genuine Dialogues with Great Books

For that is really great which bears a repeated examination, and which it is difficult or rather impossible to withstand, and the memory of which is strong and hard to efface. In general, consider those examples of sublimity to be fine and genuine which please all and always. For when men of different pursuits, lives, ambitions, ages, languages, hold identical views on one and the same subject, then that verdict which results, so to speak, from a concert of discordant elements makes our faith in the object of admiration strong and unassailable.

(Longinus 1967: 69)

The classics are those books which come to us bearing the aura of previous interpretations, and trailing behind them the traces they have left in the culture or cultures (or just in the languages and customs) through which they have passed.

(Calvino 1999: 5)

PART II

Some Genuine Dialogues with Great Books

CHAPTER

5

The Sacrifice Scene – Kierkegaard and Levin

The following three chapters focus on dialogues with *the* canonical text in the West, the one for which the word canon and its derivations (canonized, canonization, canonicity) are used in the basic (not extended, metaphorical) sense – the Bible. Reading dialogues with the Bible is an excellent opportunity not only to get acquainted with interesting texts but also to re-examine some assumptions about canon formation, especially those associated with the power party. Prima facie, the Bible seems to offer the power party an ultimate proof: here is a collection of books that at some point in history were assembled, sealed and declared sacred by an authorial (religious), institutional hegemony. For the Jewish canon of the Hebrew Bible, this was probably a long process, continuing over five or six centuries (from 400 BCE to 200 CE) and involving various political, priestly and other religious authorities. Whereas the Torah (Pentateuch) achieved a stable status relatively early, the process of canonization of Nevi'im (Prophets) and Ketuvim (Writings) is less self-evident. Barton (1988) evokes in this context T. S. Eliot's description of the dynamic formation of the canon of English literature, where there was a consensual body of books constituting the essential corpus of classics but without excluding new candidates, and McDonald adds: "as new books with a demonstrated stature were written, they were immediately placed in relationship to the existing canon ... This sort of even-new inclusion seems to have occurred as the Prophetic collection was gradually recognized and added to the well-established 'classics' of the Torah" (McDonald 2007: 186–87). The canonization process of the New Testament was somewhat shorter and has better determined focal points, especially the decisions taken in three synods: one in Hippo (393), and twice repeated and confirmed in Carthage (397 and finally 419), with a decisive role played by St. Augustine (Metzger 1987: 236–38; McDonald 2007: 205). The rigid model of Christian canon formation was tacitly adopted by scholars of literature, fostering "a tacit notion of a kind of synod of cultural authorities who have dictated a list of 'genuine and inspired' writers" as Robert Alter points out (Alter 2000: 22). The canonicity of the Hebrew Bible, with its ambiguous, dynamic and over determined aspects proves to be, according to Alter, a more useful model for the complicated, fluid and multifarious process in which "certain works become popular beyond their own times and are anthologized, reprinted, cherished by readers, even included in curricula" (Ibid).[1] Note, however, that even Alter's critique of the adoption of the rigid model of Christian canon by literary scholars does not comment on an important difference between the biblical canon – Jewish and Christian alike – and the literary canon: whereas the former is defined as a closed set of (sanctioned) texts, the latter presents a basically open body of works, even for those who struggle to keep it as closed as possible. Thus, when applying the metaphor of biblical canon to literature, we are calling attention to similar processes of status-gaining, inclusion and exclusion, but we should not forget that this metaphor also breaks down in (at least) one fundamental aspect. And this openness unavoidably implies an ongoing dynamics of change and re-structuring.

According to the logic of the power party, the ultimate authoritative decree (no matter how complicated and drawn-out the process leading to it) has caused the Bible to be read, studied, interpreted and re-interpreted, and has generated various dialogues throughout the ages – some even formally commissioned by the religious establishment. And, *up to a point*, the institutionalized sanctioning of the Bible can indeed explain the dissemination of the text, especially in the form of echo-dialogues (e.g. simple translations, basic commentaries). Furthermore, when we remember that the very teaching of reading and writing in Europe was for centuries in the hands of the clergy, the connection between social power, texts and (echo-) dialogues with texts becomes evident. But using canonization as the one and only explanation for the number and diversity of dialogues stimulated by the Bible has at least one serious shortcoming.

If authoritative canonization explains the procreation of dialogues, why is it that some parts of the Bible have evoked a huge number of diverse dialogues while others have produced relatively few, and even fewer genuine dialogues? Even without any empirical search, it is clear, for instance, that the Sacrifice scene in Genesis 22 has initiated far more echoes and dialogues than, say, the description of Abraham's victory over Chedorlaomer in Genesis 14.

The intuitive answer to the question why some parts of the Bible have instigated more dialogues than others is that these parts have more attractive or profound or beautiful or meaningful elements. This intuitive answer might sound a bit circular (they inspire more dialogues because they are more inspiring) and it needs an explication that will make it less circular (such an explication will shortly be offered). But even if at this point we cannot satisfactorily explain why some parts are more "inspiring" than others, it is clear that using canonization as the only basis for generating dialogues is inadequate or, at best, very partial. Canonization can explain why the Bible has a good "starting point" – compared to similar but non-canonized texts – in competing for the attention of authors, artists and interpreters. But by no means can it explain the differences in the generative potential of its separate parts.

The idea that canonization, in and of itself, can predict the generation of dialogues can be undermined from another angle. Let us compare the references and echoes generated by a book of consensual canonical status with a book that has a shakier standing within the canon. If we rely on canonization alone, the latter book would have a weaker position in such a comparison. However, a look at the results obtained in searches for the book of the prophet Nahum, included in the biblical canon by Judaism and by all Christian denominations, with the book of Judith, excluded by Jews and Protestants but not Catholics, clearly shows that the *less*-canonized text generates *more* references on all search engines than does the undisputed canonized text.

TABLE 5.1
Results of Searches of Judith and Nahum

	Google	Google-Image	Clio	IMDb
Judith	2,720,000[2]	167,000	17[3]	6
Nahum	1,810,000	19,200	14	0

We might disregard the results obtained on the IMDb – the book of a minor prophet with no coherent story is no match in cinematic terms for the story of seduction, heroism and death told in the book of Judith. Still, it is symptomatic that in all search engines – including Clio, representing scholarly interests – the book of Judith gained significantly more references. But even if the comparison of the book of Judith and the book of Nahum has some methodological flaws, it still allows us to conclude that a consensual canonization of a text does not guarantee this text the generation of more dialogues than a text with a questionable canonical status. There is a difference between acknowledging canonization as an important factor in explaining the dynamic of generating dialogues – first and foremost in providing a privileged "starting point" – and claiming that the dialogues inspired by a text are a direct function of its canonic status.

To accept the argument that canonization cannot explain procreation is to undermine a basic assumption of the power party. Does the weakening of the power party result in strengthening its rival, the beauty party? Not necessarily. The sacrifice story in Genesis 22 is well known for its density and concision, but it is difficult to argue that this aesthetic quality, in and of itself, can explain the attraction the text has had for so many readers, interpreters and artists.

If neither canonicity nor aesthetic qualities can explain why a story has called forth many and diverse dialogues, what then endows a biblical story – or for that matter any other story – with a high inspirational potential? Three things seem to recur in some famous biblical texts.[4] (1) The central character represents an apex in a human domain (beauty, courage, cunning, leadership, bravery etc.); while this apex is not common, it is perceived as representing the limits of human experience. (2) There is a significant tension between some traits of the main character (he is extremely strong but has a weak point; she is attractive but dangerous). (3) The actions of the main character are related to some perennial human hopes (e.g. to be strong and loved) and fears (e.g. to become weak and be rejected).

In the Sacrifice scene, Abraham demonstrates his readiness to sacrifice his beloved son, showing an extraordinary degree of faith; his willingness to sacrifice something dear to him is a recognizable human situation (thus, #1); there is an almost unbearable tension between Abraham's status as a parent and as a servant of God (thus, # 2) and Abraham's actions are related to humanity's high aspiration to serve God's will (or any other larger-than-life vocation) but also the deep fear of losing something very dear on the way (thus # 3). The three principles do not of course provide a simple formula for predicting the capacity of a story to initiate dialogues but only heuristic guidelines for estimating its potential. However, there is good reason to believe that, *ceteris paribus*, a story with these characteristics will procreate more than a story which lacks them.

Kierkegaard's Abraham: Imaginary Poetic Variations

Throughout the ages the sacrifice of Isaac has called forth innumerable dialogues with interpreters and artists. It raises theological issues in a most acute way and exemplifies the highly concise method of telling a story (Auerbach 1953: 7–25). Some of these dialogues stand out as intellectual or artistic achievements and contemporary readers of the biblical story are sometimes influenced by these post-biblical representations. In the visual realm one can think of the depiction by Rembrandt. And of modern interpretations, there can be little doubt that Kierkegaard's *Fear and Trembling* is a most powerful and original response to Genesis 22.

Kierkegaard's originality gives rise, among other things, to the difficulty of categorizing his text and applying to it a specific set of expectations and criteria. The subtitle, "Dialectical Lyrics," suggests different, sometimes conflicting expectations: It is a philosophical treatise, developing some arguments against the Hegelian system with regard to ethics and metaphysics. It is also an elaborated exegetical work, offering a careful reading of the original biblical story. It is also a poetical reaction, playing with the identities of the writer (presented as "Johannes de Silentio"), intertwining imaginary scenes and parts of legends into a loose net of associations. It is also a satirical exposure of contemporary bourgeois, complacent readings of the story by the official Church. Furthermore, let us not forget that the work is a hidden personal confession about the author's dealing with the question of whether to get married. To illustrate Kierkegaard's rich and unpredictable (hence genuine) dialogue with the biblical sacrifice scene, let us focus on a passage close to the opening of the book. After the preface by the invented authorial persona, Johannes de Silentio, the writer expresses his desire to accompany Abraham and Isaac on their three days' journey to Mount Moriah. Perhaps by being there, the writer muses, he will be able to really understand what happened during this otherwise inexplicable, mysterious event. As part of his attempt to understand what happened there, he offers four imagined scenarios. Each invention concludes with an analogy (or an elaborated simile) to a weaning of a child. After quoting Genesis 22: 1–2, here is how Kierkegaard presents the first scenario:

> It was early morning. Abraham rose in good time, had the asses saddled and left his tent, taking Isaac with him, but Sarah watched them from the window as they went down the valley until she could see them no more. They rode in silence for three days; on the morning of the fourth Abraham still said not a word, but raised his eyes and saw afar the mountain in Moriah. He left the lads behind and went on alone up the mountain with Isaac beside him. But Abraham said to himself: 'I won't conceal from Isaac where this way is leading him.' He stood still, laid his hand on Isaac's head to give him his blessing, and Isaac bent down to receive it. And Abraham's expression was fatherly, his gaze gentle, his speech encouraging. But Isaac could not understand him, his soul could not be uplifted; he clung to Abraham's knees, pleaded at his feet, begged for his young life, for his fair promise; he called to mind the joy in Abraham's house, reminded him of the sorrow and loneliness. Then Abraham lifted the boy up and walked with him, taking him by the hand, and his words were full of comfort and exhortation. But Isaac could not understand him. Abraham climbed the mountain in Moriah, but Isaac did not understand him. Then he turned away from Isaac for a moment, but when Isaac saw his face a second time it was changed, his gaze was wild, his mien one of horror. He caught Isaac by the chest, threw him to the ground and said: 'Foolish boy, do you believe I am your father? I am an idolater. Do you believe this is God's command? No, it is my own desire.' Then Isaac trembled and in his anguish cried: 'God in heaven have mercy on me, God of Abraham have mercy on me; if I have no father on earth, then be Thou my father!' But below his breath Abraham said to himself: 'Lord in heaven I thank Thee; it is after all better that he believes I am a monster than he lose faith in Thee.'
>
> * * *
>
> When the child is to be weaned the mother blackens her breast, for it would be a shame were the breast to look pleasing when the child is not to have it. So the child believes that the breast has changed but the mother is the same, her look loving and tender as ever. Lucky the one that needed no more terrible means to wean the child! (Kierkegaard 1985: 45–46)[5]

This imagined first variation (like the three that follow), could have happened; it does not directly contradict any specific detail of the original biblical story. According to this scenario, Abraham decides to reveal to Isaac what he is going to do to him: "I won't conceal from Isaac where this way is leading him". Abraham is trying to soften the blow as much as he can: "Abraham's expression was fatherly, his gaze gentle, his speech encouraging... his words were full of comfort and exhortation." Abraham is trying to maintain a harmonious atmosphere in the midst of a horrific scene: to follow God's command, to maintain his care for Isaac and make him accept his fate. Abraham's attempt to produce such a mollifying effect fails, as is evident from Isaac's repeated reaction: "But Isaac could not understand him ... But Isaac could not understand him." Isaac's inability to understand is quite comprehensible and indirectly represents both Kierkegaard's and the reader's inability to understand Abraham's attitude and the situation as a whole: how is it possible to reconcile the command to sacrifice your son and continue to be a loving and protecting father. And from Isaac's perspective: how can he continue to love his father and the God who orders this father to kill him? These conflicting demands are too much to sustain and can be contained by neither father or son.

Abraham realizes that he cannot maintain harmony in this situation; there is no way to eat the cake (or your own son ...) and have it too. This realization brings him to a dramatic choice: if someone has to lose Isaac's love, he will be the one, provided Isaac does not lose faith in God. At that point, the story becomes a story of *Abraham's* self-sacrifice. To obtain his objectives – executing God's command while preserving Isaac's faith in God – Abraham opts for a highly inventive move: "He caught Isaac by the chest, threw him to the ground and said: 'Foolish boy, do you believe I am your father? I am an idolater. Do you believe this is God's command? No, it is my own desire.'" By thus staging the scene, pretending to be a murderous idolater, Abraham achieves his purpose: Isaac falls for the pretence, distances himself from his father and addresses a loving prayer to God.

This first imagined scenario offers a rational conclusion for the sacrifice story, in keeping with logical and psychological verisimilitude. The problem is – as becomes clear from the rest of Kierkegaard's work – that this scenario (and also the other three) did not happen. The riddle posed by the sacrifice story becomes a torturing enigma for Kierkegaard precisely because such a logically sound and psychologically credible scenario did not take place. A crucial element in this variation is an attempt on the part of Abraham to explain God's command to Isaac. But, according to Kierkegaard, this is not an option because Abraham *cannot* talk about God's command. One can talk about things pertaining to the public, discursive domain: something shared by a community thanks to some common language, concepts, logic, norms and laws. If the killing of Isaac had been a means for achieving some greater good – saving the nation, complying with a higher law – Abraham's deed would have been part of what Kierkegaard calls the realm of ethics. Kierkegaard conjures up the stories of Agamemnon and Iphigenia, Jephthah and his daughter, to illustrate situations where a tragic hero is torn between an obligation to protect one's own child and the need to sacrifice that child in the name of a higher ethical demand. But Abraham's situation is different:

> The difference between the tragic hero and Abraham is obvious enough. The tragic hero stays within the ethical. He lets an expression of the ethical have its

telos in a higher expression of the ethical; he reduces the ethical relation between father and son, or daughter and father, to a sentiment that has its dialectic in its relation to the idea of the ethical life . . . With Abraham it is different. In his action he overstepped the ethical altogether, and had a higher *telos* outside it, in relation to which he suspended it . . . How could any point of contact ever be discovered between what Abraham did and the universal other than that Abraham overstepped it? (Kierkegaard 1985: 87–88)

The ethical realm is characterized by logic, discourse and disclosure: "The ethical is as such the universal; as the universal it is in turn the disclosed" (109). The tragic hero, who acts within the realm of ethics, is thus required to disclose the logic and motivation of his deed. In fact, disclosing the reasons for his action is part of his heroism: "His heroic action requires courage, but part of that courage is that he shirks no argument . . . ethics required disclosure and found satisfaction in the tragic hero" (114). But Abraham is *not* a tragic hero, who is performing his deed because of some greater good like the good of the nation (Isaac is, after all, the promised nation . . .). In following God's command, Abraham is not directed by any reason, by any universal, justifiable law.

The command Abraham, this "knight of faith," received from God is not, and cannot become part of public discourse; what characterizes it is precisely its private, absolute nature, transcending the universal, discursive realm of the ethical. The reception of God's command is something that happened exclusively between God and Abraham and cannot – by definition and in principle – be "translated" into a public discourse. The moment we imagine an attempt to communicate this absolute private experience to the public sphere, we understand the futility of such an undertaking. Suppose Abraham says to someone "God told me to kill my son; a son I love very much" and suppose that person says to Abraham "then why sacrifice him?" Abraham cannot answer such a question in any intelligible way (98). All he can say to this or to a question like "How do you know that it was God and not Satan?" is to resort to his private, inner, ultimately incommunicable experience.[6]

Faith cannot be mediated to others: "So Abraham's story contains a teleological suspension of the ethical. He has, as the single individual, become higher than the universal" (95) and, furthermore, "The paradox of faith has lost its intermediate term, i.e., the universal . . . Faith itself cannot be mediated into the universal, for in that case it would be cancelled. Faith is this paradox, and the single individual is quite unable to make himself intelligible to anyone" (99). Abraham, then, cannot provide any satisfactory, even intelligible answer to the question why he intends to sacrifice his son, precisely because his action stems from the realm of faith, overstepping the realm of universal, discursive ethics.

What is so frightening in Abraham's situation, says Kierkegaard, is that faith in God resembles – from without – the situation of temptation by a demon or Satan: both are characterized by overstepping the boundaries of universal ethics (Kierkegaard 1985: 96–98).

The invented scenario could smooth out some enigmatic qualities of the sacrifice story, since it complies with basic assumptions about human psychology (e.g. Abraham's wish to make things easier for his son). But these unresolved enigmatic qualities are precisely what make the biblical story attractive to Kierkegaard. Each of his four invented scenarios has a dramatic structure; sometimes more realistic, sometimes demanding a stretch of imagination. But all, even the most fanciful, comply with basic norms of human nature and social convention. And it is precisely from such norms that the sacrifice scene of Genesis 22 departs, leaving the reader in a state of awe and stupefaction, of fear and trembling.

The concluding passage of the first scenario, an analogy between the sacrifice scene and the process of weaning a child adds an unexpected dimension. Some of its aspects are rather strange, especially when we try to concretize the elements of an analogy which makes Abraham correspond to a mother's breast. There is a tension between a vehicle which is part of a natural, common chain of events – the weaning of a child – and the exceptional, extraordinary event of Genesis 22. But beyond the specific way we may make the connection between the vehicle and the tenor of this extended simile, it is interesting to see how through the vehicle of a mother Kierkegaard brings back into the discussion the biblical character that has been omitted from the sacrifice scene altogether: Sarah, Isaac's mother.

By adding a detailed scene in which Abraham and Isaac discuss things, Kierkegaard indirectly highlights the terse biblical style of telling the story. The reader's need to expand on things left unsaid can be found in many dialogues with Genesis 22, starting with some original and thought-provoking Midrashic re-tellings of the story.[7] Nonetheless, Kierkegaard's scenario, despite its inventiveness (e.g. Abraham's desperate move to masquerade as a murderous idolater), still complies with the basic story told in the Bible: Abraham intends to execute God's command and Isaac is not killed at the end.

My next example of a genuine dialogue with Genesis 22 differs from Kierkegaard's *Fear and Trembling* in almost every respect. As against Kierkegaard's deeply serious tone, it is a satirical, comic sketch, presenting a dialogue between Abraham and Isaac; unlike Kierkegaard's deeply religious, Christian concerns, it was written in the secular atmosphere of the city of Tel Aviv in Israel in 1970. But both dialogues – even the contemporary, modernist one – do not deviate from the basic biblical story line.

The Satirical Version of Hanoch Levin

The sacrifice scene, known in Hebrew as the *Akedah* (literally the binding), has promulgated a great number of dialogues in Hebrew literature throughout the ages (Kartun-Blum 1999: 17–65). When Hanoch Levin's *The Queen of the Bathtub* was staged by the Cameri (Chamber) Theatre in 1970, the young writer was still trying to make his name in Israeli theatre and had only two short, satirical fringe productions to his credit. Over the next three decades he was to become the most productive, popular and respected playwright in the country. The production of *The Queen of the Bathtub* was overshadowed by a public scandal: in response to some harshly unfavorable reviews and some public protest, the board of the Cameri Theatre decided, after only 19 performances, to take the play off the stage. Levin's satire criticized Israeli policy towards the Arabs and implied that Israel was sending its youth into unnecessary wars. In the still pervasively euphoric atmosphere of the post-Six Day War (June 1967) period, together with the war of attrition against Egypt which took casualties every day, such a satire was too much for the Israeli public to swallow. Add to this Levin's attack on the highly sensitive social issue of dead soldiers and bereavement and one can understand the heated reaction the play triggered at the time.

Here is the skit entitled "The *Akedah*" from *The Queen of the Bathtub*:

ABRAHAM: Isaac my son, do you know what I'm going to do to you now?

ISAAC: Yes, father, you're going to slaughter me.

ABRAHAM: God commanded me.

ISAAC: I have no complaints against you, father, if you need to slaughter, so slaughter.

ABRAHAM: There has to be slaughter, I'm afraid there is no choice.

ISAAC: I see. You don't have to make things difficult for yourself, simply get up and flourish the knife over me.

ABRAHAM: I'm doing this only as a messenger of God.

ISAAC: Sure, father, as a messenger. Get up like a messenger of God and wave the knife like a messenger of God over your only son whom you love.

ABRAHAM: Very nice, Isaac, make things harder on your poor father, make him depressed, as if it is not enough for him as things are.

ISAAC: Who is making things harder, father, get up quietly and liquidate your unhappy son in one fatherly stroke.

ABRAHAM: I know, the easiest thing is to blame me. Never mind, never mind, blame your lonely father.

IBRAHIM: Why blame, when you are only God's messenger, aren't you? And when God tells you to slaughter your own son like a dog, you have to run and slaughter.

ABRAHAM: Good, good, this is what I deserve in my old age. Put all the blame on me if it suits you, on me, your old and broken father, who, in his old age, has to climb up the mountain with you, to bind you to the altar, to slaughter you, and then to tell everything to mother. You think I've got nothing better to do at my time of life?

ISAAC: I simply understand you, father, really and truly I don't complain, they tell you to slaughter me, to cut off the future of your dynasty with your own hands, to wash your hands with your own blood - I am prepared, please, slaughter, father, slaughter.

ABRAHAM: Thus, dear son, you play with the feelings of a father soon to become bereaved. Break, break my heart, a gifted son who respects his parents, look at me with your big eyes, my dear son, and shorten the one or two years left to your father, caught in the pincers of the decree, to outlive you.

ISAAC: I don't get it, father, you can see that it's all right by me. If you are prepared to murder me in cold blood, me the son of your old age, the dandled child that you miraculously received at the age of 90, your only solace in life, if you are prepared - will I be the man to say "no"? They tell you to slaughter, father, then jump to your feet and slaughter, and God forbid you should have any remorse. For what is going on here after all? Slaughtering of a child. Big deal to slaughter a small and feeble child? And what is it, after all, slaughtering a child, what is a child anyway? Especially when the slaughterer is his father, and he is a qualified slaughterer and in addition to that only a messenger?! Get up and thrust the knife's blade into my young flesh, daddy, and slash my throat till the blood bursts out and spurts on the ground like a cow's blood. Make me a cow, daddy, and when my eyes stare and almost start from their sockets, and my tongue turns blue and lolls out with my last broken scream - then, daddy, you will turn the knife in my throat while I, your own flesh and blood, jerk my legs convulsively on the altar and struggle my last dying struggle. Well, daddy, they told you to slaughter - slaughter.

ABRAHAM: Yes, yes, this is how it goes. What can be done, I was born to be a victim. I am a victim. What is the reward that you get after you invest all your life and soul in your children? Spit in your face. Why not dance on my conscience if you can? Why not bring me down to *Sheol* in grief when all I am trying to do is merely to fulfil what has been decreed from above? Why not, in fact? An old, exhausted man, with one foot in the grave. So maybe, Isaac darling, loyal son, maybe you should suddenly get up from the altar and run away altogether? Maybe you make me run after you with my failing knees?! Or maybe you also snatch the knife from me, huh?! Why not?! Maybe you take the knife and slaughter me?! Slaughter, slaughter your weak father, exactly what I deserve.

ISAAC: *You* will slaughter, merciful and gracious father, slaughter me, virtuous father.

ABRAHAM: Kill your father, robber! Kill him!

ISAAC: Slaughter, model father, father with a warm Jewish heart, slaughter!

ABRAHAM: Bury your only father, you scum!

ISAAC: Cut up, dear old Dad, cut up the meat and bring it to mother!

ABRAHAM: Murderer!

[Holding Isaac by the throat]
Lie down!

ISAAC: A voice! A voice! I hear a voice!

ABRAHAM: What voice? Lie down!

ISAAC: A voice from heaven!

ABRAHAM: What voice from heaven?! Lie down!
ISAAC: I don't know. He said "Lay not thy hand upon the lad."
ABRAHAM: I didn't hear anything.
ISAAC: You've been going deaf for a long time now. Here it comes again: "Lay not thy hand upon the lad." Didn't you hear?
ABRAHAM: No.
ISAAC: I swear to you ... "Lay not thy hand upon the lad."
[Pause; Abraham relaxes his grip]
 Father, I swear to you that I heard a voice from heaven.
ABRAHAM [after a while]: Well, if you say you heard, so you probably did. I am, as you said, a bit deaf.
ISAAC: All's well, you know that as far as I am concerned, I was ready, but a voice is a voice. [Pause] You saw for yourself that as far as I was concerned I was in the clear. [Pause] Both of us were in the clear, weren't we, father? [Pause] Weren't we? [Pause] Everything turned out well, father, why are you sad?
ABRAHAM: I am thinking what if other fathers have to slaughter their children, what will save *them*?
ISAAC: A voice could always come from heaven.
ABRAHAM [with resignation]: Well, if you say so.
(Levin 1987 [1970]: 89–91. My translation, in collaboration with Mira Reich)

The skit, which can be described as a modern Midrash (Jacobson 1987: 7–8) or even better, as a *re-dramatization* of the biblical model (Kartun-Blum 1999: 17) differs from the original story on at least three levels. First, it makes the biblical narrative into a dialogue. In Genesis 22, there is only one very short exchange of words between Abraham and Isaac: "And Isaac spake unto Abraham his father, and said, My father: and he said, Here am I, my son. And he said, Behold the fire and the wood: but where is the lamb for burnt offering? And Abraham said, My son, God will provide himself a lamb for a burnt offering" (Genesis 22: 7–8). Isaac's naïve question and Abraham's enigmatic answer of the Bible became in Levin's version a long dialogue.

The second significant difference is the decision to endow Isaac with a voice. To a certain extent, this is an outcome of the wish to tell the story in the form of a dialogue. Every adaptation of a story into a new genre has some consequences (Stanford 1954: 5); transforming a story into a dialogue entails giving a voice to characters instead of telling about their deeds or words. But here it goes beyond the outer dimension of giving a voice. An author can technically endow Isaac with a voice, but not necessarily in the sense of an independent voice. In one Midrash, for example, Isaac is worried that he might move involuntarily during the sacrificial act, thus making himself unfit according to the laws of sacrifice. Hence, he encourages Abraham to be decisive and swift in his action: "Father, make haste, bare thine arm, and bind my hands and feet securely, for I am a young man ... I may perchance begin to tremble at the sight and push against thee, for the desire unto life is bold. Also I may do myself an injury and make myself unfit to be sacrificed" (Ginzberg

1968: 280).[8] Some medieval Hebrew poets, reacting to horrific events taking place during the Crusades in some Jewish communities, represented Isaac as encouraging Abraham to pursue the killing in the name of mutual belief in God (Elizur 1998). In Levin's version, however, Isaac is far from accepting his father's plan and when he uses encouraging words, they are heavy with sarcasm and intended to produce the opposite effect. Towards the end of the dialogue it is Isaac, not Abraham, who hears the voice from heaven (or perhaps he is making it up?) and pushes Abraham to forgo the planned killing. Isaac has a voice not only technically, he has an independent voice and he assumes the part of an active leader in the whole scene – a complete reversal of roles, compared to the original biblical story.

Thirdly, in terms of the content, attitude and tone of the two interlocutors in the dialogue, there is an exchange of recriminations, indirect accusations and a ping-pong game of attempts to arouse guilt feelings. This is related to the intention of giving Isaac an independent, oppositional stance vis-à-vis Abraham's compliance, but it is not necessarily an outcome of such an intention. Levin – or any other writer – could have presented a confrontation between father and son that uses an entirely serious tone, with no ironic, comic or grotesque effects. Further, as part of the comic dimension, some expressions and intonations Levin uses ("with one foot in the grave" "my failing knees") evoke in the audience associations with a typical self-pitying motherly Jewish discourse. This effect is closely related to other anachronisms in the dialogue ("You've been going deaf"), which do not attempt to preserve the impression that we are listening to an authentic biblical conversation; on the contrary, we are constantly aware that we have here a modern, contemporary Abraham and Isaac, at least in the linguistic dimension. Other Israeli phenomena are effectively treated in the piece – the circularity and repetitiveness of a typical Israeli argument; the dialogue-of-the-deaf duets in many local exchanges, private and public.

All these modifications serve Levin in conveying his harsh criticism of the older Israeli generation – represented by Abraham – as rigid, almost senile and ideologically driven, with no real appreciation of the young lives that are going to be sacrificed. The grotesque tone that dominates the skit – where laughter is checked by horror and shock is mixed with hilarious, exaggerated descriptions of blood and entrails – becomes elegiac in the next scene, where an Isaac-like, fallen son addresses his bereaved father from the grave (translated and discussed in Kartun-Blum 1999: 56–59).

❋ ❋ ❋

Despite the enormous differences between Kierkegaard and Levin – in magnitude, tone, intention and, of course, language, culture and historical context – they both illustrate the genuine type of dialogue. Both authors have attentively read the original biblical text and both attempt to express their deepest concerns through the lenses of the biblical sacrifice scene; these are genuine dialogues because it is difficult to imagine how they could express what they had to express without the tense and intimate dealing with the original story. We can of course compose a summary of what the two authors were trying to say without referring to Genesis 22 – e.g. "in *Fear and Trembling* Kierkegaard is coping with questions of faith and ethics," or "in The *Akedah* from *The Queen of the Bathtub* Levin is criticizing the elderly Israeli generation." Such brief summaries, while truthful, nevertheless miss an essential part of the texts. To summarize genuine dialogues while ignoring the crucial part played by the initiating text is like paraphrasing a poem without making any reference to the specific images it uses.

CHAPTER

6

Samson – Jabotinsky, DeMille and Milton

The biblical story of Samson is a great generator of dialogues, probably the most fertile in the Book of Judges. Using the four search engines introduced in Chapter 4, we can compare references to two stories from Judges, those of Gideon and of Samson (Table 6.1). Both characters are judges (i.e. in the Book of Judges the term means primarily military leaders) and their stories evolve around their heroism in fighting people who oppress the Israelites; thus we can neutralize as much as possible factors that might distort a comparison (say, comparing the story of Samson with that of Ruth). To the extent that the databases represent traces and dialogues generated by the two stories, Samson appears to be a clear winner.

TABLE 6.1
Results of Searches of Samson and Gideon

	Google	Google-Image	Clio	IMDb
Samson	1,980,000[1]	93,300	120	20[2]
Gideon	1,190,000	51,600	48	3

Note that Samson scores much higher than Gideon, especially in visual representations (Google-Image), in exegetic, interpretative and scholarly work (Clio) and in cinematic adaptations (IMDb), all areas that demand a high degree of investment of energy (whether literary, artistic or interpretative) – unlike the superficial traces of the all-inclusive Google; in other words, Samson has the upper hand in areas closer to the top of the pyramid presented in Chapter 4.

Why does the story of Samson score much higher in these areas? There is no reason to assume, for example, that it necessarily presents more aesthetic qualities than that of Gideon. If we adopt a narrow understanding of the term aesthetic qualities (e.g. unity of action), we can even argue that Gideon's story is better shaped. And the two stories have the same canonical status since they are both part of the Book of Judges. A more promising way to explain the gap is to look at the three factors suggested in Chapter 5 for measuring a character's potential to generate dialogues. Both Samson and Gideon were gifted warriors, thus fulfilling the criterion of excellence in some area, but Samson surpasses Gideon. He is almost superhuman in strength and kills swarms of enemies single-handedly; he is also more audacious, taking the gates of a city on his shoulders (Judges 16: 3). If Gideon can be likened to a commander of an elite unit, Samson is more of a Rambo with characteristics of Superman. Moreover, when we come to the second factor – the tension between some traits of the character – it is clear that Samson has more to offer: he is extremely strong, but he has a fatal weakness for treacherous lovers; he is a devout Nazarite, but he spends his time in feasting and with foreign women.[3] As for the third factor – to evoke perennial human hopes and fears – Samson's story resonates with more such deep emotions than the story of Gideon: to be loved (or betrayed) by a beloved woman, to be embraced (or rejected) by one's people and by God – to name but a few themes evoked by his story. Thus, the three parameters that signal a character's high potential to initiate a rich and varied body of dialogues are nicely fulfilled in the case of Samson.[4] To illustrate the diversity of dialogues generated by the Samson story, I will focus first on two modern examples – Jabotinsky's novel *Samson* (1927) and Cecil B. DeMille's film *Samson and Delilah* (1949) – and then add a comparative note on Milton's play *Samson Agonistes* (1671).

Jabotinsky's novel and DeMille's film had a great impact on contemporary readers and movie-goers and although they differ in many significant ways, they are also, unexpectedly, connected because the movie is partly based on the novel. When Cecil B. DeMille's *Samson and Delilah* was first released in 1949, and immediately turned out to be one of the first big blockbusters in the history of movie theater, not many viewers paid attention to the film's titles saying that the script was based not only "upon the history of Samson and Delilah in the Holy Bible, Judges 13–16," as would be expected, but also "from original treatments by Harold Lamb and Vladimir Jabotinsky" (referring to Jabotinsky's novel *Samson*). And if viewers did make a note of this, the name Vladimir (Ze'ev) Jabotinsky probably did not tell them very much.

Jabotinsky's Samson: A Secular National Hero

Jabotinsky's name, unknown to most American movie-goers, was quite familiar to many contemporary Jews, but not necessarily as the author of a work of fiction. Jabotinsky was associated first and foremost with the political and ideological leadership of the right wing Revisionist Zionist movement and its Beitar youth offshoot in the 1920s and 1930s. He died in 1940.

Vladimir (Ze'ev) Jabotinsky, born in Russia in 1880, began his career as a promising man of letters – a poet, a translator of poetry and a writer of stories and review articles[5] – before devoting most of his time and energy to the Zionist movement. During the late twenties, at the time that Jabotinsky was preoccupied with the founding of the Revisionist party, he was also writing *Samson*. The novel, originally composed in Russian, was published in 1927 and was almost immediately translated into Hebrew, German and English (the translation was also printed under the titles *Samson the Nazarite*, *Judge and Fool* and *Prelude to Delilah*). The English translation received critical acclaim (Katz 1996: 1053–54) and Hollywood bought the rights to the novel. Shmuel Katz, in his voluminous biography of Jabotinsky, comments that "Characteristic of Jabotinsky's business sense is his sale of the film rights for only $2,500" (Katz 1996: 1057).

Jewish readers in the Diaspora and in Palestine, especially those associated with the Revisionist party, enthusiastically embraced Jabotinsky's *Samson*, the writer's most politicized literary piece, with its advocacy of Jewish nationalism and portrayal of Samson as a model hero for contemporary Jews. The impact of the novel on the Jewish community in Palestine during the 1930s and 1940s is evoked in Amos Oz's *My Michael* (1968). The scene where Jabotinksy's *Samson* is mentioned actually takes place later in 1956, during the Sinai war (better known as the Suez Canal operation). Chana Gonen, the heroine of Oz's novel, is visited by two elderly rightwing neighbors who try to cheer her up when her husband, Michael, is mobilized. One of them, Mr. Kadishman, delivers this patriotic speech:

> Israel is no longer "as scattered sheep"; we are no longer a ewe among seventy wolves, or a lamb being led to the slaughter, we have had enough. "Among wolves, be a wolf." It has all happened as Jabotinsky foretold in his prophetic novel, *Prelude to Delilah*. Have you read Jabotinsky's *Prelude to Delilah*, Mrs. Gonen? It is well worth reading. And especially now that our army is pursuing the routed forces of Pharaoh and the sea is not divided for the fleeing Egyptians. (Oz 1972 [1968]: 168)

For these two elderly Revisionists, Jabotinsky's *Samson* did not function as a simple novel: its main character is a model hero, a mythical symbol, and the book provides historical guidance and a blueprint for contemporary politics.

To further grasp the novel's role as a catalyst and a focal point of national Jewish sentiments during the 1930s and 1940s we may look at the novel's most famous scene. Samson, blinded and in a Philistine prison, before the dramatic finale in the temple of Dagon, receives a visitor in his cell, one of his former warriors. In a chapter titled "Farewell" (or "The Will" or "Testament") Samson asks this visitor to deliver the following message to the Children of Israel:

> Tell them two things in my name – two words. The first word is iron. They must get iron. They must give everything they have for iron – their silver and wheat, oil and wine and flocks, even their wives and daughters. All for iron! There is nothing in the world more valuable than iron ... The second word they will not understand yet, but they must learn to understand it, and that soon. The second word is this: a king! Say to Dan, Benjamin, Judah, Ephraim: a king! A man will give them the signal and of a sudden thousands will lift up their hands. (Jabotinsky 1986 [1927]: 330–31)[6]

These formulations encapsulate Jabotinsky's belief that the most important factors determining a nation's fate are its ability to gather its vital forces and translate them into military might and unified political action. However, before the messenger leaves, Samson has an afterthought: "I have changed my mind. Tell them three things in my name, and not two: they must get iron; they must choose a king; and they must learn to laugh" (Jabotinsky 1986 [1927]: 331). This addition offers a mitigating factor to the Spartan message of military power and national unity embodied in the first two words. It advocates a sense of joie de vivre that the Israelites seem to lack (something the Philistines, their conquerors and neighbors, have). Samson's last message has become emblematic of Revisionist ideology, often learned by heart by followers of Jabotinsky.

Thanks to such memorable formulations Jabotinsky's Samson became a model hero for the Revisionist faithful and acquired mythical status. Even H. N. Bialik, the leading Hebrew poet of the early twentieth century, notwithstanding political disagreements with Jabotinsky, admitted that in writing *Samson* Jabotinsky had succeeded in doing what many authors might aspire to – creating a modern myth (Katz 1996: 1054–55).

Apart from the political ramifications of the novel, two interesting modifications are introduced into the biblical story. The first and perhaps the most provocative from a religious point of view is the re-telling of Judges from a radically secular perspective. In re-writing a traditional hero, every choice of genre has its implications (Stanford 1954: 5). Thus, perhaps the very attempt to re-write a biblical story in the form of a novel (and not, say, a long poem), implies a secular perspective: the great realist and naturalist tradition of the nineteenth-century novel, which Jabotinsky knew and cherished, presented characters as part of a social fabric without resorting to any superhuman interventions. Adopting the perspective implied by the decision to write a novel, Jabotinsky deliberately elaborated on the secular dimension, demonstrating that every event of the biblical story could be given a realistic explanation, based on social, ethnic, psychological and economic factors. Moreover, he particularly wanted to expose biblical references to God or to angels as the fabrications of interested parties.

Samson's strength, then, was not supernatural; he was simply an extremely resourceful warrior. Some of the so-called facts that come to us from the Bible are in fact legendary embellishments or elaborations. A small but representative example: the foxes with fiery tails that Samson loosed into the Philistines' crops were in fact a bunch of young fighters nicknamed "foxes" (or "jackals") led by Samson during some guerilla war against the Philistines and also helping him to solve disputes among his fellow Israelites. Another representative example: after Samson's locks were shorn and shaved by Delilah, he lost his might not because of any super-human factors associated with his status as a Nazarite but because he was ridiculed and humiliated by the Philistines. He quite naturally lost his confidence and self-respect. The supernatural event is thus explained in very simple psychological terms. Finally, the most iconoclastic element of all: Samson's birth is described as the result of adultery: the man who came to Samson's mother in the field (Judges 13) was no angel of God, but Samson's real father.

Let us take a closer look at how Jabotinsky conveys the notion that the biblical account of Samson's birth is based on fabrications intended to promote various characters' self-interest. When Samson's mother describes to Machbonai Ben-Shuni, a traveling Levite (a character Jabotinsky added to the story) how she met a stranger in the field it is clear that she is trying to obscure her cheating on her husband. She is using words that inadvertently give away the true nature of the events that took place that night:

> During the night she had been unable to sleep, for the air was very close; so she had slipped out of the house and taken a bucket to the well, intending to pour cold water over herself – at that time she was still very young and often did queer things. The stranger had arisen out of the thicket; his voice had been like the soughing of the wind in the leaves, and his words unlike any words spoken among her neighbors – but she could not recall the words he had spoken. Then she had turned faint and her heart stood still, for she realized that Jehovah Himself was with her, and she lost consciousness. (45)

Machbonai the Levite, like the reader, understands perfectly well what happened that night, but when he himself later reports these events in a prayer addressed to God, he joins Samson's mother in concealing their true nature:

> Finally, he reminded Jehovah of the story of Samson's birth as it is generally narrated: And the angel of the Lord appeared unto the woman and said unto her, "Thou shalt conceive and bear a son." And the woman hastened at once to her husband and told him of it. And Manoah arose and went after the man of God, and he took a kid and a meat-offering and offered it upon a rock unto the Lord, but the Angel ascended in the flame of the altar. (49)

It is clear why Samson's mother wants to conceal what really happened that night: to avoid Manoah's wrath and retribution and the stigmatizing of Samson as a bastard. The Levite has his own agenda for re-iterating the mother's cover-story: it is he, the Levite, who represents Jehovah on earth, and it is he who collects "meat-offering" in his role as a priest and the official chronicler and scribe of the family's history. Repeating the mother's cover-story is instrumental in building his political and economic power. Thus, Jabotinsky offers a radical secular, perhaps cynical, perspective on the biblical story and exposes religious functionaries as participating in the dissemination of self-serving lies. The critique of institutional religion was important to Jabotinsky, who was trying to promote the idea of a secular modern Jewish national identity as something distinguishable from traditional Judaism as a religious practice and set of beliefs.

In addition to the many contemporary ideological implications, Jabotinsky also introduced some highly imaginative new elements into the story. First, he proposed that Samson's first Timnath woman (called Semadar in the novel) and Elinoar, who later changed her name to Delilah, were half-sisters. In the Bible, the stories of these two women run on parallel lines. Both betray a secret Samson has told them to the Philistines, his enemies, but there is no reason to assume that they are related. By making them half-sisters, Jabotinsky added a plausible psychological motivation to Delilah's betrayal of Samson, beyond the greed presented in the Bible (Judges 16:5). Elinoar/Delilah is envious of her sister, with whom Samson is in love, and wants him to love her. The fact that Semadar, the beloved sister, is a legitimate daughter of the lady of the house and Elinoar/Delilah is the illegitimate daughter of a servant of inferior ethnic background, only fuels her hatred and adds social dimension to the psychological story of sibling envy.

Another added element is seen in the tragic culmination in the temple of Dagon: Jabotinsky makes Samson and Delilah meet again, this time after the consequences of her betrayal – he is imprisoned and blinded – have been revealed. A quick, emotionally charged exchange of words is taken place between the two. Elinoar/Delilah, still filled with vengeance and the will to humiliate Samson, taunts him by posing a series of riddles (a practice he himself had been fond of in the past):

> "Here is another riddle," she cried. "From the outcast came a conqueress, and the eyes that once looked on her with contempt will never see again. Do you know the answer to that riddle?" (340)

When Samson attempts to ignore her and briefly responds "Elinoar? Who is she? I don't remember her", she moves to her next riddle. This time the riddle is not made up only of words: Delilah carries a baby with her and makes Samson feel and touch it. Only then, after he asks her "Whose child is that?" she triumphantly formulates her final and fatal riddle:

> Guess! It will grow brave and strong like its father and I, since my milk has turned to poison, shall teach it to hate its father's race. And so, out of the judge and protector will come an enemy and destroyer. (341)

Hearing these words and realizing that Delilah is going to raise his child as an enemy of his people, Samson undergoes a frightening transformation:

> Then from the giant's throat came a strange gurgling sound that had little resemblance to a human voice. Stretching out his hands, he stepped forward, but collided with one of the pillars that supported the roof above the figure of Dagon and the sacrificial altar. The woman stood her ground, laughing and pressing to her breast the child, which was now crying plaintively again ... his excitement subsided, the smile came back to his face, and he said in his former voice, but very loudly and slowly: "Now you can all guess Samson's last riddle: In his lifetime he slew many, but more still in the hour of his death – who is that?" (341–42)

After the formulation of the last riddle comes the moment when Samson brings down the temple of Dagon on himself and on all who are present – first and foremost Elinoar/Delilah and his own child. The motivation for his suicidal act is thus presented as an outcome of his outrage on hearing that his own son was to be turned against his people. Throughout the novel, Samson is quite friendly with the Philistines, joins in their festivities, tells jokes and riddles, takes part in athletic competitions and of course makes love to Philistine women. Even after he is captured and blinded, the Philistines and he still maintain a reasonably amicable relationship. Only here, when he is faced with a dire and irreconcilable conflict between his role as a national leader and his role as a father, does he revert to basic tribal loyalties and destroys the temple, himself, Delilah, the child, and the Philistines in a fatal outburst of rage.

DeMille's Samson: A Christian, Forgiving Lover

If movie-goers expected that Cecil B. DeMille's *Samson and Delilah* (1949) would faithfully follow the biblical story in Judges 13–16, only fleshing out some details, some surprises awaited them. To be sure, the movie does not explicitly *contradict* anything told in the Bible but it does stretch the boundaries of the original story, notably when it comes to the portrayal of Delilah. Since the script was based not only on the original biblical story but also on Jabotinsky's *Samson*, a good starting point for commenting on the film's special outlook is to examine what the movie borrowed from the novel, what it ignored – and why.

DeMille adopted Jabotinsky's idea that Semadar (Angela Lansbury), the first Timnath woman, and Delilah (Hedy Lamarr) were half-sisters fighting for Samson's (Victor Mature) attention. As in the novel, so in the movie this element provides Delilah with a psychological motivation, explaining why she wanted to tempt and betray Samson, thus making the story in DeMille's words "a drama rather than a narrative" (DeMille 1959: 398) . But one can detect an interesting shift in this borrowed element. Whereas Jabotinsky underscores the social, ethnic and economic dimensions involved in the sisters' competition for Samson's heart, what matters to DeMille is Delilah's personal ambition to be the loved one; in Jabotinsky we learn of the inferior ethnic and social status of Delilah's mother; in DeMille we simply know that Delilah is Semadar's younger sister (not half-sister). Thus, DeMille replaces Jabotinsky's interest in the role of social reality as motivating people's actions with a timeless, romantic love story.

Ignoring Delilah's social background is on a par with DeMille's skipping over other important social and political dimensions of the novel. A great part of Jabotinsky's *Samson* revolves around the ideas of Jewish nationalism and the necessary political strategy for constructing national power. This historical and political dimension is almost totally forgotten in the film.

In its stead, DeMille develops two important elements. First and foremost, the movie becomes an elaborate love story. DeMille tells in his autobiography how he was trying to sell the idea of the biblical story of Samson and Delilah to the executives of Paramount Pictures:

> I asked Dan Groesbeck to draw a simple sketch of two people – a big, brawny athlete and, looking at him with an at once seductive and coolly measuring eye, a slim and ravishingly attractive young girl.
>
> When the executives trooped in, ready to save me and Paramount from the ruinous folly they were sure I had in mind, I greeted them, saw them to their seats, and brought out the Groesbeck sketch.
>
> "How is that," I asked them, "for the subject of a picture?"
>
> They were enthusiastic. That was movies. That was boy-meets-girl – and what a boy, and girl!
>
> "That, gentlemen," I said, "is *Samson and Delilah*." (DeMille 1959: 398–99)

In the script and production DeMille fleshed out the theme of a romantic love story to the end. In addition to the story of Samson and Delilah, taken in unexpected directions, we encounter other love stories: between Samson and Semadar (his beloved Timnath, first woman), between Lord Achtur (Henry Wilcoxon), a noble Philistine, and Semadar, between Samson and Miriam (Olive Deering), a Hebrew maiden and a commendable match for Samson, and between the Saran of Gaza (George Sanders), presented as the Philistine leader, and Delilah. Some of these love stories are already present in the Bible (the first Timnath woman and Samson and Delilah) and others were taken from Jabotinsky's novel (e.g. the character of a Hebrew maiden, named Karni in the novel, who became Miriam in the film) but DeMille brought the whole issue of romantic love to a new level. To complicate the intrigue, he developed the character of the Saran as a worthy opponent to Samson in the contest for Delilah's heart: she has to choose between the wise leader of her people and the attractive Hebrew strongman; she becomes the Saran's concubine, but her heart still belongs to Samson, despite the risks involved. Amorous intrigues, unexpected plot twists, and the variations of love became the major theme of DeMille's movie: Lord Achtur's possessive love for Semadar, Miriam's devotional love for Samson, the Saran's instrumental love of Delilah, Samson's spontaneous love first for Semadar and then for Delilah, and above all Delilah's love for Samson: first as a whim and then from the depths of her heart. In Jabotinsky the love story is intertwined with the social, ethnic, economic and political background of the characters; in DeMille, the social and political context is pushed into the background, playing, at most, the role of a colorful setting for the love story (or stories).

The elaboration of love's triangle (or quadrangle) and the diminished interest in social reality do not mean that there are no references to history in DeMille's film. These references, however, take the form of mythical history – as opposed to Jabotinsky's deep interest in concrete ethnic, political and economic life. In the opening scene, for example, we see a group of Israelite villagers, oppressed by the Philistines, reminiscing about the Exodus from Egypt, daydreaming of a new Moses who will liberate them from contemporary bondage. History is presented as cyclical – Pharaoh is made equivalent to the Philistines, the Israelites in Egypt are the same people as the tribes in the Land of Israel – without any real interest in the historical specificity of the Philistines and the Israelites.

Furthermore, to connect Samson's story to mythical history, DeMille adds a prologue to the movie: while we watch images of the earth, hurried by winds and clouds, alarming idols and the trampling boots of conquering legions, we hear, in dramatic voice-over, the following narration:

> Before the dawn of history, ever since the first man discovered his soul, he has struggled against the forces that sought to enslave him. He saw the awful power of nature arrayed against him: the evil eye of the lightening, the terrifying voice of the thunder, the shrieking wind-filled darkness – enslaving his mind in shackles of fear. Fear breeds superstition, blinding his reason. He was ridden by a host of devil-gods; human dignity perished on the altar of idolatry. And tyranny rules; grinding the human spirit beneath the conqueror's heel. But deep in man's heart still burns the unquenchable will for freedom. When this divine spark flames in the soul of some mortal, whether priest or soldier, artist or patriot, lover or statesman, his deeds have changed the course of human events and his name survives the ages. In the village of Zorea in the land of Dan, one thousand years before the birth of Christ, lived such a man. In him the elements had fused greatness and weakness, strength and folly. But with these was a bold dream: liberty for his nation. The man's name was Samson. For forty years the Philistines had held his people in bondage. (DeMille 1949)

The prologue offers a brief account of human history. According to this narrative there is a constant, recurring battle between the forces of evil and the forces of good. DeMille packs together superstition, idolatry and tyranny on the one hand, and human dignity, belief in one God and freedom and democracy on the other. Needless to say, this brief course in history had contemporary political resonance. It was composed four years after the end of the Second World War and the beginning of the Cold War, and there is no question that DeMille is drawing a direct line from the ancient Hebrews to their Christian heirs and from there to modern democracies, notably the United States of America. By the same token, he is identifying a line connecting ancient tyrannies with contemporary non-believing and totalitarian regimes, i.e. communism and the Soviet Union.

Aside from the political implications of the Cold War, DeMille slips another interesting dimension into the mythical narrative of the prologue: we hear the first hint that connects the story of Samson with Jesus Christ, introduced in the time reference: "one thousand years before the birth of Christ lived such a man." This is not the only such suggestion in the film. In fact, when we first see Samson, in the second scene of the movie, he is carrying a lamb; in addition to making Samson a shepherd for his people (something we do not have in the Bible) it might also invoke the idea of Jesus as the Good Shepherd.

This first image of Samson is clearly associated with Jesus, as is his last appearance, in the temple of Dagon. During the concluding scene, where Samson stands between the two columns of the temple, just before he brings it down on everybody, DeMille deliberately directs Samson – with his position, his wounds and his agonized expression – so that his figure immediately evokes the figure of Christ on the cross. There is no mention of a torture scene in the Bible or in Jabotinsky's novel, such that might have caused bleeding wounds on the hero's chest, legs and arms in a way that highlights the association with Christ. Needless to say, DeMille was not the first to make a connection between Samson and Jesus; there is a rich tradition portraying Samson as a precursor of Christ, especially in medieval art (Krouse 1949; Fishelov 2000: 157–170). Instead of Jabotinsky's representation of Samson as a model hero for modern Zionism, DeMille develops Samson as a Jesus-like figure. Thus the personage is elevated above the supposedly historical chain of events and above existence as an earthly lover to a more spiritual plane. The corporeal, earthly Samson acquires a saintly Christian aura, not only through visual images but also because he nobly forgives Delilah. Samson's forgiveness is closely related to perhaps the most innovative element introduced into the film: making Delilah a penitent.

In the biblical story, Delilah plays her role as a temptress and betrayer and after she sells Samson's secret to the Philistines she simply disappears. In Jabotinsky's novel, as we saw, she meets him again after the betrayal, but only to tantalize and further torment him. DeMille's Delilah, however, plays a more central role. She is deeply in love with Samson, fighting Miriam (the proposed Hebrew bride) whom she perceives as her rival. Her passion causes her also to defy the Saran of Gaza, her benefactor and partner, and in the final scene she sacrifices herself in order to be united with her true love. This final scene has overtones that go beyond the act of a desperate woman. Samson is indirectly associated with Jesus Christ and Delilah is portrayed as a penitent and almost a martyr.[7]

After Delilah discovers, to her horror, that Samson has been blinded, she falls into a state of self-torment. In a touching scene we see her tossing sleeplessly on her bed, with the harsh words of the Saran echoing in her mind – "You cannot undo what you have done" – and we hear her addressing Samson's God in an attempt to seek help. Thus, Delilah is not only a passionate woman in love but also a born-again monotheist. Deeply remorseful, Delilah decides to visit Samson again in his prison cell, this time without the Saran and without a guard. She throws herself into his arms asking him to do whatever he pleases with her. The fact that during her secret visit to the prison cell she is dressed in a way that reminds one of a nun gives her a chaste, sincere appearance. When Samson realizes that he is holding his betrayer in his arms, his first impulse is to take revenge and crush her to death. While making his first move towards this end, his chain breaks, a sign that his legendary strength has returned, and he hesitates. There and then follows an emotional and tender moment as he recognizes Delilah's true love for him and his own love for her.

The belated lovers' union encourages Delilah to suggest that she will help him to escape from prison and both of them will flee to Egypt – representing a neutral place, far from the national and religious feuds that plague their lives and hinder their love. Samson checks her fantasizing about this happy ending, pointing out that he is, after all, blind and cannot exercise any power in the real world. At that point Samson's mind is already working on his final plan of revenge against his enemies the Philistines, this time with Delilah's help. Delilah's sentimental happy end is rejected, and there is a better, more melodramatic conclusion awaiting the audience.

Thus, as the final scene in the temple of Dagon begins, we know that Samson and Delilah will collaborate like a loving couple. When the camera zooms in on Delilah, she is seated next to the Saran like a queen, wearing a dress with a long peacock-like train. When Samson is brought into the hall – to be tormented, humiliated and eventually to be made to renounce his God and kneel before Dagon – Delilah expresses her desire to take an active part in the proceedings. The Saran suspects that she simply wants to be close to her beloved (and he is right); he warns her "if you go to him, you cannot come back to me" – but Delilah defies his threat and approaches Samson.

Pretending to participate in the mocking, whipping and tormenting of Samson, she actually helps him to reach the two columns that support the temple. At that point, Delilah perhaps suspects Samson's intention, even if he does not express it. He only says to her: "Death will come into this temple. The hand of the Lord will strike." Before he starts to push at the two pillars, he wants to make sure that Delilah will escape the fate awaiting the crowds of Philistines gathered there. He asks her to leave the place and when he repeats "have you gone?" she is still present but does not respond, giving him the impression that she has left. But she remains, hypnotized by Samson's renewed strength, willing to die, like a true martyr, with her beloved.

At this point, it might be instructive to remember how Jabotinsky concluded his novel. Whereas for Jabotinsky the reunion of Samson and Delilah helps to underscore the unbridgeable gap between the two, DeMille used the scene to overcome their national and religious differences. In Jabotinsky, Delilah wanted to celebrate her victory over Samson; in DeMille, she was willing to sacrifice herself in an ultimate romantic gesture of joint suicide. If Jabotinsky wanted to say clearly that at critical moments one cannot, and should not, break his bonds with his national roots, DeMille wanted to show that forgiveness and love can overcome ethnic loyalties. Jabotinsky wanted to promote Zionist ideas; DeMille wished to advocate American, and Christian, ideals.

Ponytail, Genuine Dialogues and Milton's *Samson Agonistes*

Structurally, Jabotinsky's and DeMille's works can nicely illustrate the ponytail model (p. 70) suggested in Chapter 4: one post-biblical dialoguing text,

DeMille's movie (DT-2), brings us back to the first, initiating text (IT) – the biblical chapters – but also makes use of an interesting dialoguing text (DT-1) – Jabotinsky's novel – without necessarily producing a significant dialogue with it. Note that Jabotinsky was not the first to devise a meeting between Samson and Delilah *after* the betrayal: two and a half centuries before Jabotinsky wrote his novel, in *Samson Agonistes* (1671) John Milton made Delilah visit Samson in his prison cell in an attempt to obtain forgiveness. In fact, Milton's entire play consists of a series of meetings between Samson, captured and blinded in the Philistine prison, and several characters, some taken from the biblical story (Manoah, Delilah) and some invented (Harapha of Gath).

When we read the first words of Milton's Dalila (= Delilah), we might get the impression that she is a true penitent. Delilah's plea to Samson is ostensibly sincere, and her speech is fraught with kind words:

> With doubtful feet and wavering resolution
> I came, still dreading thy displeasure, *Samson*,
> Which to have merited, without excuse,
> I cannot but acknowledge; yet, if tears
> May expiate (though the fact more evil drew
> In the perverse event than I foresaw),
> My penance hath not slack'n'd, though my pardon
> No way assur'd. But conjugal affection,
> Prevailing over fear and timorous doubt,
> Hath led me on desirous to behold
> Once more thy face, and know of thy estate.
> If aught in my ability may serve
> To light'n what thou suffer'st, and appease
> Thy mind with what amends is in my power,
> Though late, yet in some part to recompense
> My rash but more unfortunate misdeed. (Milton 1937: 732–47)

According to Milton, however, all Delilah's words of comfort are but a façade, a further manifestation of her artful guile and wiliness. Samson does not succumb to her rhetoric, and at some point it becomes clear that Delilah's soothing words do not express genuine repentance. Towards the end of their meeting, Samson calls her bluff and in response, she says:

> I shall be nam'd among the famousest
> Of Women, sung at solemn festivals,
> Living and dead recorded, who to save
> Her country from a fierce destroyer, chose
> Above the faith of wedlock-bands, my tomb
> With odours visited and annual flowers.
> Not less renown'd than in Mount *Ephraim*,
> *Jael*, who, with inhospitable guile

> Smote *Sisera* sleeping through the Temples nail'd.
> Nor shall I count it heinous to enjoy
> The public marks of honour and reward
> Conferr'd upon me, for the piety
> Which to my country I was judg'd to have shown.
> At this who ever envies or repines
> I leave him to his lot, and like my own. (982–96)

Thus, all her earlier pleasant words and professed love were meant to mislead and to camouflage the fact that she still takes pride in the honors conferred on her by the Philistines for betraying Samson. After these words she leaves, and Samson poignantly addresses the chorus:

> So let her go, God sent her to debase me,
> And aggravate my folly who committed
> To such a viper his most sacred trust
> Of secrecy, my safety, and my life. (999–1002)

According to Milton, Delilah's words of repentance are meant to lead Samson, and the reader, astray from true, deep Christian principles.

The three dialogues with the biblical story of Samson – by Milton, Jabotinsky and DeMille – illustrate the distinction between the very existence of an element or a motif and the function it serves: all three versions add a scene which is not part of the original story (the reunion of Samson and Delilah) but in each case this new element serves different ideological goals. Both Milton and DeMille use the reunion of Samson and Delilah to promote Christian ideas, but they assign to Delilah a totally opposite role: in Milton Delilah's pleasant words camouflage satanic temptation,[8] in DeMille she represents genuine repentance. We should also note that whereas in Milton, Christian ideas are at the play's core, in the movie Christian motifs play only a secondary role, supporting the major theme of a "bigger than life" love story. And in one aspect, Jabotinsky's secular version of the story is found unexpectedly closer to Milton than to the modern movie: both Milton and Jabotinsky use the reunion scene to emphasize Delilah's inherent wickedness and treachery.

The recurring motif of a reunion scene in all three post-biblical DTs further highlights the usefulness of the ponytail model. The model enables us to trace the appearances as well as the transformations of certain motifs in the rich history of dialogues with the biblical story of Samson and reminds us that the borrowing of an element by one DT from an earlier DT (or DTs) does not necessarily mean these DTs are engaged in a dialogue: DeMille's film is not a dialogue with Jabotinsky's novel, just as the latter is not dialoguing with Milton's play, despite the fact that all three added the same invented scene. All three, however, do conduct an active, original dialogue with the IT, namely the biblical story of Samson.

These three versions of re-writings of the Samson story can also illustrate the unpredictable nature of genuine dialogues: they differ not only in medium, language, genre and period but also in their ideological goals and in the rhetorical means they use to promote these goals. Again, the introduction of the reunion scene underscores the unpredictable nature of genuine dialogues: it is difficult not only to predict the very introduction of a new element but also the specific direction that the new motif takes. In other words, if after reading Milton's play we were told that DeMille also made Delilah meet Samson in his prison cell and then we were asked to guess the nature of their encounter, we would probably come up with the wrong answer.

The innovative dimension of the three genuine dialogues is located in different areas: deepening and complicating the spiritual struggle Samson has to go through when he encounters several characters representing different aspects of his life and psyche (Milton); re-constructing Samson as a secular, national leader, a model to be emulated by contemporary Jews (Jabotinsky); elaborating on Samson as the passionate but also forgiving lover (DeMille).

Compared with the versions of Milton and Jabotinsky, one could perhaps dismiss DeMille's film as part of popular culture, complying with many conventions of a prototypical Hollywood production. It is important, however, to caution against such a hasty dismissal. First, we should not forget that DeMille was in fact *creating* what would come to be known as a typical Hollywood production. Secondly, popularity among movie-goers or readers is not, in and of itself, a mark of bad art. The dialogic perspective advocated in this study enables us to describe DeMille's film as a genuine dialogue, without automatically relying on the value-ridden opposition of popular vs. elite culture. To be a genuine dialogue means first and foremost that it is a more complex, hence unpredictable artistic creation than an echo-dialogue and, compared to dialogue-of-the-deaf, it is still attentive to the IT. True, compared to echo-dialogues, a genuine dialogue has perhaps a better chance to become a new influential work on its own right: Jabotinsky's novel, for example, became a source of inspiration for many authors in Modern Hebrew literature.[9] Still, to label an artistic work as a 'genuine dialogue' is primarily meant to describe its relationship with an IT, not to valorize it.

CHAPTER

7

Jesus Christ – Monty Python and Saramago

The New Testament is one of the most influential texts ever composed, shaping the beliefs and sentiments of billions of people over two millennia. Its greatest appeal lies in the chief character – Jesus Christ. More specifically, I would like to argue that it is the tensions and contradictions embedded in the character of Jesus that make him so attractive to the imagination: his spiritual vision and deep moral stance elevate him above ordinary humans and regular social structures but at the same time he is inferior when it comes to actual political power. He is a social revolutionary, planning to reverse accepted hierarchies, ready to challenge social practices ("And Jesus went into the temple of God, and cast out all them that sold and bought in the temple, and overthrew the tables of the moneychangers"; Matthew 21:12) but also does not wish to confront existing social structures of power (e.g. "Render therefore unto Caesar the things which are Caesar's: and unto God the things that are God's"; Matthew 22:21); his teaching advocates forgiveness ("whosoever shall smite thee on the right cheek, turn to him the other also"; Matthew 5:39) but also severe strictness ("whosoever looketh on a woman to lust after her hath committed adultery with her already in his heart"; Matthew 5:28); he promotes an extremely compassionate attitude towards the meek, the weak, the poor, the outcast ("I am not sent but unto the lost sheep of the house of Israel"; Matthew 15:24), but also requires hardening of the heart towards our family, our closest and dearest human beings ("Who is my mother? And who are my brethren? And he stretched forth his hand toward his disciples, and said, Behold my mother and my brethren!"; Matthew 12:48–49); he is confident in his place next to the Almighty ("I say unto you, Hereafter shall ye see the Son of man sitting on the right hand of power, and coming in the clouds of heaven"; Matthew 26:64) but also has a moment of crisis ("Jesus cried with a loud voice, saying, E-li, E-li, la-ma sa-bach-tha-ni? that is to say, My God, my God, why hast thou forsaken me?"; Matthew 27:46). Also in Jesus the teacher one encounters contradictory tendencies: on the one hand he approaches everybody, talks to every one who is willing to listen, scatters his parables in the market place; but on the other, his sermons are directed to the handful of the chosen who can grasp the deep, mysterious meanings hidden in his words, making him the most egalitarian and the most aristocratic teacher of all times (e.g. Mark 4:1–20). This series of contradictions emanates from, or finds its ultimate apex in, Jesus' dual status as human being and as God.

So far, attention was called to some contradictions apparent in the character of Jesus as we know him from the Synoptic Gospels. Tension between a character's traits, as argued at the beginning of Chapter 5, is the second factor indicating a strong potential to arouse dialogue. The first factor was that the character should represent a high point in some human domain. While Jesus does not excel in beauty or as a warrior on the battlefield, there is no doubt that he represents the summit of humanity in many spheres: spirituality, depth of faith, courage in confronting political authority – to name a few that come to mind. Finally, as the third factor in estimating a character's potential, Jesus's actions are related to perennial human hopes and fears, perhaps the deepest and most persistent ones: the hope of immortality and the fear of dying forsaken and desolate, and with no afterlife.

It is precisely the high inspirational potential embodied in the character of Jesus that has attracted so many readers, interpreters and artists throughout the ages – not necessarily an authoritative ecclesiastical dictate. All these readers, interpreters and artists have tried to cope, each according to her or his sensibilities and objectives, with the story of Jesus, serving as its echo chamber, or probing it from different perspectives, or bringing to life some of its hidden meanings. In this chapter two such modern, iconoclastic dialogues with the New Testament will be examined. As with Kierkegaard and Levin in Chapter 5, these two works differ in almost every conceivable respect – genre, tone, language, culture and mode. Furthermore, whereas Saramago's *The Gospel according to Jesus Christ* is a novel, my other example is a cinematic dialogue: Monty Python's *The Life of Brian*.

Monty Python's Hilarious Parody

Our first example, Monty Python's *The Life of Brian* (1979), obviously illustrates a parodic treatment of the New Testament. The Monty Python group is known for its iconoclastic, anarchic humor, from the short sketches of their TV show *The Flying Circus* to the feature films they began to make during the seventies. The *Life of Brian* takes a further step in the direction previously followed by *The Holy Grail* (1975), an earlier feature film; whereas in *The Holy Grail* Monty Python bestow their parodic, lampooning treatment on English history and Arthurian legend, in *The Life of Brian* they direct it at the roots of Christianity. The overall parody is based on a simple idea – to tell the story of someone named Brian who lived at the same time as Jesus Christ, was involved with activities like those attributed to Jesus Christ and, finally, like Jesus, was crucified by the Romans.

The first scene of the film not only situates the story line in the time and place of Jesus (caption says "Judea A.D. 33"), but actually presents someone who is most probably Jesus himself, in the midst of preaching what sounds like parts of the Beatitudes from the Sermon on the Mount in Matthew 5:2–11.[1] After presenting Jesus – or at least a conventional representation of Jesus – the camera moves to the crowd of people listening to the sermon, including our hero Brian and his mother, and focuses on a small group at the back of the crowd. Here the Monty Python parody begins: some of the people treat the sermon as a way to pass the time, as free entertainment. Brian's mother, for instance, pushes him to find something more exciting such as a stoning to death. Some people are busy teasing other people (incited by one individual who refers to another as "big nose"), and the heated exchange of words develops into a fist fight. A contrast emerges between Jesus' words of peaceful wisdom and the pettiness and grudges of people in the audience.

Another dimension of the parody lies in the exposure of problematic aspects of the hermeneutical process: because of the distance from Jesus, his words are not heard clearly or correctly, and some people think they are hearing something totally different. Instead of "Blessed are the meek" (Matthew 5:5), someone hears "Blessed are the Greek" and a whole series of comical mistakes ensues, revolving around some famous sayings from the Sermon on the Mount. The idea of distorted hermeneutics is further exploited as the movie progresses. Words are not only misheard, leading to a series of hilarious results ("blessed are the cheese makers") but even when they are not distorted, they can be misunderstood and misinterpreted.

A nice instance of this dynamics of misinterpretation moved by people's desires occurs when Brian is followed by a crowd who believe him to be the Messiah. Brian tries to escape and push them off, and when they catch up with him in the midst of the desert he is still emphatically denying that he is the Messiah: "Would you please listen, I am not the Messiah, Do you understand? Honestly!" Their immediate response, however, shows how true believers can treat words: "Only the true Messiah denies his divinity." An explicit statement, accompanied by a forceful clarification of intentions, does not stand in the way of people who *want* to understand certain things in what they hear. The will of the interpreter easily prevails over the intentions of the speaker, taking his words to mean the opposite of what he is saying.

The tortuous, twisting ways of interpretation demonstrated by the people who follow Brian to the desert are closely associated with a larger phenomenon satirically exposed in *The Life of Brian*: the dynamics characterizing a horde of believers. Waking up at home in the morning, Brian discovers that a crowd of his followers are sitting next to the house, waiting for him to deliver his "message" to them. He is horrified and, as in the desert, tries to convince them to leave him alone, to abandon the crowd mentality, to adopt independent, individual thinking. Their response shows how naïve he is in expecting a crowd of believers to listen and absorb words of wisdom even when they come from the mouth of the very man they suppose themselves to believe in. Perhaps the most memorable exchange is Brian's exhortation: "You've got to think for yourselves. You're all individuals," to which the crowd responds enthusiastically and unanimously: "Yes, we're all individuals!" When Brian insists that they are all different, they echo: "Yes, we are all different!" To underscore the silliness of this mob of "different individuals," one dissenting voice dares to say "I'm not."

As the crowd of blind believers pursues the new "Messiah" another aspect of mob mentality is exposed: the tendency of zealous believers to split. While Brian is fleeing from the Romans and from his followers, they are busy finding "signs" in everything he does. The first thing that happens is that a schism forms between followers of Brian's gourd and followers of Brian's shoe. Needless to say, these two "sacred signs" have no hidden meanings whatsoever: Brian was forced to buy the gourd in a comic scene of haggling in the market and then simply gave it to someone, and as for his shoe – it fell off while he was trying to escape his lunatic devotees and he did not stop to pick it up lest he be caught by them.

The amoeba-like sectarian tendencies of ardent religious or ideological groups are satirized in Monty Python's representation of Judea's "freedom fighters" whom Brian has joined. When he identifies the small group of rebels in the local coliseum – they are attending a gladiatorial show and he is selling them snacks – he wants to join them in the fight against the Roman occupiers of Judea. But it seems that most of their energy is spent not in fighting the Romans but rather in distinguishing themselves from rival groups of freedom fighters, distinguished only by different grammatical constructions of the words "Judean People's Front." At some point, one of Brian's associates is so carried away by his denunciations of rival groups that he denounces his own comrades. This misdirected hatred culminates during a would-be terrorist attack on the palace of Pontius Pilate, when two competing bands meet on their way to execute a similar plan: kidnap the governor's wife and demand the dismantling of the Roman Empire. Instead of joining forces, they start to fight each other. When Brian, the naïve recruit who truly wishes to fight the Romans (for dubious personal reasons, by the way), reminds them that they should be struggling together against their common enemy, they try to guess who that common enemy might be: "The Judean People's Front?" The only person left standing after a heated battle between the two factions of freedom fighters is Brian; he is caught by the Roman legionaries, who were watching the fight all the time in amused astonishment.

Throughout the film the group of insurgents becomes a central butt of the satire: their tendency to split, their misdirected hatreds, their absorption in hollow rhetoric (instead of rushing to save Brian they are busy formulating a decision), their ridiculous version of feminism (to fight for the *right* of a group member, a man-who-wants-to-become-woman, to give birth to a child). Now what has all this got to do with the life of Jesus? The truth of the matter is that it has very little to do with the New Testament and Jesus. A great part of the satirical attack is directed at modern targets, notably the follies of national liberation fronts and some aspects of the radical left. Situating this criticism in the circumstances of Judea of the first century CE adds a comic dimension but it does not necessarily make that historical situation the main butt of the satire.

As Ben-Porat has argued (Ben-Porat 1979), parody might critically expose the parodied text *and* the social world and values embedded in that text, but at times the satirical target *is different* from the text parodied. Parody in these cases contributes to the overall comic effect, but should not be confused with a satirical attack – and this is what happens in parts of *The Life of Brian*. Even in the opening scene, where Jesus is represented, it is clear that the target of the satire is not the preaching of Jesus as such but the distorted hermeneutical modes which his teaching is made to go through – where "blessed are the meek" turns into "blessed are the Greek" – and the huge gap between the elevated content of preaching love of your neighbour and the basic instinct to punch your neighbor because of a silly remark he has made.

Monty Python's *The Life of Brian* has been introduced as an anarchic, iconoclastic film that takes many liberties with the New Testament and displays a wild parodic technique. Some of these hilarious, carnival-like effects, however, do not amount to a direct satirical criticism of the teaching of Jesus. The vehement opposition and censorship the film has encountered from devout Christians is perhaps a bit exaggerated.[2] The film does not embody a serious anti-religious attitude, and many of its comic effects have little to do with the teachings of Jesus Christ and the spiritual content of the New Testament. Still, for many believers, the very idea of producing a parody based on the sacred is considered as crossing a red line and lightheadedness is considered a sin.

Saramago's Serious Re-telling

Unlike the lightheadedness of Monty Python, the next dialogue we shall examine is a serious re-telling of the life of Jesus. Although *The Gospel according to Jesus Christ* (1991) contains many familiar elements from the New Testament, readers will be taken aback on many fronts. The first surprise is the fact that the book does not open with the expected textual passage but with a picture of a woodcut, followed by a detailed description.[3]

The movement of the observing eye is very odd, in some sense foreshadowing the major characteristics of the novel as a whole. Before we even start reading the description, we, readers-spectators, know that this is a picture of Jesus Christ, not only because of the book's title – *The Gospel according to Jesus Christ* – but mainly because we are familiar with centuries of pictorial representations of Jesus on the cross. We would expect the description to start with the most important figure in the picture, situated at the center, i.e. Jesus Christ. Instead, the description focuses first on the upper left corner of the picture and on a non-human object, the sun:

> The sun appears in one of the upper corners of the rectangle, to the left of anyone looking at the picture. Representing the sun is a man's head which sends out rays of brilliant light and sinuous flames, like a wavering compass in search of the

Dürer's "The Crucifixion"

right direction, and this head has a tearful face, contorted by spasms of pain which refuse to abate. (Saramago 1993: 1)[4]

Note how the detailed description of the sun's facial expression helps to blur the usual boundaries and hierarchies between the human and the non-human. The next sentence continues the description of the sun and introduces a new dimension: "The gaping mouth sends up a cry we shall never hear, for none of these things is real, what we are contemplating is mere paper and ink, and nothing more." This self-reflexive dimension is unexpectedly introduced, blocking us from immersion in the represented world described, keeping us watchful of the role of the reader-spectator in constructing and interpreting that world. Saramago plays with our probable expectation to encounter a story representing real or fictional life. First, by offering us an engraving instead of a text; secondly, by focusing on a marginal figure, and finally, by heightening our awareness of the whole process of representation.

After these opening manipulations, we move to a description of a person hanging on a cross (on the left side of the image). So perhaps now we shall learn about Jesus? Not necessarily:

> Beneath the sun we see a naked man tied to a tree trunk with a cloth tied round his loins to cover those parts we call private or the genital organs, and his feet are resting on a piece of wood set crosswise, to give him support, and to prevent his feet from slipping, they are held by two nails driven deeply into the wood. Judging from the anguished expression on the man's face, and from his eyes which are raised to heaven, this must be the Good Thief. (1)

The identification of the Good Thief is presented as the conclusion of a hypothetical line of reasoning, based on a series of clues ("Judging from... and from"). The author could, of course, have adopted an authoritative, omniscient stand from which there would have been no need to justify statements about the identity of certain figures. By limiting the range of his knowledge to that of an ordinary spectator, trying to decipher the engraving and using inductive logic, the author alerts us to the crucial role of any reader or spectator in understanding and interpreting a picture and, by implication, any artistic representation or any representation of reality. The hesitant tone reinforces the preceding comment about the status of a picture, an engraving, as artifact, putting the reader on the alert.

So perhaps after the assumed Good Thief we shall finally move to the person who interests us most? Once more Saramago frustrates our expectation and the next human figure described is a man with a long beard situated below the Good Thief:

> Richly attired in loose, flowing robes, he is looking upwards but not towards heaven. This solemn posture and sad countenance must surely belong to Joseph of Arimathaea, because the only other person who comes to mind, Simon of Cyrene, after being forced to help the condemned man to carry his cross, as was the practice when these executions took place, went about his own affairs, much more anxious about a business transaction which called for an urgent decision than about the sufferings of a miserable wretch about to be crucified. (1–2)

Note, again, the modalities ("must surely") and the long explanation intended to corroborate the hypothesis about the figure's identity ("because the only person....") in which the speaker suddenly assumes an omniscient stance, reporting Simon of Cyrene's actions as if he has privileged knowledge of Simon's whereabouts and state of mind ("anxious about a business transaction"). All these long explanations, the hypothetical guesswork and shift in point of view put the reader on the alert about the validity of the description and perhaps of any description of what is "really" represented in a work of art.

The narrator goes on to elaborate a bit on Joseph of Arimathaea, and while doing so introduces a subtle critical comment on the Church's system of honours: "Now then, this Joseph of Arimathaea is that affluent and good-hearted man who donated a grave for the burial of the greatest criminal of all, but this act of generosity will be to no avail when the time comes to consider his beatification, let alone canonisation" (2). From Joseph of Arimathaea the narrator moves on to describe a woman kneeling below Joseph, presumably named Mary, followed by a detailed discussion regarding the question which Mary this is, and offering some compelling arguments in support of the claim that this one is Mary Magdalene:

> The kneeling woman must be Mary because, as we know, all the women gathered here have this name, with one exception, for she is also called Magdalene. Anyone viewing this picture, who is aware of the elementary facts of life, will swear at first sight that this is precisely the woman called Magdalene for only someone with her disreputable past would have dared to turn up at such a solemn occasion wearing a low-cut dress with a close-fitting bodice to emphasize her ample bosom, which inevitably attracts the lewd stares of passing men, putting their souls at grave risk, dragged to their perdition by that sinful flesh. Yet the expression on her face is one of sad contrition and her wilting body conveys nothing other than her sorrowing soul, which we cannot ignore, even if it is concealed by tempting flesh, for this woman could be completely naked, had the artist so chosen to portray her, and she would still be deserving of our respect and veneration. Mary Magdalene, if that is her name, is holding to her lips the hand of another woman who has collapsed on to the ground as if bereft of strength or mortally wounded. (2)

As with the identification of other figures in the painting, by exposing his considerations, hesitations and decisions, the narrator only arouses the reader's more acute attention. To make sense of the represented scene we cannot allow ourselves to remain in a state of uncertainty as to the figures' identities, so we accept the narrator's decision that this is indeed Mary Magdalene. But only a few lines later on, after focusing on what seems to be Mary the mother of Jesus, the narrator suddenly calls into question the assumption that he has established, raising the possibility that Mary Magdalene is in fact another woman:

> Reclining on her left side, Mary, the mother of Jesus, rests her forearm on the hip of another woman, also kneeling and also called Mary, and who might well be the real Mary Magdalene although we can neither see nor imagine the neckline of her tunic. Like the first woman in this trinity, she wears her long tresses hanging loose

down her back, but to all appearances they are fair, unless it is only by chance that the pen-strokes are different, more delicate ... We are not trying to prove that Mary Magdalene was, in fact, blonde, but simply conforming to the popular belief that women with blonde hair, whether it be natural or dyed, are the most effective instruments of sin and perdition. So Mary Magdalene who, as everyone knows, was as wicked a woman as ever lived, must have been blonde if we are to respect the firm opinion held, for better or worse, by half of mankind. However, it is not because this third Mary has fairer skin and hair than the first one that we are suggesting ... that she is the Magdalene. The overwhelming evidence which confirms her identity is that this third Mary, who is distractedly supporting the limp arm of the mother of Jesus, is looking upwards and her enraptured gaze ascends with such power that it appears to elevate her entire being like a bright aureole capable of outshining the halo already encircling her head and of suppressing every thought and emotion. Only a woman who had loved as much as we believe Mary Magdalene to have loved could possibly have such an expression, conclusive proof that it is her and no other, and thus excluding the woman standing beside her. (3)

A kaleidoscopic effect is systematically built into these descriptions: every movement in perspective, every rearrangement of certain details and every shift in some background knowledge may produce a new hypothesis, corroborate a different organizing principle and invalidate a previous interpretation. When popular assumptions about blond women are also brought into the picture – and questioned – the kaleidoscopic effect gains an almost comic effect. Note that the new hypotheses about the "true" identity of Mary Magdalene are not less convincing than the ones adduced a few lines earlier to support a different identification. Thus we are left wondering "Which woman is Mary Magdalene?" a question that underscores the deep epistemological question of how true knowledge can be achieved when it is based on a fallible, partial and sometimes biased series of conjectures. True, some conjectures may be more compelling than others, but the moment we read that we have "overwhelming evidence which confirms her identity" we are keenly aware that the previous section brought us no less "overwhelming evidence" and "conclusive proof" and the next sentences might bring with them other "overwhelming evidence" establishing a different identity.

After exhausting the description of the four women at the base of the engraving – all turn out to be different "Marys" – the narrator moves to a youth identified as John (or is he?) and from him, after a parenthetical sentence about Joseph of Arimathaea, to the crucified figure on the right, identified as the Bad Thief:

> Thin and smooth-haired, his head turned towards the earth that will devour him, condemned to both death and hell, this pathetic creature must be the Bad Thief, an upright man when all is said and done, who, free from divine and human laws, was honest enough not to pretend to believe that sudden repentance suffices to redeem a whole lifetime of evil or a mere moment of weakness. (4)

Into what appears to be a neutral description of the figure, Saramago sneaks a critical comment aimed against some practices of the Church. The narrator moves on to describe the moon above the Bad Thief, and the figures of horsemen in the background, and only then, after a long wait, does he come to the central – literally and metaphorically – figure of Jesus Christ.

At this point the reader assumes that the compositional logic of the long passage is that of movement from margin to center: the narrator began with the peripheral characters in order to conclude with an elaborate and in-depth description of the most important character, namely Jesus Christ. If the reader makes such an assumption, however, she/he is going to be frustrated. First, when we at last get to the description of Jesus Christ, it is not necessarily more elaborate or deeper or more insightful than the descriptions of the other characters. And, what is even more striking, this long opening section of the novel does not conclude with the figure of Jesus but rather moves again – against the reader's expectations – to a new character. This personage, who by all regular standards occupies a marginal position in the traditional scene of the Crucifixion, suddenly becomes the apex of the passage:

> Further back, in the same field where the horsemen execute one last manoeuvre, a man is walking away but looking back in this direction. In his left hand he is carrying a bucket and in his right a staff. On the tip of the staff there ought to be a sponge, not easy to see from here, and the bucket, one can safely wager, contains water with vinegar. (5–6)

By focusing on this marginal character, Saramago calls into question not only some assumptions about who deserves to be in front and who "further back" but also challenges some negative judgments of this character, supposedly based on mistaken assumptions and lack of relevant knowledge:

> One day, and forever more, this man will be much maligned and accused of having given Jesus vinegar out of spite and contempt when he asked for water, but if truth be told, he offered him vinegar and water because at that time it was one of the best ways of quenching thirst. (6)

Only then does Saramago conclude the passage, with this statement emphasizing a human, earthly perspective – as opposed to the religious or metaphysical – that we can, and should, adopt when trying to decipher perhaps the most influential story ever told:

> The man walks away, does not wait for the end, he has done all he could to assuage the mortal thirst of the three condemned men, and made no distinction between Jesus and the Thieves, for the simple reason that these are things of this Earth which will persist on Earth, and from these things the only possible history will be written. (6)

Make no mistake. Recommending a perspective that puts "things of the Earth" in the center does not mean that Saramago will stick to a realistic or naturalistic assumption in his re-telling of the story of Jesus' life and death. In his version of the story we encounter magical objects hidden in the ground, unidentified angels who walk the earth, Satan in various disguises and even God, all partaking in the story line of *The Gospel according to Jesus Christ*. Still, the opening passage represents, in miniature, Saramago's major artistic and ideological perspective throughout the novel, which can be summed up as four characteristics: (1) Playful frustration of the reader's expectations as to the identity of certain figures: Saramago establishes some assumptions in the reader's mind only to pull the rug out from under her/his feet; the most striking, almost shocking reversal of expectations in the novel regards the identity of God and Satan (e.g. the memorable scene where Jesus, God and Satan meet to talk in a boat on the Sea of Galilee, pp. 280–300). The play on the reader's expectations and the inversion of identities is closely related to (2) Reversal of expected and accepted hierarchies and judgments: who is, and who should be at the center, who should be praised, with whom we should identify and why out of the gallery of represented characters (Jesus or perhaps Devil-Pastor?); all these questions – hinted at in the opening passage – are elaborated in the novel. (3) Shooting some satirical arrows towards institutionalized religion, whether Jewish priests who delight in sacrificial rites (e.g. the memorable graphic description of sacrifices in the Temple, pp. 65–70) or the institutional Church absorbed in power and wealth. Perhaps "only a bigot or a fool would judge Saramago's *Gospel* to be blasphemous," as Bloom suggests (Bloom 2001: 155), but it is quite obvious that the novel radically shakes some accepted religious notions, especially those associated with the idea of a benevolent God. Alongside the satirical attack one can find a deep humanistic "refusal to acquiesce in unreasonable cruelty" (Fokkema 1999: 397).[5] (4) Calling attention to the act of representation and to the role of conventional cultural assumptions in reaching certain conclusions about "what was really going on then and there" (and also here and now). Saramago's novel, however, goes far beyond a playful meta-fiction dealing with questions of literary representation because, as Duarte argues, it treats the sacred source text as a mere genre to which one can add another "gospel" or "pseudo-gospel," thus provoking conservative Catholicism (Duarte: http://www.docstoc.com/docs).

Parody and Re-writing

Artists can produce a funny parody on a text using the dual structure of comic imitation and deviation, but without necessarily calling into question ideas and ideals related to the parodied text.[6] Monty Python's *The Life of Brian* showed how a hilarious parody can wage a satirical attack on phenomena that are not related to the parodied text. Some of the targets of the satire in the film – modern factions of liberation organizations, the tendency of their followers to disagree on nonsensical issues and to forget their original goal – are not part of the New Testament and its world. But it would be misleading to present *The Life of Brian* as innocent slapstick. The absurdity of the quarrel between followers of the shoe and followers of the gourd as to who carries more faithfully the master's legacy evidently refers to the history of Christianity. Moreover, the anarchic spirit of *The Life of Brian* and the very decision to re-tell the life of Jesus Christ in a burlesque style could arouse the antagonism of many devout believers (and it did). We can thus decide to see the movie as an iconoclastic attack on Christianity or as a hilarious but harmless parody (or a mixture of the two), and such a decision would undoubtedly be influenced by personal beliefs. But no matter what we ultimately decide, it is useful to keep the distinction between parody as the manipulation of texts, and satire as the criticism of social reality (Ben-Porat 1979; Hutcheon 2000 [1985]: 43–49).

In Saramago's *The Gospel according to Jesus Christ* we can detect the structure of parody – imitation and substitution, reversal of hierarchies – but without the comic effect. Saramago's novel can be described as a prototypical case of re-writing where the juxtaposition of the two texts "involves not only the construction of the best possible (for any actual reader) mental representation (schema) of the new text, but also changes in the previously constructed schema of the source text" (Ben-Porat 2003: 94). Two general conclusions can be drawn from these two examples of genuine dialogue with the New Testament. First, the technique and effects of parody are more multifaceted than generally assumed and, secondly, modern dialogues with the Scriptures tend to be iconoclastic, whether composed in secular, flippant Britain or in Catholic Portugal emerging from a long repressive dictatorship.

CHAPTER

8

Horace in Pushkin, Owen and Diderot

The number and diversity of dialogues conducted with classical Greco-Roman literature has undergone dramatic shifts through the ages, moved by changing ideological and aesthetic considerations. The Renaissance and Neo-classical periods, for example, brought Greek and Latin works back to literary life through translations, imitations, allusions and re-writings, and made some of them an indispensable acquisition for an educated person. Today, classical literature still enjoys a high status and is taught at university level but it no longer plays the role of a common cultural language.[1] Thus, one can question whether classical literature (in the historical sense of the word) is still classical (in the sense of a great book), especially from the perspective of the dialogic approach, because this approach requires that a work should generate many and diverse dialogues. If classical literature's dissemination is declining, perhaps it is losing its standing as a collection of great books.

My task here is neither to eulogize classical literature nor to rebuke the impoverishment of contemporary culture; rather, to study the ways some Greco-Roman texts have been and still are generating dialogues, thus reflecting and maintaining their reputation.

Special attention may be given in this context to the role played by certain expressions taken from classical texts. These expressions, which have become part of what can be described as an extended dictionary, help keep classical works circulating in contemporary culture. When someone uses one of these expressions this does not mean that she or he has read the text in which the expression originated. It also does not mean that the writer or spectator recognizes and activates the IT (initiating text). Still, as there is a good chance that someone who introduces the expression "My kingdom for a horse" into discourse knows that it comes from Shakespeare's *Richard III* and wants his audience to think of Shakespeare's play, so when someone says "*dulce et decorum est pro patria mori*" she or he wants to evoke Horace's ode. Such expressions indicate that at some level classical literature still circulates in contemporary culture, but this circulation can be very superficial. If we recall the pyramid model introduced in Chapter 4, these expressions belong to the lowest level of the pyramid, representing the most minimal and passive form of dialogue. In many cases their use does not indicate an invocation of the IT with its specificity, thus making a genuine literary allusion with a network of meaningful, bi-directional relations (Ben-Porat 1978). It may be used simply to emphasize a point and at the same time signal that the writer or speaker is an educated person. Perhaps the historical source is the IT, but the reference is absorbed into a linguistic-cultural complex of associations.

As in the case of using the adjective 'quixotic' to designate certain qualities in an action or a character without necessarily evoking Cervantes' text, so by introducing the expression *"quis custodiet ipsos custodes?"* when talking about the regulation of the money market we may simply want to call attention to the fact that there cannot be a foolproof, trustworthy system of regulation, not to evoke Juvenal's Satire 6 (the IT of this expression). How can we know whether the specific IT is evoked? Actually, we cannot know in advance and have to examine the context of using it: the nature of the author and her/his audience (academic conference of classicists or newspaper article), the overall tone (a Juvenal-like diatribe or a balanced discussion) and other aspects of the discourse, notably references to distinctive topics of the IT (women in Juvenal's Satire 6). Another interesting factor is whether the expression is used in its original Latin form or in a translated version (e.g. "who will guard the guardians?"). There is a better chance that the specific IT would be evoked when one cites the Latin expression than if an English translation is used; *ceteris paribus*, that is.

Table 8.1 gives results obtained in the four search engines for a few famous Latin expressions taken from Horace.[2]

TABLE 8.1
Results of Searches for Latin Expressions Taken from Horace

	Google	Google-Image	Clio	IMDb
Dulce et decorum est pro patria mori (Odes 3.2)	97,200; 14,200	6,800; 689	3	1[3]
Exegi monumentum (Odes, 3.30)	45,900; 3,470	3,160; 368	2	0
Dulce et utile (Ars Poetica)	18,200; 4,170	6,650; 220	0[4]	0

To conclude these introductory notes: Horace lives in contemporary literature and culture not only in translations and re-writings of some of his texts (Harrison 2007: 344–46) but also in expressions that have become part of our cultural baggage, some of which still function as literary allusions, i.e., a form of genuine literary dialogue. In this chapter three texts that evoke Horace by using direct quotations will be examined. Despite the similar technique for activating the Latin text, the intentions of these three texts differ greatly.

Horace's Glorious Monument in Pushkin

The dialogic approach to literature emphasizes the ability of texts and authors to survive through dialogues they generate with different authors and in different periods. Authors may differ in the way they estimate the power of their works to outlive them by reaching many people. Historically, we can detect a shift from a belief in the power of literature to a more skeptical attitude. The prevalent modernist approach casts doubt on belief in the power of literature, as part of its deep suspicion of language as a truthful and reliable modus of communication. This, however, was not always the case. Authors in the classical age had faith in language and in the power of literature. A typical example of this self-confident attitude can be found in Horace, Book 3, Ode 30; his poetry, Horace asserts, will reach posterity and defeat, at least partly, death:

> I have completed a monument more lasting than brass, and more sublime than the regal elevation of pyramids, which neither the wasting shower, the unavailing north wind, nor an innumerable succession of years, and the flight of seasons, shall be able to demolish. I shall not wholly die; but a great part of me shall escape Libitina. I shall continually be renewed in the praises of posterity, as long as the priest shall ascend the Capitol with the silent [vestal] virgin. Where the rapid Aufidus shall murmur, and where Daunus, poorly supplied with water, ruled over a rustic people, I, exalted from a low degree, shall be acknowledged as having originally adapted the Aeolic verse to Italian measures. Melpomene, assume that pride which your merits have acquired, and willingly crown my hair with the Delphic laurel. (Horace 2004, in prose translation)

Note how Horace in fact introduces some humble remarks among his self-confident assertions. First, he mentions his origins in "rustic people" and "low degree"; true, he has been "exalted" but he presents his current, elevated state as a result of the generosity of other people. Secondly, when defining his claim to fame he points out that he brought "Aeolic verse to Italian measures," a comment which presupposes reverence for Greek poetry. He thus assigns himself the role of a successful importer of foreign goods, not that of inventor of poetic forms.

A critical reader might think Horace's statements about touching posterity boastful. Such a reader may be reminded that Horace's self-confidence was in fact grounded in reality: his poetry did indeed outlast the life of its composer and whenever someone reads this ode, she or he brings it to life again.[5] Horace's unapologetic belief in the power of his poetry appealed to the Romantic Russian poet, Aleksandr Pushkin, who used the opening words of Horace's ode, "Exegi monumentum," as the title for a poem:

> I have erected a monument to myself, one not built by hands,
> To which the people's path shall never become overgrown with weeds.
> Its noble head is held higher
> Than Alexander's column.

> No, not all of me shall die – my soul, dwelling in the sacred lyre,
> Shall survive my ashes and resist decay,
> And I shall be famed, so long as in the sublunary world
> At least one poet still remains.
>
> Tidings of me shall travel throughout the breadth of great Russia,
> I shall be known in every language that is spoken in its bounds,
> By the proud grandson of the Slavs, and by the Finn, and by the Tungus,
> As yet untamed, and by the Kalmyk, friend of the steppes.
>
> I shall be ever beloved by the people,
> For having aroused kind feeling with my lyre,
> For having, in my cruel age, extolled freedom,
> And called out for mercy to the fallen.
>
> Oh Muse, obey the will of God,
> Fear not insult, ask not for laurels;
> Accept both praise and slander with equanimity
> And do not contradict the fool.[6]

While continuing the Horatian motif of the poet's belief in the power of his poetry, Pushkin's variation differs from Horace in at least two respects. First, we do not find in Pushkin any humble comments like those we found in Horace. It is "*my* sacred lyre." The poet is not indebted to any foreign language or literature. Secondly, and more strikingly, Pushkin adds to his version an indirect and still quite bold political statement: according to his self-portrayal, he will be "beloved by the people for having aroused kind feeling with my lyre, for having, in my cruel age, extolled freedom, and called out for mercy to the fallen." Whereas Horace dwelt on certain poetic qualities endowing him with the Delphic laurel bay of fame (but he also qualified his poetic originality), Pushkin moves the emphasis to the social calling of the poet, advocating freedom, justice and compassion, and exemplifying the Russian tradition where the poet holds the place of the ancient prophet.

Still, despite these changes, Pushkin's poem follows Horace's model on both the micro (borrowing certain expressions) and the macro levels (the underlying tone and sentiment). This cannot be said about our next example, where the poet focuses on one expression from the IT and uses it as the butt of his critical comments.

The Glory of Dying for One's Country: Owen vs. Horace

When Wilfred Owen titled one of his poems "Dulce Et Decorum Est" he was using a direct quotation from one of Horace's odes (Ode 2 of Book 3). Let us look at the first sixteen lines of the ode (in prose translation):

> Let the robust youth learn patiently to endure pinching want in the active exercise of arms; and as an expert horseman, dreadful for his spear, let him harass the

fierce Parthians; and let him lead a life exposed to the open air, and familiar with dangers. Him, the consort and marriageable virgin-daughter of some warring tyrant, viewing from the hostile walls, may sigh— Alas! let not the affianced prince, inexperienced as he is in arms, provoke by a touch this terrible lion, whom bloody rage hurries through the midst of slaughter. It is sweet and glorious to die for one's country [*dulce et decorum est pro patria mori*]; death even pursues the man that flies from him; nor does he spare the trembling knees of effeminate youth, nor the coward back. (Horace 2004).

The lines contain an enthusiastic description of a young soldier and the perturbation he evokes among female spectators in the enemy's camp. This introduction presents a soldier's way of life as an educational experience with some positive consequences that have nothing to do with one's country, like "learn patiently to endure pinching want." Only after the excursion to the enemy's womenfolk does Horace introduces the statement "It is sweet and glorious to die for one's country," and hastens to put this statement into perspective: since death hunts down everybody, patriotic fighters and fleeing cowards alike, it is better to end life as part of the former category.

Owen, who experienced the trenches of World War I (he was killed on November 4, 1918) detests the patriotic sentiment presented in Horace.[7] Here is the second half of Owen's poem:

> If in some smothering dreams you too could pace
> Behind the wagon that we fling him in,
> And watch the white eyes writhing in his face,
> His hanging face, like a devil's sick of sin;
> If you could hear, at every jolt, the blood
> Come gargling from the froth-corrupted lungs,
> Obscene as cancer, bitter as the cud
> Of vile, incurable sores on innocent tongues, –
> My friend, you would not tell with such high zest
> To children ardent for some desperate glory,
> The old Lie: Dulce et decorum est
> Pro patria mori.
>
> (Owen 1973: 79)

Owen portrays the actual face of Horace's presumably sweet death. The death in the poem is a result of a poison-gas attack ("Gas! GAS! Quick, boys!" says one of the preceding lines), thus neutralizing the personal bravery of the individual soldier that was central to Horace's ode. The reader is horrified by the description of death and is led to reject any association between *dulce* and *mori*. Owen directs his main thrust not necessarily at Horace's ode but at those who "tell with such high zest / To children ardent for some desperate glory." In other words, even when he presents Horace's line as an "old lie," his main interest is mainly with teachers, educators and politicians who cynically use Horace's lines when they address young soldiers.

As we saw at the beginning of this chapter, to use a Latin expression (originating in a specific IT) does not always mean that this specific IT is evoked by that use; sometimes the expression has become part of our extended vocabulary and we need no precise intention to activate our knowledge of the IT. Owen's anti-militaristic poem with its allusion to Horace's ode illustrates another interesting situation where one DT (dialoguing text), can be seen as an IT (initiating text) for other texts.[8] Consequently, when we encounter the expression *dulce et decorum est pro patria mori* in a contemporary poem or song we should not assume automatically that the Latin quotation directs us to Horace and not to Owen or to Horace filtered through Owen. The answer to the question "Which is the relevant IT at hand?" can be given only after we examine case and context.

Should we, for example, describe the *Dulce and decorum est pro patria mori* of the young contemporary author-singer Regina Spektor, presenting the Latin expression as a lie repeated through the years (see Spektor in http://www.lyricstime.com), as a DT with Horace or with Owen? The answer to the question how we should describe Spektor's song vis-à-vis Horace and Owen lies in some details of the song: Spektor introduces the Latin quotation in the way it was introduced by Owen, namely as a lie repeated through the years; furthermore, the song presents young people's lives from an existential humanistic perspective. Owen's poem is clearly the primary IT here and Horace's ode may be regarded as only a secondary IT, filtered through Owen. In fact, Spektor's song is very likely representative of many of today's uses of the *Dulce et decorum est* expression, echoing Owen rather than Horace.

The Epigraph for *Le Neveu de Rameau* as an Association Generator

The epigraph to Diderot's *Le Neveu de Rameau* (*Rameau's Nephew*) is taken from Horace's Satire 2.7: "Vertumnis, quotquot sunt, natus iniquis (born under the evil influence of every Vertumnus)."[9] Like any good literary allusion, the epigraph resembles a stone thrown into water: while the stone hits the surface at some specific point, its effectiveness lies in the beautiful concentric circles that are produced.

The immediate context in Satire 2.7 from which the epigraph is taken is a description of Priscus, a senator notorious for his instability. Nial Rudd sums up the description of "the senator whose life was a jumble of absurd contradictions. On reading Horace's description of him, one is reminded of the French diplomat's comment on one of his English counterparts: 'Quel homme étrange! Son centre n'est pas au milieu.' Or perhaps we should say that Priscus had no center at all" (Rudd 1982: 138). These same words can apply verbatim to the hero (or better, the anti-hero) of *Le Neveu de Rameau* (the nephew of the famous French composer). Here, with the analogy between Priscus and the nephew, the epigraph starts to function, but this is by no means where it ends. The nephew resembles also the character of the slave, Davus, in his vehement attacks on the "I" ("Moi") of the dialogue. And of course the "I" of Satire 2.7, supposedly Horace himself, holds a position similar to the "I" of *Le Neveu de Rameau*. In both cases, one should not mechanically identify this "I" with the biographical author of the works, yet this "I" does represent him somewhat and the question (especially in Diderot's text) is to try to determine to what extent.

In addition to the analogies between the nephew and Priscus, the nephew and Davus, Horace and the "I", there is the fact that Satire 2.7 is set during the Saturnalia (December 17–19) during which slaves had the license to speak against their masters. While in *Le Neveu de Rameau* there is no official festivity, the "I" tells us that characters like the nephew "interest me once a year when I run into them" (Diderot 1966: 35).[10] Here too there is a kind of cyclical occasion, like a feast. It is not only that these kinds of meetings occur once a year; the nature of the encounter where an inferior character challenges the morals of his superior establishes an analogy between the two situations. There is also a resemblance between specific themes in the two works: food, women, hypocrisy, art and art criticism.

So far some analogies between *Le Neveu de Rameau* and Horace's Satire 2.7, the source of the epigraph, were pointed out, but we should not confine ourselves to Satire 2.7. The epigraph can and should remind us of various themes and characters that occur repeatedly in other satires of Horace. This move is perfectly justified because 2.7 contains in an encapsulated form some of the dominant themes of Horace's satires, or as Niall Rudd puts it: "2.7 is the most inclusive of all the diatribes. It contains the discontent of 1.1, the adultery of 1.2, the inconstancy of 1.3, the subservience of 1.6, and the gluttony of 2.2. The most important comparison, however, is offered by 2.3. Both poems have a Saturnalian setting. They open with a dialogue in which the poet is in a good humor, proceed to a central section in which a stoic paradox is expounded at second or third hand, and end with an exchange in which Horace shouts the speaker down" (Rudd 1982: 194).

To this list one might add the satires in which the relationship between Horace and his patron and protector, Maecenas, is discussed (especially 1.6 and 2.6), because one of the points on which Davus attacks Horace is his alleged groveling before Maecenas. In short, Diderot was felicitous in his chosen epigraph not only because it brings us back to a very important and amusing aspect of Horace but also because it evokes some of the most central and prevailing themes of Horace the satirist.

Now, after noting some parts of the network of textual resemblances that the epigraph suggests, one has to inquire into the meaning of the comparison between *Le Neveu de Rameau* and Satire 2.7 (or, as we have seen, many of Horace's satires). E. R. Curtius, for example, after noting only a small part of the associations, comes to the conclusion that "the basic theme – contrast between the fool, enslaved by want, necessities, lusts, and passions, and the self-sufficient and therefore only free man, the sage – is identical in the two works" (Curtius 1953: 582). This interpretation, which stresses the antithesis between the stoic notions of the sage as a free man and the fool as a slave evoked an extremely critical comment from Herbert Dieckmann:

> Now, this antithesis certainly occurs in the course of the dialogue, but it is far from being predominant and it certainly does not give us the meaning of the *Neveu de Rameau* ... The Moi upholds at one point the ideal of the sage who has no needs and is therefore free, but the Moi cannot possibly be identified with the stoic conception of the sage. The nephew, on the other hand, is undoubtedly the victim of desires, passions, and vices, but he has many redeeming features, not only thanks to Diderot's art but also in Diderot's opinion. He is not a fool in the stoic sense, but in a modern sense, which presupposes the Renaissance. One does justice to neither Horace nor Diderot if one exaggerates in such an apodictic manner what has always been recognized as an interesting resemblance. One even destroys the wealth of meaning and the rich texture of the *Neveu de Rameau* by reducing the exchange between the two persons to the kind of antithesis which Professor Curtius imposes upon the work. The exchange is essentially a dialectic relationship which was totally alien to Horace and which alone gives the meaning of the form which Diderot chose for the Satyre 2nde. (Dieckmann 1952: 25)

Though it is debatable whether any kind of dialectic relationship was "totally alien to Horace," there is no doubt that Dieckmann's criticism of Curtius is basically valid. Dieckmann is quoted at length because his discussion recognizes the close affinities between Horace and Diderot, but at the same time is sensitive to the differences, sometimes even contrasts, between the two. Thus, the meaning of the later work should not be mechanically equated to that of the earlier, despite the many allusions that connect them. In order to demonstrate the significant difference between the two works, let us focus on one aspect: the way the two authors deal with emotions and more specifically with the excessive emotions displayed by the characters in the two dialogues. This aspect may serve as a litmus-test to reveal some of the deepest artistic sensitivities and inclinations of the two. We will start with a an analysis of the relatively easy case, Satire 2.7, and go on to the more complex and evasive work of Diderot.

Anger and Excitement in Horace's *Satire 2.7*

In the case of Horace's Satire 2.7, the two most conspicuous emotions the characters reveal are anger on the part of Horace ("Horace" the speaker in the dialogue, who is not to be entirely identified with the author), and excitement on the part of Davus.

The case of Horace is very clear: he expresses himself very briefly and only a few times during the dialogue, mostly to rail at Davus with increasing degrees of anger. Horace's first utterance is a very neutral one. He wants to identify the speaker of the opening sentence and asks "What, Davus?" The question might reflect the fact that Davus was speaking from a distance or from a dark corner, or it might indicate a derogatory tone on the part of Horace. However, if such an implication exists at all, it is concealed at this point. In his second utterance, Horace grants Davus the right to speak freely, since it is the Saturnalia. But Horace adds a short explanation to his permission: "since our ancestors would have it so." This subordinate clause, which seems very innocent at first reading, can be interpreted, at least retrospectively, as an indication that Horace complies with the custom of granting free speech in the Saturnalia against his will and only because of the force of tradition, as if he were saying: As for myself, I am not enthusiastic about all this, but "since our ancestors would have it so," have your say.

If there is some implicit sign of discontent in Horace's second statement, it becomes very explicit and sharp when he responds to Davus' first speech: "Will you not tell to-day, you varlet, whither such wretched stuff as this tends?" The most striking thing about this is that Horace's vehement reaction seems totally disproportionate and unjustified. Perhaps Horace is right in urging Davus to come to the point, but there is no reason for him to insult Davus. It is an obvious case of an unprovoked offense, and in such a moment, Horace has alienated himself from the reader. Davus answers Horace's attack with the rhetorical claim that all these stories can be applied to Horace himself: "Why, to you, I say." While there is some provocation, or at least a challenge, in the statement, Horace's reaction is again unreasonable, unjustified, and rude: "In what respect to me, scoundrel?" But his most vehement reaction comes, of course, at the end of the satire after Davus describes how a "gloomy companion presses" upon Horace. Horace bursts into a rage and utters a series of threats, and this brings the dialogue to an abrupt end: "Where can I get a stone? . . . Where some darts? . . . If you do not take yourself away in an instant, you shall go [and make] a ninth laborer at my Sabine estate." These exclamations and threats violate the rules of the game of the Saturnalia: suddenly Horace can not take it any more, so he exercises his power and revokes the *libertas Decembri* granted earlier to Davus. In addition to this violation of the religious and cultural code, Horace is cast in this scene in a ridiculous light because the exaggerated terms that he uses when he rails at Davus are terms that belong to the battlefield (a stone, arrows) and not to a domestic scene.

But it is by no means Horace the ridiculous railer against Davus the dispassionate and pious philosopher that we have in this satire. Davus has moments of excitement too in which he scores badly in the rhetorical game. The case with him, however, is more subtle than what we have with the open ranting of Horace. After he tells Horace that all the unstable characters that he depicted earlier apply to Horace himself, he launches a direct attack on his master, claiming him to be an unstable person: "At Rome, you long for the country; when you are in the country, fickle, you extol the absent city to the skies," and even a hypocrite who praises simple food only because no one invites him to a good dinner: "Should Maecenas lay his commands on you to come late, at the first lighting up of the lamps, as his guest; 'Will nobody bring the oil with more expedition? Does any body hear?' You stutter with a mighty bellowing, and storm with rage."

This is a very funny description, yet it seems that the reader has every reason to suspect its truthfulness. We should remember that Satire 2.7 comes just after 2.6, the famous satire about the country mouse and the town mouse, and in this satire Horace's negative feelings toward the city, as well as his cherishing of his life on the Sabine farm, are very clearly stated. Moreover, in the scene that takes place on the Sabine farm, there is no mention of any longing for city life, as Davus claims, but rather the opposite: we have a pastoral picture of Horace with his friends, which is followed by Cervius' story of the country mouse and the town mouse. And the story is intended, of course, to illustrate the disadvantages of the city life.

There is another reason to suspect Davus' description of Horace's relationship with his patron, Maecenas. Needless to say, Horace was grateful for the honor of being in Maecenas' circle (see Satire 1.6, for instance), but it is a long way between being grateful and being a hypocrite and groveler as Davus describes him. As a matter of fact, Horace's connections with Maecenas were a source not only of pride but also of pain and disturbance. Satire 1.9, with the bore who tries to be introduced to Maecenas through Horace, is one example, and again the scenes from city life described in 2.6, preceding our satire, stress the annoyance, nagging, and discomfort Horace suffered as a result of his close relationship with Maecenas. People harass Horace in the street, trying to get some favor or service with regard to Maecenas, and what was only one ridiculous pest in 1.9 becomes the general rule in 2.6.

All these descriptions indicate Horace's ambivalent feelings with regard to his relationship with Maecenas. So it seems that Davus' accusations are not reliable. But after starting his series of attacks, Davus cannot stop himself. He goes on, and his description of Horace's behavior becomes more and more extravagant. He opened by claiming that Horace has a fickle character, but now he says that Horace is an adulterer. Here, after a vivid description of his affair with a married woman, Davus quotes Horace's reaction: "I am no adulterer," and we have good reason to believe him. Throughout the two books of satires, Horace presents himself as a very moderate character who recommends the famous (Horatian) golden mean, and it is difficult to see this kind of man risking everything in a dangerous love affair. Moreover, Horace devoted a whole satire (1.2) to the recommendation of a very cautious and practical attitude with regard to love, and one of the specific things he cautioned against (from a utilitarian, not necessarily moral point of view) was a love affair with a married woman.

So again, Davus has uttered a groundless accusation, and this time Horace has rightly protested. Will Davus take back what he has just said and apologize? It seems that now Davus is not capable of such a move. He is in the midst of a self-accelerating process and Horace's remark, instead of cooling him down, throws him into another phase of excitement and accusation. This time he says: well, maybe you are not an adulterer but it is only because you are a coward. Using this tortuous way of argument, Davus, of course, will never be caught.

So far, Davus has exposed himself as unreliable, both on factual grounds and in his method of arguing. But the more his accusations are found to be baseless, the more vehement they become. In his next assault on Horace, this time on his presumptive good taste, Davus addresses Horace as "mad one." And this should signal a red light: we might recall a scene from the preceding satire, 2.6, in which Horace has been harassed in the street, and addressed also as a "madman." Needless to say, the analogy between Davus and the man who accosts Horace in the street does not flatter Davus. Davus' rhetoric might also recall Satire 2.3 in which Damasippus, the newly converted stoic, tries to prove to Horace in a very zealous and un-stoic way, that Horace is a madman. Damasippus' accusation of insanity has a boomerang effect: the more he claims that Horace is a madman, the more he reveals his own unreasonable and over-zealous attitude. Or, as William Anderson puts it: "So Damasippus tries to convict the satirist of insanity, by the most extreme of charges, of which the last is that our mild little satirist feels passion for a thousand girls and a thousand boys! After all this ranting the satirist makes his comment in a single verse: O major tandem parcas, insane, minori! O you who are a greater madman, spare at last a lesser one!" (Anderson 1982: 45) Horace could have used this line in Satire 2.7 to refer to Davus, but he chose to let the readers make the inference for themselves.

Before the dramatic conclusion of the satire, Davus again launches a vehement and groundless attack on Horace which culminates with the picture of a "gloomy companion" haunting and pursuing Horace's soul, and at that point Horace bursts out with the threats that put an end to the dialogue. While this disproportionate reaction exposes Horace in an ironic light, it is less clear to what extent we are supposed to take Davus' entire speech as serious or ironical. Niall Rudd, for example, thinks that the fact that Horace puts the stoic doctrine that every man is a slave in the mouth of Davus the slave does not necessarily make it less effective: "Horace may have had reason to believe that he could get his message across *more* effectively in this way. It is as if he were saying... 'Truth, after all, is found in some unlikely quarters.' So instead of a sermon, the preacher has presented a sort of comic morality-play. But the message is still there" (Rudd 1982: 196). On the other hand, William Anderson, although he does not directly discuss Satire 2.7, makes some general remarks on the nature of Book 2 of the Satires in which he stresses the irony with which Horace treats the preaching figures: "The satirist and we are obliged to listen to a series of slightly distorted precepts... Perhaps we can make the distinction between Books I and II by describing the chief character (the man speaking to the virtually silent satirist) as a *doctor ineptus*. He is a teacher who fails to grasp the implications of his own precepts and thus ends as a figure of fun" (Anderson 1982: 46).

In such an overall debate Anderson's argument which stresses the ironic perspective of Horace is more persuasive. But even without adopting a definite position on the overall irony issue, there should be no argument on two points. First, that there are moments in the dialogue in which the characters, both Horace and Davus, are exposed in an ironic light. And second, that these moments occur when the characters get excited. In other words, there is a direct proportion between the level of the mental excitement of the character and the level of the irony exercised on him: the more vehement and extravagant he is in words and actions, the more he is exposed to ironic comment and alienates himself from the reader. Thus the satire conveys, through its rhetorical structure, the importance of being moderate and self-composed and the ridiculous aspects of being excited and stirred up.

Excitement and Self-Acceleration in *Le Neveu de Rameau*

If in Horace's satire the two main emotions which the characters revealed were anger (Horace) and excitement (Davus), the picture in Diderot's work is much more complicated. There is a larger variety, moving from amusement to fear and from high excitement to an almost catatonic paralysis, and sometimes to a mixture of different, even opposing, emotions. There is also no one typical emotion for each character: both get excited or depressed, angry or elated at different stages of the dialogue. But the most important point is that, unlike Horace, there is no one simple formula (the more you get excited, the more you alienate yourself from the reader) that accounts for every case in which a character reveals some excess of emotion. But before we move to any general conclusions, let us look at some specific cases.

The first is the story of the renegade of Avignon. This rascal convinced a Jew to trust him and to give him all his money, before betraying him to the Inquisition. The nephew is very enthusiastic about this story, and about its main character: "You are about to see the advantage that a fertile brain would be able to take of this admission... Usually greatness of character comes from a natural balance between several opposing qualities" (Diderot 1966: 94). But even more than in these explicit declarations, the nephew reveals his excitement and emotional involvement in the way he tells the story. When he gets to a critical point, he suddenly breaks into the narrative; while reporting an exchange of words between the renegade and the Jew, the nephew interjects a comment: "'Come along, calm yourself,' said the Jew, instead of saying: 'You are a barefaced rogue; I don't know what you have to tell me, but you are a barefaced rogue and simulating terror'" (94–95). This comment is striking not so much because the nephew apparently puts himself on the side of the Jew (it is only in order to increase the dramatic tension that he does this, not from any moral stand) but because his deeper emotional involvement in this "masterpiece of evil" brings him almost to transgress the boundaries between fiction and reality in the prompting he offers to the Jew. While telling the story, the nephew shows a deep level of emotional involvement, verging on sadistic enjoyment.

When Moi ("I") reacts at the end of the story: "I don't know which strikes me as more horrible, the villainy of your renegade or the tone in which you talk about it" (96), we share his sentiments. Ironically enough, in praising the artfulness of the renegade the nephew had said: "Too much eagerness might ruin the project"(94), but in telling the story he falls into this very trap by revealing the foul fire within himself, and thus his excess of excitement causes Moi's, as well as our, negative reaction. So this first example, although very different from Horace in subject matter and tone, and in the extremity of the reported circumstance, shares with Satire 2.7 the basic rhetorical structure in which the more a character is excited the more he removes himself from the norms of the work.

The second example is of another kind. Here, it is not storytelling, but the medium in which the nephew is at his best: miming and imitating. If there is any dramatic peak to the work, it is in this grandiose scene in which the nephew imitates operatic-spectacles of various sources and genres: "He sang thirty tunes on top of each other and all mixed up: Italian, French, tragic, comic, of all sorts and descriptions" (102). He sketches an imitation of the different kinds of characters and their typical expressions: "Here we have a young girl weeping, and he mimes all her simpering ways, there a priest, king, tyrant, threatening, commanding, flying into a rage, or a slave obeying. He relents, wails, complains, laughs, never losing sight of tone, proportion, meaning of words and character of music" (102). But this is just the beginning. The nephew becomes more and more excited, more absorbed in this self-inflaming process, and his imitations become more intense and more ambitious; he imitates all the musical instruments and all the roles on stage: "a one-man show featuring dancers, male and female, singers of both sexes, a whole orchestra, a complete opera-house, dividing himself into twenty different stage parts, tearing up and down, stopping, like one possessed, with flashing eyes and foaming mouth" (103). The more he appears possessed, the more his performance expands, and we get the impression that he is no longer imitating the theatrical scene but rather the whole range of human feelings: "He wept, laughed, sighed, his gaze was tender, soft or furious: a woman swooning with grief, a poor wretch abandoned in the depth of his despair" (104), and then he becomes the entire universe: "birds falling silent at eventide, waters murmuring in a cool, solitary place or tumbling in torrents down the mountain side, a thunderstorm, a hurricane, the shrieks of the dying mingled with the howling of the tempest and the crash of thunder; night with its shadows, darkness and silence, for even silence itself can be depicted in sound. By now he was quite beside himself" (104). From this, the highest point of excitement, he collapses into a catatonic-like paralysis.

Regardless of the outcome of this scene, the process itself fascinates the reader (as well as the Moi), and the more excited the nephew becomes, the more we are attracted and impressed by his virtuosity. Leo Spitzer analyzes this passage together with other passages of self-acceleration and self-potentiation in Diderot's works and his analysis stresses the self-destructive mechanism of the uncontrolled artistic talent that dominates such passages. Yet he admits that in this specific and powerful instance: "no mechanism is allowed to seize our attention; rhythm is lost in meaning" (Spitzer 1948: 161).

So far, one instance agreed with the principle governing Horace's satire: the more one is excited, the more one is subject to irony and criticism, while the second indicated a different rhetorical situation: the more the character becomes ardent, the more we are fascinated with him and the more he represents the innermost sensibilities of the author. These two examples illustrate two points. First, Diderot's work has come a long way from the values of the golden mean so dear to Horace. And the second point is that while it is impossible to formulate a simple correspondence between being excited and being wrong, it is equally impossible to state an opposite formulation. Both such generalizations would be false, and instead of one general principle governing the rhetoric of the entire work, we have to judge each scene separately, on its own merits. Thus, the work becomes more complex, and readers should be more alert, more active, and more flexible in their responses.

In both cases the nephew is our main interest, and if we compare him to Moi, there can be no question that he is by far the livelier and more interesting and attractive character. His centrality is reflected in the simple fact that his words, and not the philosopher's, occupy the greatest part of the text. Nevertheless, Moi is an interesting figure and he, too, sometimes reveals an excess of emotion, albeit on a much quieter scale. In some of these cases we can detect a good deal of the complexity of the work.

A relatively simple example in which Moi gets excited and is carried away by his own words occurs when the two discuss the relative advantages and disadvantages of being a genius as opposed to being a wealthy merchant. The nephew claims that it would have been much better for Racine and for his family if he had been a prosperous citizen rather than the author of literary masterpieces, and he imagines pleasant scenes from such a life: "We should have had some excellent meals at his home, played for high stakes, drunk excellent liqueurs and coffee, gone for excursions into the country."(41) To this description Moi starts to respond in a calm, philosophical tone: "No question about that, provided he hadn't made dishonest use of the wealth he had acquired in legitimate trade,", but then his tone changes and he proceeds to a self-accelerating attack: "that he had kept out of his house all these gamblers, these parasites, these dull toadies, idlers and useless rakes, and provided that he had got his shop boys to wallop the officious person who comforts husbands with a nice change from the usual cohabitation with their wives." (41) As in the self-acceleration processes of the nephew, here too the philosopher is *possessed* by his growing animosity toward the scenes that the nephew has just pictured. As in similar cases, it is "le style coupé" ("all these ... these ... these") which governs the passage. And then, just as Moi reaches the peak of his excitement, the nephew makes an ironic remark: "Wallop, sir, wallop! You don't wallop people in a well regulated city." (41) This remark has the effect of pricking Moi's rhetorical balloon. At first, we respect his moral protest, but when the protest becomes subject to the mechanical process of self-acceleration, it becomes difficult to identify with him, and then comes the ironical remark of the nephew which exposes Moi as ridiculous. Part of the irony emerges from the sudden inversion of roles: the calm, self-composed philosopher reveals himself as subject to an emotional outburst, while the pleasure-loving nephew soberly reproaches him in the name of law and order.

Thus our response to Moi's emotional flare-up is hesitant: we share some of his moral values, yet we can not help ridiculing him when he expresses these values in hyperbolic terms. This kind of ambivalent response becomes almost perplexing when we come to our next example.

Here, again, Moi is enticed by an argument and brings it, with self-propelling enthusiasm, to a new peak. Interestingly enough, the basic argument which Moi vehemently develops was suggested by the nephew. Toward the end of the dialogue, the nephew starts to mime "the admiring man, the supplicating man, the complaisant man" (120), and when he ends his presentation he claims, in a way typical of his course of thought, that this kind of flattery and posing is shared by many people: "That is my act, about the same as that of flatterers, courtiers, flunkeys and beggars" (121). Moi, attracted by this argument, starts to imagine some implications of the nephew's claim, and tries to make a universal statement based on the nephew's position: "But by your reckoning there are lots of beggars in this world, and I can't think of anybody who doesn't know a few steps of your dance" (121). The nephew, suddenly confronted with this general statement, admits its truth but makes one exception: "You are right. There is only one man in the whole of a realm who walks, and that is the sovereign. Everybody else takes up positions"(121). Moi, set on fire by this reservation, launches into a sweeping attack:

> The sovereign? But then isn't there something else to be said? Do you think he doesn't find himself from time to time in the vicinity of a dainty foot, a little lock of hair, a little nose that makes him put on a bit of an act?... The king takes up a position with his mistress and his God; he performs his pantomime step. The minister executes the movements of courtier, flatterer, flunkey or beggar in front of his king. The mob of place-seekers dance your step in a hundred ways, each more vile than the one before, in front of the minister. The abbé of noble birth puts on bands and long cassock at least once a week when he calls on the keeper of the list of benefices. (121)

Again, we can observe the repetitive structure which reflects the self-accelerating process (a little ... a little ... The king ... The minister ... The mob ... The abbé) which leads Moi to the statement that behind various disguises everyone is in fact like the nephew, at least in essence: engaged in the art of posing and bending the spine. Facing this vehement rhetoric, the reader is a bit perplexed. There is something very alluring here, yet there are some factors which make it difficult, if not impossible, to identify with Moi when he talks in this way. Our response is to be a bit suspicious, first and foremost, because these excited statements seem to belong to the nephew and not to the calm and composed philosopher. When we are told that the nephew was mimicking the types of people that Moi was referring to ("But while I had been talking he had been mimicking in a killing way the positions of the types as I mentioned them," 122), we realize that we see the nephew imitating Moi who is, in a way, imitating the nephew but without realizing it. Again, as in the previous example, the nephew's response (here not a verbal one) is an ironical comment on the enthusiastic argument of Moi.

After Moi has concluded his vehement attack on the notion that there could be an exception to the rule that everyone poses in one way or another, he proposes an exception. This time it is not the king (as the nephew suggested) but a Diogenes-like philosopher: "And yet there is one person free to do without pantomime, and that is the philosopher who has nothing and asks for nothing ... Diogenes laughed at his needs" (122). At this point, the reader may remember that early in the dialogue the nephew compared himself to Diogenes: "I should look better between Diogenes and Phryne. I am as impudent as the one and I am fond of consorting with the other" (37). When we add this detail to Moi's speech adopting the nephew's attitude, we get the impression that a total exchange of identities occurs between the nephew and Moi toward the end of the dialogue. Thus, the reader has a highly ambivalent response to Moi's excited speech. There is some truth in it, but this truth is mixed with ambivalence and irony.

The complex response to the character in a state of excitement, usually the nephew but at times also the Moi, can be disentangled if we observe a recurring pattern in many of Diderot's works, one which reveals his fascination with the process of self-acceleration. Leo Spitzer, who thoroughly analyzed these kinds of moments, concluded that Diderot's "most effective or conspicuous passages, those in which one feels the vibrations of Diderot's own nature, will always be those which describe the emotional movement of an individual 'hors de lui-même'" (Spitzer 1948: 151). On another level, we can understand this special combination of fascination with and dissociation from the characters when they reveal themselves in an extreme light, if we take into account Diderot's ambivalent attitude toward his two main characters in the dialogue. Arthur Wilson sums up this point: "both Lui and Moi are aspects of Diderot and represent conflicting elements in his personality. One element represents Diderot the *philosophe*, the other represents Diderot the Bohemian, the Diderot that was (or the Diderot that came close to being) in those wild and disordered days of his early life in Paris. According to this Faustian view: 'Two souls, alas! dwell in my breast' – the dialogue signifies a conflict of irreconcilable impulses in Diderot's own psyche" (Wilson 1972: 420).

The explanation for Diderot's complex dialogue may well be found in his unsettled, conflicted psyche. But from a literary, not a psychological perspective, the text's complexity forces us to become more active in our responses. We have to evaluate and re-evaluate our attitude toward the characters at every moment. Our sympathy for one character at one point may be reversed the next moment, and our attitude toward the argument of one character could be changed when the same argument is echoed in the words of the other character at another point in the dialogue. In short, readers have to be on their guard, ready to change positions and sides as required. The second point is that not only do we have to switch our responses constantly, but sometimes we have to remain ambivalent: there are times, though few in number, when the text is straightforward; there are times when the text is unequivocally ironic; but there are many other times when we are not sure whether, and to what extent, irony is present. In these cases sympathy is inseparably linked to irony and it is difficult to determine to what extent we should identify with a character and a vehement argument or reject them. This last point makes *Le Neveu de Rameau* a very modernistic text, and it goes hand in hand with Diderot's decision to leave the end open, in the sense that there is neither a clear winner of the dialogue nor any other closure. Thus, the epigraph of *Le Nevue de Rameau*, which reminds us of the work's affinities to the classical, composed Horace, also underlines the innovative nature of the text. While Diderot is still connected to classical and neo-classical attitudes, his work clearly expresses Romantic and Modernist sensitivities in his fascination with twisted but genius-like characters and in cultivating an ambivalent and watchful reader.

Quotations: Form, Function and Genuine Dialogue

Pushkin, Owen and Diderot all introduced into their texts a short quotation from Horace and all three produced genuine literary dialogues. But a direct quotation, in and of itself, is neither a necessary nor a sufficient condition for creating a genuine literary dialogue. An author can generate an interesting relationship with an IT (initiating text) without using a direct quotation (as some examples in this book illustrate) and some direct quotations may not generate genuine dialogues. Furthermore, to identify the formal method an author uses to activate an IT (e.g. a direct quotation), does not mean that we can predict the specific rhetorical, aesthetic and ideological purposes this formal method serves. Pushkin's *Exegi monumentum* basically continued the spirit of Horace's ode 3.30, and took it to some new directions, expressing Romantic sentiments and advocating political freedom. Owen's *Dulce et decorum est* used the phrase from Horace's ode 3.2 to reject the patriotic sentiment underlying Horace's text, substituting the adulation of military life by rejection of the glorification of war. Diderot used a short quotation from Horace's Satire 2.7 but the implications of this tangential point are far richer than its immediate meanings and create a rich network of analogies between *Le Neveu de Rameau* and Horace's satires. And, as against Horace's treatment of excitement (the more a character gets excited the more he is criticized), Diderot presents a complicated attitude towards a character who goes 'hors de lui-même' (beyond himself).

These three examples illustrate variations on genuine literary dialogues: they all create a dialectical relationship with an IT, paying tribute but at the same time taking it to new, unpredictable territories. They also illustrate how sometimes a DT (dialoguing text) can itself become a powerful IT, as Owen's anti-militaristic *Dulce et decorum est* has done since it was published.

CHAPTER

9

Juvenal's *Satire 10* – Johnson and Swift

When applied to our present example, Juvenal, the question to what extent his works are still part of our "cultural baggage" becomes urgent, since even during the flourishing of classical education, Juvenal was considered an enfant terrible.

As far as the search engines introduced in Chapter 4 can detect, the number of echoes generated by Juvenal is on a lower scale than that of most works representing the hard core of great books, apparently refuting his claim to be included in the great writers' club. But before leaping to a hasty conclusion, we should remind ourselves of the stipulation attached to the requirement of a large number of dialogues: this large number should be understood in the context of the relevant cultural community and the context of neighboring works, i.e., works of the same genre and period. There is no sense, for instance, in comparing the number of references, echoes and genuine dialogues produced by a successful novel to those generated by a lyrical poem: the former is going to encounter, for one, a significantly higher number of readers (= passive echo dialogue) than the latter can ever aspire to.

Likewise, when tracing references to Roman authors, it is necessary to factor in the relevant comparative dimension. Thus, we should measure a Roman author against another Roman author who wrote in roughly the same genre and not a modern English one. A good candidate to set against Juvenal's dissemination would be Persius (Table 9.1). These two Roman satirists belong roughly to the same period (they were both born in the fist century CE) and, assuming that the four searches are indicative of an author's dissemination, it is clear that Juvenal has a small but consistent advantage over Persius (and in the undifferentiated Google he has a big advantage):

TABLE 9.1
Results of Searches of Juvenal and Persius

	Google	Google-Image	Clio	IMDb
Juvenal	241,000[1]	685	110	1
Persius	88,600	647	102	0

To factor in relevant comparisons is crucial when considering the quantifiable dimension of the dialogic approach: were we to choose only one Roman satirist of the first century CE, Juvenal would be the one. Were we to choose only one Roman satirist, without restricting ourselves to a specific period, most chances are that Horace would be the one.[2] We might prefer Juvenal, arguing that he was a much more powerful satirist. But if we try to put aside personal preferences and adhere to the logic of the dialogic approach, we would have to admit that Horace has gained more readers, editions, translations, adaptations and allusions throughout the ages. And, were we to choose only one Roman author, without restricting ourselves to any specific genre (satire or any other), Virgil and Horace would be close contenders: the results obtained in the all-inclusive search engines of Google and Google-Image are almost a tie, but the other two solid databases, especially Clio as representative of the accumulation of editions and scholarly and critical work, clearly favor Virgil.[3]

Perhaps Greco-Roman authors do not enjoy a vast readership when compared to contemporary authors, but it would be premature to eulogize their reputation and dissemination: it is a safe bet that people who respond to satire are acquainted with Swift and Voltaire; and those who are truly drawn to the genre have read, or at least heard of Aristophanes, Horace and Juvenal.

Another dimension of Juvenal's dissemination has to do with some expressions from his works. As we saw in the previous chapter, such expressions play an important role in the way classical literature is present in today's culture. Table 9.2 is a particularly interesting result of searches done with an expression taken from Juvenal Satire 10, compared to two Latin expressions taken from Virgil's *Aeneas*: the three opening words, stating the topic of the poem and the beginning of the saying "*Timeo Danaos et dona ferentes* (I fear the Greeks even if they bring gifts)."[4] According to searches results, when it comes to composing memorable phrases, Juvenal has a very good standing, surpassing Virgil, the greater Roman poet:

TABLE 9.2
Results of Searches of Memorable phrases from Juvenal and Virgil

	Google	Google-Image	Clio	IMDb
Mens sana in corpore sano (from *Satire 10*)	671,000; 29,300	20,700; 1,830	4	0[5]
Arma virumque cano (from *Aeneas*)	25,800; 5,580	3,110; 323	5	0
Timeo Danaos (from *Aeneas*)	81,000; 2,650	3,660; 336	4	0

Juvenal's Self-Propelling Explosion in *Satire 10*

In reading Juvenal's Satire 10 we are reminded that human prayers have not changed much during the past two thousand years. It seems that people in Rome of Juvenal's time (he was active in the late 1st and early 2nd century CE[6]) were praying for pretty much the same things that we pray for today: strength, glory, wealth, eloquence, beauty, longevity. Juvenal exposes people who pray for these things not because they are unattainable (i.e. do not waste time on cultivating hopes that will not be realized) but rather because there is something inherently wrong with the content of these prayers: when people get the things for which they have prayed, they discover that these things are, in Gilbert Highet's words, "useless – or, even worse, dangerous" (Highet 1961: 125). In other words, instead of bringing happiness, they bring trouble.

One striking characteristic of Satire 10 is Juvenal's fascination with these troubles. Whereas the conventional wishes themselves are only briefly mentioned, the disastrous outcomes are fully expanded. At times, one gets the impression that the conventional prayers serve Juvenal as a springboard or an excuse to linger on his long descriptions of the disastrous effects of fulfilled prayers where he can fully develop his poetic inventiveness. Juvenal's treatment of the prayer for strength and glory is representative of his poetics:

> Some men are hurled headlong by over-great power and the envy to which it exposes them; they are wrecked by the long and illustrious roll of their honours: down come their statues, obedient to the rope; the axe hews in pieces their chariot wheels and the legs of the unoffending horses. And now the flames are hissing, and amid the roar of furnace and of bellows the head of the mighty Sejanus, the darling of the mob, is burning and crackling, and from that face, which was but lately second in the entire world, are being fashioned pipkins, pitchers, frying-pans and slop-pails! (Juvenal 1940: 197; lines 56–64)[7]

But Juvenal is not satisfied with the effect of this grotesque reflection of Sejanus' downfall. He goes back to the execution of the strongman, as if he had been present at the time and place where Sejanus' body was dragged on the streets of Rome: "Up with the laurel-wreaths over your doors! Lead forth a grand chalked bull to the Capitol! Sejanus is being dragged along by a hook, as a show and joy to all!" (197; 65–67). This cry, in turn, seems to propel Juvenal to compose a mini-drama, full of exclamations and short dialogues, where the mob's hubbub and fickleness are brilliantly captured: "What a lip the fellow had! What a face!"—"Believe me, I never liked the man!"—"But on what charge was he condemned? Who informed against him? What was the evidence, who the witnesses, who made good the case?" (197–99; 67–70). This self-propelling dynamics is the hallmark of Juvenal's poetics. The drive to explore more and more striking illustrations for the ruinous outcomes of fulfilled prayers seems to overshadow everything else. Here lies Juvenal's most powerful poetic strength, and here is the source of the readers' enjoyment of his poetry.

The basic rhetorical structure of the Sejanus exemplum is typical of the whole poem. Satire 10 can be graphically depicted (from a rhetorical point of view) as a rising and falling curve, where the apexes stand for the content of human prayers while the sharply falling descents (on which Juvenal likes to linger) represent the pernicious outcomes. Whenever the reader tries to cling to a comforting and conventional prayer, she/he finds that Juvenal has prepared the same disillusioning mechanism. To use the image of the graph-like curve: while individuals in the world described by Juvenal experience in their lives the ironic zigzags of fate, the reader experiences similar ups and downs in the reading process, moving from high hopes to new depths of disillusionment.[8]

Let us look now at Juvenal's treatment of the prayer for old age, perhaps the deepest and most universal wish of mankind, expressing our greatest fear: that of death. Juvenal introduces this prayer immediately after he has undermined (or, to be more precise, smashed) the hopes associated with military glory. The reader's first impression is that, in contrast to the bloody tumult of the battle field, we are now moving to a peaceful, serene, and more promising prayer: "Give me length of days, give me many years, O Jupiter!" (207; 188). Needless to say, this first impression does not last very long. In accordance with the rhetorical structure favored by Juvenal, the brief mention of the prayer triggers a remarkably long list of pictures, arguments and episodes, all portraying the physical disintegration of old age (lines 189–203). This introduces but by no means ends the long list of old age miseries. After referring to impotence (lines 204–9), weakening senses (lines 209–16), diseases and ailments (lines 217–32), and when the reader thinks he has reached the depths, Juvenal holds some deeper agonies in store, related to losing one's mental capacities:

> But worse than any loss of limb is the failing mind which forgets the names of slaves, and cannot recognise the face of the old friend who dined with him last night, nor those of the children whom he has begotten and brought up. (211; 232–36)

Then comes one of the most telling parts of the poem: Juvenal admits the possibility that, despite what he has just described, an old man can remain in a state where "his mental powers are still alert" (211; 240). Perhaps there is, after all, a sense of hope in Juvenal's world; maybe old men have to suffer all the physical ills, but at least they can preserve their *mens sana* and consequently their human dignity. But, alas, this rising curve of hope is harshly dashed in the next lines:

> And though the powers of his mind be strong as ever, yet must he carry forth his sons to burial; he must behold the funeral pyres of his beloved wife and his brothers, and urns filled with the ashes of his sisters. (211; 240–2)

This total reversal of expectations represents in an encapsulated form what Juvenal wants the reader to learn throughout the poem: humans wishes, as well as the reader's own optimistic expectations, are basically vain. The reader will therefore not be surprised to meet in the following lines a catalogue of *exempla* representing degraded old age; or, in the next conventional prayer (lines 289–345), to see how beauty turns into a death trap. Even the famous aphorism in the concluding section (*mens sana in corpore sano*; line 356) can be read, at best, as a cliché providing a formal coda rather than a serious didactic statement (Fishelov 1990). To become attuned to Juvenal's satirical temper means to learn to enjoy the explosion of true or invented catastrophes that he enumerates.

Johnson's Taming of Juvenal's Explosiveness

In *The Vanity of Human Wishes*, Samuel Johnson made a free translation-adaptation of Juvenal's Satire 10 or, as this genre was known in eighteenth-century England, an imitation. As the opening lines of Johnson's version immediately show, he was tailoring Juvenal to suit contemporary English readers, transforming "In all the lands that stretch from Gades to the Ganges" (193; 1–2) into "Survey Mankind, from China to Peru" (1974: 115; 2).[9] The guiding principle of an imitation can be described as the sacrifice of a faithful replication of concrete units in order to preserve their overall function.[10] The specific geographical places mentioned by Juvenal (Cadiz and Ganges) are accordingly replaced by names familiar to Johnson's readers (China and Peru) as marking far away places and thus preserving the perceived overall function of the opening lines: a survey from a bird's-eye-view of the known globe.[11] Johnson makes many more such changes. Some of them can be explained by the organizing principles of a translation-imitation; others, however, stem from his poetic sensibilities, quite different to those of Juvenal.

Let us look at Johnson's treatment of Juvenal's prayer for old age. First, Johnson dramatically shortened Juvenal's initiating text: Juvenal devotes 101 lines to the topic (lines 188–288), whereas Johnson is satisfied with 64 (lines 255–318). This shortening cannot be explained as due to a general tendency to abbreviate. In fact Juvenal's Satire 10 and Johnson's *The Vanity of Human Wishes* are roughly of the same length: Juvenal's 366 lines compared to Johnson's 368. However, there are apparently some things in Juvenal's text that Johnson preferred to bypass. And, indeed, Johnson decided to leave out a few things. Perhaps the most conspicuous omitted element is Juvenal's explicit treatment of sexual impotence. To illustrate the deteriorating senses of old age, Juvenal first briefly refers to loss of joy in food and wine: "Their sluggish palate takes joy in wine or food no longer" (209; 203–4). Then, he moves to the loss of sexual functioning, describing in detail the efforts to arouse the old man's organ that despite the treatment it gets all night is lying still (lines 204–9).[12] Johnson decided to omit any reference to the topic of sex, leaving no trace of these graphic descriptions.[13]

Perhaps less conspicuous than the reluctance to include the lines on sexual impotence, but still symptomatic, is Johnson's omission of Juvenal's description of the physical appearance of old age. Immediately after introducing the prayer for longevity and saying that it brings miseries, Juvenal goes on to depict the face of old age. The delineation has a peculiar effect: while describing in a concrete, graphic manner *different* kinds of physical deformity that characterize old age, Juvenal insists on *the same* (appalling) face of old men, in contrast to the variety of youth. Thus we get one big, nameless, hideous face but are not spared the rich possibilities of the repulsive details:

> Look first at the misshapen and ungainly face, so unlike its former self; see the unsightly hide that serves for skin; see the pendulous cheeks and the wrinkles like those which a matron baboon carves upon her aged jaws in the shaded glades of Thabraca. The young men differ in various ways: this man is handsomer than that, and he than another; one is stronger than another: but old men all look alike. Their voices are as shaky as their limbs, their heads without hair, their noses drivelling as in childhood. Their bread, poor wretches, has to be munched by toothless gums. (207–9; 191–200)

What does Johnson reproduce from this long, grotesque representation? As a matter of fact, he omits the entire passage, presumably because it violates accepted standards of decorum. Thus, in addition to the guiding principle of translation-imitation (preserving function, altering details) Johnson was guided by further set of principles. A central one was adherence to the ideal of poetic decorum, entailing the omission of explicit sexual passages and graphic, grotesque descriptions.[14]

The ideal of maintaining poetic decorum goes with an attempt to produce a "smoother," more "organized" version of Juvenal.[15] To understand how Johnson accomplishes this, let us read the passage in Juvenal on the diseases of old age. To underscore the fact that these diseases are innumerable, Juvenal presents a series of analogies, saying it would be easier to count such large-scale phenomena than to enumerate old age's maladies:

> Diseases of every kind dance around him in a body; if you ask of me their names, I could more readily tell you the number of Oppia's paramours, how many patients Themison killed in one season, how many partners were defrauded by Basilus, how many wards corrupted by Hirrus, how many lovers tall Maura wears out in a single season; I could sooner run over the number of villas now belonging to the barber under whose razor my stiff youthful beard used to grate. (209–11; 218–26)

These lines illustrate a central characteristic of Juvenal's jovial poetics: the use of a handy occasion to make satirical remarks about various targets not related to the formal topic under discussion. The formal topic here is, we may remember, the list of diseases that accompany old age, but Juvenal's attention is caught by other things that come in large numbers. Needless to say, these other things are not innocent, neutral examples, but rather more manifestations of Juvenal's inclination to exploit any opportunity to aim satirical arrows at almost any possible target in Roman society. These opportunistic attacks do not all have the same moral weight or social significance (for example, moral corruption in commerce and education as against the speaker's nouveau riche former barber). But Juvenal is the last to care about the logical consistency of his catalogues or the relative social significance of his examples, so long as they provide him with an opportunity to exhibit his satirical temper and poetic inventiveness.

This temporary deviation from the main road into some dark alleys of Roman society is only a prelude to a long list of the various diseases of old age that Juvenal after all provides. What does Johnson make of the list of "irrelevant" comparisons to phenomena that come in multitudes? In accordance with his poetic norms that made him omit indecorous themes and descriptions, so here Johnson attempts to create textual consistency and coherence in places where Juvenal "went astray":

> Unnumber'd Maladies his Joints invade,
> Lay Siege to Life and press the dire Blockade;
> But unextinguis'd Av'rice still remains,
> And dreaded Losses aggravate his Pains;
> He turns, with anxious Heart and crippled Hands,
> His Bonds of Debt, and Mortgages of Lands;
> Or views his Coffers with suspicious Eyes,
> Unlocks his Gold, and counts it till he dies.
> (Johnson 1974: 128–29; 283–90)

Rather than follow Juvenal's free imagination, Johnson structures the passage, omits all the satirical forays and in their stead adds a moralistic note about avarice, indicative of man's inability to focus on what really matters (i.e. morality).

This is not the only added passage in *The Vanity of Human Wishes*. When Juvenal introduces the theme of praying for old age, the conventional prayer is followed by a short sentence summing up the ails lying in wait: "yet how great, how unceasing, are the miseries of old age!" (207; 190–91). After this warning, Juvenal moves swiftly to the graphic descriptions that so interest him. Johnson, however, is not content with Juvenal's short summary and decides to elaborate on the prayer:

> Enlarge my Life with Multitude of Days,
> In Health, in Sickness, thus the Supplicant prays;
> Hides from himself his State, and shuns to know,
> That Life protracted is protracted Woe.
> Time hovers ov'r, impatient to destroy,
> And shuts up all the Passages of Joy:
> In vain their Gifts the bounteous Seasons pour,
> The Fruit autumnal, and the vernal Flow'r,
> With listless Eyes the Dotard views the Store,

> He views, and wonders that they please no more;
> Now pall the tasteless Meats, and joyless Wines,
> And Luxury with Sighs her Slave resigns.
> (128; 259–66)

These lines, which compensate for the omission of Juvenal's grotesque description of the hideous face of old age (quoted above, lines 191–200), represent Johnson's distinct tendency for symmetrical structures. In addition to the rhyming scheme of the heroic couplet, there are parallels within the poetic line: the "fruit autumnal" is matched by in "vernal flower" and "tasteless meat" is echoed in "joyless wines." Here Johnson shows himself a studious disciple of the poetical principles cultivated by the Augustan poets, especially Alexander Pope.

This emphasis on symmetrical, structured elegance is precisely what distances Johnson from Juvenal's tendency to follow a line of thought even when it does not fit nicely into the declared topic of discourse, or perhaps precisely because it does not fit. Whenever Juvenal's self-propelling imagination leads him into some dark side alleys, Johnson sticks to the main road and hastens to add a paved, well-lit section to the freeway he is constructing.

Whereas *The Vanity of Human Wishes* follows Juvenal's Satire 10 fairly closely, our next example, a section from Swift's *Gulliver Travels*, is a free variation on Juvenal's theme of praying for old age.

Swift's Narrative Variation on a Theme

The third book of *Gulliver's Travels* is generally considered the least consistent or coherent of the four. The other three books are organized around one unifying voyage, one central image, a single visited land and usually one major theme: the giant Gulliver among the tiny Lilliputians; Gulliver turned into a tiny creature compared to the giant Brobdingnags; and Gulliver caught between the admired Houynhnms and the despicable Yahoos in the fourth and last book. In the third book, on the other hand, Gulliver travels to different places (a flying island, the underworld, and Japan, among others) and meets different kinds of people with no one shared conspicuous trait. The book is also diversified in themes and tone: hilarious satirical presentation of modern science, sardonic critique of kings' cruelty, and, atypically, some serious words of wisdom pronounced by revered figures of the past.

Among the many places Gulliver visits in the third book, there is the kingdom of Luggnag. After describing some customs prevalent at the court of this kingdom, notably that of licking the dust before His Majesty's footstool (when the king wants to execute one of his nobles, the floor is strewn with a deadly powder). While spending time in this kingdom, Gulliver is asked "by a Person of Quality, whether I had seen any of their *Struldbruggs* or *Immortals*" (Swift 1973: 177).[16] When Gulliver responds that he has not yet met them, his interlocutor explains that these immortals can be detected when they are born because they have "a red circular Spot in the Forehead, directly over the left Eye-brow, which was an infallible Mark that it should never die" (177). The man goes on to describe this spot and the changes it undergoes in size and color until the bearer reaches the age of forty-five; in the whole kingdom there are no more than eleven hundred of these *Struldbruggs*.

Gulliver is not particularly interested in all these physical and statistical details; he is mesmerized by the astonishing information about the existence of immortals on earth. A reader aware of Juvenal's Satire 10 and of its treatment of longevity might immediately be put on guard, but Gulliver does not seem to have read it. Thus, Gulliver reports how he received the news:

> I freely own my self to have been struck with inexpressible Delight upon hearing this Account ... I cryed out as in a Rapture; Happy Nation, where every Child hath at least a Chance for being immortal! Happy People who enjoy so many living Examples of ancient Virtue, and have Masters ready to instruct them in the Wisdom of all former Ages! But happiest beyond all Comparison are those excellent *Struldbruggs*, who being born exempt from that universal Calamity of human Nature, have their Minds free and disengaged, without the Weight and Depression of Spirits caused by the continual Apprehension of Death. (178)

The reader may remember that the last time Gulliver was carried away and delivered an enthusiastic speech, trying to explain the advantages of using gun powder to the king of the giant Brobdingnags (Book II, chapter 7), he was exposed as someone who cannot get his values right. The reader's suspicion that Gulliver-the-enthusiast does not represent Swift's views on the present occasion either will soon be validated.

The gentleman to whom Gulliver has delivered this speech barely hides his ironic amusement. He translates Gulliver's remarks to other local people in their company and tells Gulliver that they "were very much pleased with the judicious Remarks I had made on the great Happiness and Advantages of immortal Life; and they were desirous to know in a particular Manner, what Scheme of Living I should have formed to my self, if it had fallen to my Lot to have been born a *Struldbrugg*" (179). It seems that this gentleman, who listens to Gulliver with the smile "which usually ariseth from pity to the ignorant," is offering Gulliver a further opportunity to make a fool of himself. Gulliver, in one of his most gullible moments in the book, seizes the opening and goes on with his excited speech, fantasizing about the possibility that he was born a *struldbrugg*:

> That, if it had been my good fortune to come into the World a *Struldbrugg*; as soon as I could discover my own Happiness, by understanding the Difference between Life and Death, I would first resolve, by all Arts and Methods whatsoever to procure myself Riches: In the Pursuit of which, by Thrift and Management, I might reasonably expect in about two Hundred Years, to be the wealthiest Man in the Kingdom. In the second Place, I would from my earliest

> Youth apply myself to the study of Arts and Sciences, by which I should arrive in time to excel all others in Learning. Lastly, I would carefully record every Action and Event of Consequence that happened in the Publick, impartially draw the Characters of the several Successions of Princes, and great Ministers of State; with my own Observations on every Point. I would exactly set down the several Changes in Customs, Languages, Fashions of Dress, Dyet, and Diversions. By all which Acquirements, I should be a living Treasury of Knowledge and Wisdom, and certainly become the Oracle of the Nation. (179)

On one level, this speech expresses humanity's perhaps deepest dream: to achieve immortality. On another level, the speech associates this dream with some ideals of the Enlightenment: to work hard in order to increase personal and national wealth; to study the arts and sciences and to treasure the obtained knowledge (note, however, Gulliver's good old pride as he indulges in the fantasy of becoming "the oracle of the nation"). Another fantasy is the prospect of joining forces with the other *Struldbruggs* in order to improve the morals of human society:

> These *Struldbruggs* and I would mutually communicate our Observations and Memorials through the Course of Time; remark the several Gradations by which Corruption steals into the World, and oppose it in every Step, by giving perpetual Warning and Instruction to Mankind; which, added to the strong Influence of our own Example, would probably prevent that continual Degeneracy of human Nature, so justly complained of in all Ages. (180)

Gulliver goes on and on with his fantasy about the possibility of bringing mankind to a perfected stage with the help of the *Struldbruggs*, the new Platonic philosophers guiding kings and rulers. He is absorbed in his own happy dream that he does not take the trouble to stop and ask about the actual nature and conduct of the *Struldbruggs*. Thus, when he finishes his animated speech structured around the leitmotif of "if I were a *Struldbrugg*," there comes the reaction: "When I had ended, and the Sum of my Discourse had been interpreted as before, to the rest of the Company, there was a good Deal of Talk among them in the Language of the Country, not without some Laughter at my Expense" (180). After some general observations about man's fear of death, the gentleman conversing with Gulliver provides a sobering description of the *Struldbruggs*:

> When they came to Fourscore Years, which is reckoned the Extremity of living in this Country, they had not only all the Follies and Infirmities of other old Men, but many more which arose from the dreadful Prospect of never dying. They were not only opinionative, peevish, covetous, morose, vain, talkative; but incapable of Friendship, and dead to all natural Affection, which never descended below their Grand-children. Envy and impotent Desires are their prevailing Passions. But those Objects against which their Envy seems principally directed, are the Vices of the younger Sort, and the Deaths of the old. By reflecting on the former, they find themselves cut off from all Possibility of Pleasure; and whenever they

see a Funeral, they lament and repine that others have gone to a Harbour of Rest, to which they themselves never can hope to arrive. They have no Remembrance of anything but what they learned and observed in their Youth and middle Age, and even that is very imperfect; And for the Truth or Particulars of any Fact, it is safer to depend on common Tradition than upon their best Recollections. The least miserable among them, appear to be those who turn to Dotage, and entirely lose their Memories; these meet with more Pity and Assistance, because they want many bad Qualities which abound in others. (181–2)

The gentleman provides some more depressing and even repulsive details about the *Struldbruggs*, but the basic picture is already clear: in making his enthusiastic speech about the immortals, Gulliver forgot to take into account some basic facts about human nature and its limitations. Hence, he was carried away by vehement vapors of the imagination, based on unrealistic assumptions about mankind, animated by self-love and delusion, forgetful of man's fallen state, fantasizing about creating a paradise-like society on earth.

Some details in this description of the *Struldbruggs* (e.g. losing all memory is seen as a blessing) make it clear that when Swift invented the *Struldbruggs* and the encounter between them and Gulliver, he probably had in mind Juvenal's treatment of man's prayer for longevity in Satire 10. It seems that Swift dramatized Juvenal's rhetorical structure, showing how someone who is carried away by a fantasy of old age, even longing for it, is made to face the actual face of old age – with its many forms of indignity and degeneration.

Johnson and Swift – Form and Spirit

Johnson in *The Vanity of Human Wishes* is closer to Juvenal's Satire 10 than Swift in Book Three of *Gulliver's Travels*. In terms of form or genre, Johnson's text, like the initiating text of Juvenal, is a poem, Swift's a narrative fiction. When we set aside the changes, omissions, additions and transformations made by Johnson, we can maintain that *The Vanity of Human Wishes* follows Juvenal's poem quite closely in its themes, arguments and basic rhetorical stand. Swift, on the other hand, wrote an independent story, which can be seen as a very free variation on Juvenal's theme of praying for old age, but not as a reproduction or an imitation of Juvenal's poem.

But despite Swift's apparent distance and Johnson's seeming proximity to Juvenal, we can still argue that when it comes to satirical temperament Swift, and not Johnson, is a direct heir to Juvenal: in their sarcasm, their sardonic humor and their tendency to give free rein to the imagination, Juvenal and Swift display the same poetic and satirical disposition. Probably T. S. Eliot was right when he doubted "whether Johnson was the right man for satire. He was a moralist, and he lacked a certain divine levity" (Eliot 1957: 179).[17] Johnson may have been drawn to negative qualities – that was why he wrote *The Vanity* – but he was also trying to fight and check them and, as we saw earlier, with some success.

As for the dialogic perspective, Johnson's text represents a more typical case of literary dialogue, explicitly presenting itself as an imitation: *The Vanity of Human Wishes* is subtitled "The Tenth Satire of Juvenal Imitated" (Johnson 1974: 114–15). The reader is openly invited to compare the two texts and some of Johnson's intended effects are related to such a comparison. Swift, on the other hand, does not mention Juvenal in his text, and the reader can understand and enjoy the story about the *Struldbruggs* without being acquainted with Juvenal's text. But the moment we start reading Gulliver's encounter with the *Struldbruggs* as a variation on Juvenal, it enriches our understanding of Swift's text, its goals and achievements, making it an implicit, but not less effective literary dialogue. As for the specific type of literary dialogue these two texts are engaged in, the dialectic of borrowing and inventing that characterizes genuine dialogue is quite evident in the case of Swift. With Johnson this is less obvious because *The Vanity* has also the characteristics of an echo-dialogue. But the many changes Johnson introduced clearly take it out of the category of a simple, predictable imitation of Juvenal (hence, not a typical echo-dialogue) placing it somewhere between echo- and genuine dialogue. These two texts illustrate the variety of options practicable within the heterogeneous field of genuine and echo-dialogue.

CHAPTER

10

Ovid's Pygmalion in Shaw & *My Fair Lady* via Molière

In this chapter we shall focus on the story of Pygmalion, as it is told in Ovid's *Metamorphoses* Book X, Molière's L'*École des femmes*, Shaw's *Pygmalion* and Lerner and Loewe's musical *My Fair Lady*. After presenting the initiating text and some of the conspicuous transformations the story underwent in adaptation to later genres, periods and sensibilities, some questions raised by this chain of IT (initiating text) and DTs (dialoguing texts) will be addressed.

The classical version of the story of Pygmalion can be found in Book X (lines 243–97) of Ovid's *Metamorphoses* (completed in 8 CE). Pygmalion, a sculptor, falls in love with a statue of a beautiful woman which he has made; he prays to Venus to bring the statue to life, the goddess grants his request, which brings the story to a happy conclusion. Pygmalion and his beloved statue-turned-into-woman unite and beget a child. This basic story-line is what one usually remembers when the name Pygmalion is evoked. It is useful though to look at the often neglected beginning of the story, telling us what triggered the whole chain of events:

> Pygmalion had seen them, spending their lives in wickedness, and, offended by the failings that nature gave the female heart, he lived as a bachelor, without a wife or partner for his bed.[1] (lines 243–46)

Thus, Pygmalion is depicted as a man suffering from deep sexual anxiety, fearful of women's treacherous ways, absorbed in a typically misogynistic attitude. Because of this anxiety he undertakes to create a statue of a woman, a partner who cannot by definition betray him. But the moment he finishes his creation, something unexpected happens:

> The features are those of a real girl, who, you might think, lived, and wished to move, if modesty did not forbid it. Indeed, art hides his art. He marvels: and passion, for this bodily image, consumes his heart. Often, he runs his hands over the work, tempted as to whether it is flesh or ivory, not admitting it to be ivory. He kisses it and thinks his kisses are returned ... Now he addresses it with compliments, now brings it gifts that please girls ... He dresses the body, also, in clothing; places rings on the fingers; places a long necklace round its neck ... All are fitting: but it appears no less lovely, naked. He arranges the statue on a bed on

which cloths dyed with Tyrian murex are spread, and calls it his bedfellow, and rests its neck against soft down, as if it could feel. (lines 250–69)

When we take into account Pygmalion's motivation for creating the statue it makes much sense that he would fall in love with a woman-like statue, not a real woman who could threaten him. But despite everything he thinks he knows about women and against the driving force of his character he is not content to spend his life next to inanimate statue; he longs for a woman of flesh and blood. So he prays to Venus for a bride "one like my ivory girl." The goddess of love grants his prayer and when he returns home, lies down next to the statue and starts kissing it (a habit he has developed together with dressing her in women's garments), the wondrous metamorphosis takes place:

> She felt warm: he pressed his lips to her again, and also touched her breast with his hand. The ivory yielded to his touch, and lost its hardness, altering under his fingers, as the bees' wax of Hymettus softens in the sun, and is moulded, under the thumb, into many forms, made usable by use. The lover is stupefied, and joyful, but uncertain, and afraid he is wrong, reaffirms the fulfilment of his wishes, with his hand, again, and again.
>
> It was flesh! The pulse throbbed under his thumb. Then the hero, of Paphos, was indeed overfull of words with which to thank Venus, and still pressed his mouth against a mouth that was not merely a likeness. The girl felt the kisses he gave, blushed, and, raising her bashful eyes to the light, saw both her lover and the sky. The goddess attended the marriage that she had brought about, and when the moon's horns had nine times met at the full, the woman bore a son, Paphos, from whom the island takes its name. (lines 281–97)

Love wins and Pygmalion's sexual anxiety, which started the whole chain of events, is totally forgotten. The story does not leave any space for his fears because the moment the statue comes to life he and it/she (with its/her "timid eyes") instantly make love. The nine months of pregnancy are explicitly cited, removing any doubt as to the identity of the father. All we know of his beloved statue-turned-into-woman is that she loves him and bears his child. In fact, in this version of the story Ovid develops a male fantasy of creating a beloved woman and controlling her subjectivity and sexuality. As against the beginning of the story with its emphasis on insecurity, anxiety and misogyny, the end is joyful and harmonious. It will be instructive to see how future dialogues with the Pygmalion story treat this happy ending.

The first example resembles the non-declared dialogue that we saw in the case of Juvenal and Swift in Chapter 9: Molière's *L'Ecole des femmes* is a genuine dialogue with Ovid's story of Pygmalion, despite the fact that Pygmalion's name is not once mentioned in the comedy.

A Non-Declared Dialogue: Molière's *School of Wives*

The reasons for reading Molière's *L'Ecole des femmes* as a dialogue with the Pygmalion story can be found in the play's story line as well as in some significant details. In terms of the basic, abstract narrative, Molière re-tells the same story of male fantasy: a man who tries to play God, to mold a woman according to his liking so that he can marry a creature of his making and under his absolute control, and then he falls in love with his creation. Besides this shared story line, there are some significant details that tighten the connection between the two stories. First and foremost, Arnolphe, Molière's Pygmalion, is impelled by the same motivation that drove Pygmalion.

In the opening scene we listen to a heated debate between Arnolphe and a friend of his, Chrysalde; Chrysalde objects to Arnolphe's plan to marry the young woman he has had brought up, as we learn later, in isolation and under strict control, in an attempt to avoid the thing that terrifies him the most, namely to become a cuckold:

> ARNOLPHE: Yes, and I mean to have it all over and done with tomorrow.
> CHRYSALDE: We are alone here and I think, or so it seems to me, that we could talk together without fear of being overheard. Would you like me, as a friend, to tell you exactly what I think? What you are proposing makes me terribly afraid for you. Whichever way you look at it, for you to get married would be a very rash step.
> ARNOLPHE: Very true, my friend. Perhaps it's because you have grounds for fear on that score in your own marriage that you are alarmed at my prospects. It seems to me that your forehead has a look about it that suggests that a cuckold's horns are the universal, inevitable accompaniment of marriage.
> (*L'Ecole des femmes* 1.1; Molière 2000: 7)[2]

Chrysalde warns Arnolphe that "Such things happen as the result of chance and there's nothing anyone can do about it" but Arnolphe boasts that he has learnt all about women's cheating tricks and nobody can fool him. After a long and quite funny diatribe exposing men's stupidity that makes them cuckolds, Arnolphe argues that his solid line of defense against such a threat is not to marry a smart, capable woman:

> I won't have anything to do with a wife with a mind of her own, who writes more than she needs to. I am determined that mine, sublimely untouched by knowledge, won't even know what a rhyme is. And if the occasion should rise when she's playing party games and gets asked what the cat sat on, I hope she answers 'a custard pie'. In other words, I want her to be utterly ignorant. To be blunt, it will be fine by me if she can say her prayers, if she loves me and knows how to sew and spin. (*L'Ecole des femmes* 1.1; Molière 2000: 9)

Arnolphe's expectation of a passive, loving wife does not differ much from what Pygmalion actually gets. In fact, there is no difference between Arnolphe's ideal woman and a woman-statue. And, as Pygmalion, Arnolphe seems to be guided by the anxiety that a living, lively woman will exercise her sexual independence and make him a cuckold.

To make the analogy even stronger, at some later point in the play Arnolphe uses a very telling image. He gives Agnes, the young woman he wants to marry, the "Maxims for Marriage" he has composed for her, and after listening to her reading these maxims, he says to himself: "I couldn't do better than have her for my wife. I can mould her into exactly what I want. She's like a piece of wax in my hands: I can turn her into whatever shape I like" (*L'Ecole des femmes* 3.3; Molière 2000: 29). The image of molding a woman like a wax is unmistakably Pygmalion-like. Furthermore, the specific metaphor of wax is used by Ovid: "The ivory yielded to his touch, and lost its hardness, altering under his fingers, as the bees' wax of Hymettus softens in the sun, and is moulded, under the thumb, into many forms" (lines 283–86; Kline's translation). In Ovid, the context is the description of the statue's coming to life, but the idea of molding someone like wax is evident in both cases.

Molière transforms the Pygmalion story into an unexpected, elaborate comic drama and through the complex re-telling process introduces some major changes. The most conspicuous and significant change is that the couple of "sculptor" and "statue" (Arnolphe and Agnes) are not united in a happy ending. There is certainly a happy ending to the play (it is after all a comedy) but those who participate in the lovers' union are not Arnolphe and Agnes but rather Agnes and Horace: these two fall in love despite Arnolphe's indefatigable efforts to block this. As with the typical fate of a blocking figure in comedy, Arnolphe is tricked and left outside, cheated and heart broken, at the traditional happy ending. He has learned the hard way that love overcomes authority and rigid maxims and that his hubris at the beginning of the play, where he claims that nobody could trick him, was a bit premature. The more he contrives new devices and manipulations, the more they come back to him with a boomerang effect. The only way in which Arnolphe's fate differs from that of a typical blocking figure is that at some points we feel sorry for him.

The notion of the woman-statue coming to life is a point where one can see what Molière took from Ovid but also what he changed. In Ovid, the statue's coming to life serves the real union of Pygmalion and his creation. In Molière, Agnes' coming to life takes a different form and has a different function. First, it is not a myth telling of the magical metamorphosis of a statue; Agnes is a living person and she comes to life metaphorically: from a passive, statue-like creature she starts to ask questions, look around, form her own opinion, thus liberating herself from the cast in which Arnolphe has set her. Second, and most important, her process of coming to life or self-emancipation is closely associated with her falling in love with young Horace, thus crossing the red line Arnolphe feared all along. If in Ovid's story the coming to life was a step towards a close, true, complete union of sculptor and statue-woman, in Molière it marks their separation.

While this process is taking place, with many comic moments, tricks and counter-tricks, there is an unexpected, moving moment. Arnolphe realizes that he cannot satisfy the emotional needs of this blooming young woman and that all his skills and social power cannot stop her loving Horace. After exhausting the language of threats, he suddenly shifts his tone and pleads with her:

> Just hear me sigh for love, see the languishing look in my eyes, consider the man I am, and forget that sniveling wretch and the love he [=Horace] offers you. He must have cast a spell on you: you'll be so much happier with me. You love being smartly dressed and elegantly turned out – and of course you always will be, I swear. I'll not stop billing and cooing day and night. I'll pet you, I'll cuddle you and I'll gobble you up. You shall do exactly as you please. I won't say another word because, well, I've said it all. (*L'Ecole des femmes* 5.4; Molière 2000: 51)

When we remember Arnolphe's greatest fear, the one that pushed him to contrive his complicated scheme to raise and educate a statue-like woman, we can better appreciate this love-propelled, unexpected twist: in this emotional moment Arnolphe actually gives Agnes a carte blanche to cheat on him; the man whose greatest fear was becoming a cuckold invites his beloved to make him one, provided she stays with him!

In Ovid, Pygmalion did not plan to fall in love with a statue, a love that drove him to perform some irrational acts (kissing her, lying next to her etc.). To bring such a peculiar love story to a happy ending we needed the divine intervention of Venus. In Molière, Arnolphe did not plan to fall in love with Agnes, a love that drove him to defy his greatest anxiety. But Molière does not operate in a mythical world but in the world of comedy, where the love of a young couple, signifying a fertile union, is bound to prevail. Both authors demonstrate the power of love, but the moment Molière chose to make Pygmalion an elderly, authoritative, controlling figure, trying to stifle the dynamic forces of life and love, the character is doomed to fail, and love will emerge triumphant.

Shaw: Pygmalion as a Sculptor of Speech

Whereas in Molière's case we needed some argument to show the connection between the classical tale and the modern comedy, in Shaw the connection is stated in the title.[3] Shaw's version of Ovid's story makes the sculptor a professor of phonetics and the statue is a flower seller in the streets of London at the beginning of the twentieth century. Shaw anchors the mythical tale in a concrete social reality, exploiting the mechanisms of the English class system and the role of language registers and dialects in maintaining social differentiation and social order. Professor Higgins is an endearing character in many respects but he is also highly insensitive to Eliza's needs and individuality. For him she is an object to be molded (like wax...) according to his educational plans.

In both Ovid and Molière, the major male character is driven to create a young woman because of an unresolved fear of women; the molding process serves their wish to love and be loved without taking the risks associated with real women. In Shaw, the basic motivation of the Pygmalion-like character seems to be different. The idea to transform Eliza from a common cockney girl into someone who can be presented as a woman of high society by changing her speech (and clothes) is presented as part of a wager between Higgins and his friend, Colonel Pickering, concerning Higgins' abilities as a teacher:

> PICKERING. Higgins: I'm interested. What about the ambassador's garden party? I'll say youre the greatest teacher alive if you make that good. I'll bet you all the expenses of the experiment you cant do it. And I'll pay for the lessons.
> LIZA. Oh, you are real good. Thank you, Captain.
> HIGGINS [*tempted, looking at her*] It's almost irresistible. She's so deliciously low – so horribly dirty –
> LIZA [*protesting extremely*] Ah-ah-ah-ah-ow-ow-oo-oo!!! I aint dirty: I washed my face and hands afore I come, I did.
> PICKERING. Youre certainly not going to turn her head with flattery, Higgins.
> MRS PEARCE [*uneasy*] Oh, don't say that, sir: theres more ways than one of turning a girl's head; and nobody can do it better than Mr. Higgins, though he may not always mean it. I do hope, sir, you wont encourage him to do anything foolish.
> HIGGINS [*becoming excited as the idea grows on him*] What is life but a series of inspired follies? The difficulty is to find them to do. Never lose a chance: it doesnt come every day. I shall make a duchess of this draggletailed guttersnipe.
> LIZA [*strongly deprecating this view of her*] Ah-ah-ah-ow-ow-oo!
> HIGGINS [*carried away*] Yes: in six months – in three if she has a good ear and a quick tongue – I'll take her anywhere and pass her off as anything. We'll start today: now! this moment! Take her away and clean her, Mrs. Pearce.
> (Shaw 1941: 40–41)[4]

At face value, only an intellectual wager seems to be at stake. A closer look at Professor Higgins' life style may show that the old motif of sexual anxiety has not vanished altogether but has been transformed or sublimated. Pygmalion's shunning of real, sexual women and Arnolphe's heated diatribe against women's cheating techniques take in Shaw the form of clinging to a mother figure. During a conversation with his mother, Higgins solemnly states his love for her and his unwillingness to substitute it with any attachment to a young woman:

> Oh, I cant be bothered with young women. My idea of a loveable woman is somebody as like you as possible. I shall never get into the way of seriously liking young women: some habits lie too deep to be changed. [*Rising abruptly and walking about, jingling his money and his keys in his trouser pockets*] Besides, theyre all idiots. (70)

The question whether Higgins suffers from the same sexual anxiety as Pygmalion and Arnolphe is related to the larger issue of his relationship with Eliza. To see how Higgins differs from his classical forebear, we may look at the play's conclusion, the point where actions and characters reach closure; its specific nature can explain certain choices.

As we saw earlier, Ovid offers only one option for a happy ending: Pygmalion and his statue-turned-woman unite happily in love. Molière, while maintaining a happy ending, gave it to his version of the statue-turned-alive and a young lover, Horace, leaving the disheartened Arnolphe-Pygmalion outside. The nature of the relationship between Higgins and Eliza can be formulated in the question "Will Higgins and Eliza be united and get married?" Since Shaw introduces the character of Freddy, a young man of the middle class who falls in love with Eliza (a Horace-like character) the question can be reformulated thus: "Will Shaw opt for an Ovid-like or a Molière-like happy ending?" By introducing the character of Freddy, Shaw gives us good reason to believe that he is heading for a Molière-like happy ending where the egoistical Higgins will be left behind, heart-broken, witnessing the blooming, independent young woman getting married to Freddy.

And, indeed, in the afterword to the play Shaw made his intention clear: Eliza will marry Freddy. Since the play itself *does not* conclude with the typical happy ending of a comedy, namely a marriage festivity, Shaw, after a long discussion of social and emotional considerations related to the issue of marriage, answers the question that tantalizes every reader of the play and every theatre goer: "Who will Eliza finally marry, Higgins or Freddy?"

> This being the state of human affairs, what is Eliza fairly sure to do when she is placed between Freddy and Higgins? Will she look forward to a lifetime of fetching Higgins's slippers or to a lifetime of Freddy fetching hers? There can be no doubt about the answer. Unless Freddy is biologically repulsive to her, and Higgins biologically attractive to a degree that overwhelms all her other instincts, she will, if she marries either of them, marry Freddy.
>
> And that is just what Eliza did. (Shaw 1941: 144)

Note, however, that this conclusion takes place in an afterword that is not part of the presented action. In other words, Shaw's epilogue attempts to answer a question which is left open in the play itself. But this afterword does not prevent a reader from wondering what would happen between Higgins and Eliza after the curtain falls. The fact that Shaw introduces the modal phrase ("There can be no doubt about the answer") and the fact that there are a few hypothetical clauses ("Unless Freddy... and Higgins.... ") before giving his definite answer might only reinforce the doubt in the reader's mind whether marrying Freddy is indeed the plausible option for Eliza.

These doubts can be corroborated in the concluding lines of the play as it was presented on stage. On the outer level of the dialogue, Eliza leaves Higgins, signaling her plans to marry Freddy. But when we listen carefully to the nuances behind the spoken statements, something else may be going on:

LIZA. Then I shall not see you again, Professor. Goodbye. [*She goes to the door*].

MRS HIGGINS [*coming to Higgins*] Goodbye, dear.

HIGGINS. Goodbye, mother. [*He is about to kiss her, when he recollects something*]. Oh, by the way, Eliza, order a ham and a Stilton cheese, will you? And buy me a pair of reindeer gloves, number eights, and a tie to match that new suit of mine. You can choose the color. [*His cheerful, careless, vigorous voice shews that he is incorrigible*].

LIZA [*disdainfully*] Number eights are too small for you if you want them lined with lamb's wool. You have three new ties that you have forgotten in the drawer of your washstand. Colonel Pickering prefers double Gloucester to Stilton; and you dont notice the difference. I telephoned Mrs Pearce this morning not to forget the ham. What you are to do without me I cannot imagine. [*She sweeps out*].

MRS HIGGINS. I'm afraid youve spoilt that girl, Henry. I should be uneasy about you and her if she were less fond of Colonel Pickering.

HIGGINS. Pickering! Nonsense: she's going to marry Freddy. Ha ha! Freddy! Freddy!! Ha ha ha ha ha!!!!! [*He roars with laughter as the play ends*]. (139)

The heated exchange of words between Higgins and Eliza, full of tension but also intimacy has an endearing, tender quality that we cannot envision with any other person. The emotional intensity between Higgins–Pygmalion and Eliza–Galatea,[5] the silent understanding between the two, makes it almost impossible not to imagine some kind of reunion between them.

In his last retort Higgins does not seem to be alarmed or threatened by the idea that Eliza is thinking of marrying Freddy, his young rival. Higgins is also not threatened when Eliza gains self-confidence and starts to challenge his authority. Unlike Arnolphe in Molière's play, the emergence of a free young woman with an independent, lively spirit is not a source of anxiety for him:

LIZA [*defiantly non-resistant*] Wring away. What do I care? I knew youd strike me some day. [*He lets her go, stamping with rage at having forgotten himself, and recoils so hastily that he stumbles back into his seat on the ottoman*]. Aha! Now I know how to deal with you. What a fool I was not to think of it before! You cant take away the knowledge you gave me. You said I had a finer ear than you. And I can be civil and kind to people, which is more than you can. Aha! [*Purposely dropping her aitches to annoy him*] Thats done you, Enry Iggins, it az. Now I dont care that [*snapping her fingers*] for your bullying and your big talk. I'll advertize it in the papers that your duchess is only a flower girl that you taught, and that she'll teach anybody to be a duchess just the same in six months for a thousand guineas. Oh, when I think of myself crawling under your feet and being trampled on and called names, when all the time I had only to lift up my finger to be as good as you, I could just kick myself.

HIGGINS [*wondering at her*] You damned impudent slut, you! But it's better than snivelling; better than fetching slippers and finding spectacles, isnt it? [*Rising*]

> By George, Eliza, I said I'd make a woman of you; and I have. I like you like this. (137–38)

Shaw is suggesting that these two could meet on a relatively level ground of mutual respect, a place totally different from their first meeting. Both of them have gone through a change: Eliza has obviously improved her speaking abilities and has evolved into a self-respecting, self-confident character; Higgins on his part has learnt how much he likes and needs Eliza's presence and her independent spirit. But in the epilogue, with its lengthy explanation why marrying Freddy is the plausible solution to Eliza's dilemma, Shaw, regretfully, revives and extinguishes our wishes for a possible erotic union between Higgins and Eliza:

> She is immensely interested in him. She has even secret mischievous moments in which she wishes she could get him alone, on a desert island... and see him making love like any common man. We all have private imaginations of that sort. But when it comes to business, to the life that she really leads as distinguished from the life of dreams and fancies, she likes Freddy and she likes the Colonel; and she does not like Higgins and Mr. Doolittle. Galatea never does quite like Pygmalion: his relation to her is too godlike to be altogether agreeable. (155–56)

So the reality principle pushes her to marry Freddy while the pleasure principle, the fantasy, draws her towards Higgins, a total reversal of roles from the point of view of a prototypical comedy, where the elderly, authoritative character represents the reality principle.

Recalling the two options for a happy ending for the Pygmalion story offered by Ovid and Molière, we can see how Shaw opted for an *ambiguous* ending, hovering between these two, giving good reasons to believe that each such ending has its logic but also its flaws. To marry Freddy could work out as far as real life is concerned but it will leave Eliza with some emotional discontent, some fantasies unfulfilled; to marry Higgins could perhaps be emotionally more satisfying but it could run the risk of making everyday life quite difficult. Even the afterword, which was supposed to help readers accept the reality principle, cannot make us forget the fantasy or ignore the emotionally charged tension and attraction characterizing the relationship between Higgins-Pygmalion and Eliza-Galatea.

My Fair Lady: Back to Ovid's Pygmalion

The unfulfilled, hidden wish for Eliza and Higgins to unite in a happy ending is almost fully realized in *My Fair Lady* (1956), the highly successful musical adaptation of Shaw's *Pygmalion*. Alan Jay Lerner who wrote the adaptation and Frederick Loewe who wrote the music can be said to have opted for an Ovid-like happy ending where Pygmalion and Galatea are conjoined. Well, not quite, but almost. Act Two, Scene 6 (just before the final scene of the musical) starts with Higgins' angry "Damn!! Damn!! Damn!! Damn!!" But this expression of anger immediately turns into the tender song:

> I've grown accustomed to her face!
> *She almost makes the day begin.*
> I've grown accustomed to the tune
> *She whistles night and noon* . . .
>   [*Reassuringly*]
> *I was serenely independent and content before we met;*
> Surely I could always be that way again –
>   [*The reassurance fails*]
>   and yet
>
> I've grown accustomed to her looks;
> Accustomed to her voice:
> Accustomed to her face.
>   (Lerner 1956: 125)[6]

The vacillation between contradictory feelings characterizes Higgins throughout the scene: he moves between anger and tenderness, frustration at the idea that Eliza could marry Freddy and a painful realization that he misses her very much, between dreams of revenge and fantasies of reunion. It is highly significant that towards the end, just after uttering a fuming "Marry Freddy! Ha!" (the line that concluded Shaw's *Pygmalion*) Higgins goes back to the tender "I've grown accustomed to her face" (127). In the final scene (Act Two, Scene 7), Higgins is in his study, listening to Eliza's voice and his own as they were recorded during their first meeting:

> ELIZA'S VOICE: I want to be a lady in the flower shop instead of selling flowers at the corner of Tottenham Court Road. But they won't take me unless I talk more genteel. He said he could teach me. Well, here I am ready to pay, not asking any favor – and he treats me as if I was dirt. I know what lessons cost, and I'm ready to pay.
>   [ELIZA *walks softly into the room and stands for a moment by the machine looking at* HIGGINS]
> HIGGINS' VOICE: It's almost irresistible. She's so deliciously low, so horribly dirty.
>   [ELIZA *turns off the machine*]
> ELIZA: [*gently*] I washed my face and hands before I come, I did.
>   [HIGGINS *straightens up. If he could but let himself, his face would radiate unmistakable relief and joy. If he could but let himself, he would run to her. Instead, he leans back with a contented sigh pushing his hat forward till it almost covers his face*]
> HIGGINS: [*softly*] Eliza? Where the devil are my slippers? [*There are tears in* ELIZA'S *eyes. She understands*]
>   *The curtain falls slowly* (128)

The audience is carried away by this scene. True, no wedding march plays in the background, only an old recording apparatus, but the tender moment of mutual understanding of these twin souls is unmistakable. Compared to Shaw's *Pygmalion*, *My Fair Lady* presents a less ambiguous happy ending and the scale clearly tips towards a Pygmalion–Galatea union.

Disambiguating Shaw's ending made the musical a less complex literary work and undoubtedly contributed to its career. *My Fair Lady* was enormously successful, first on Broadway, then in London, and was translated and produced around the world. Its stage success was followed by a movie musical adaptation, directed by George Cukor, starring Audrey Hepburn and Rex Harrison (1964) which had its own share of success at the box office. The happy ending can thus be partly explained as a response to audience expectations. We should remember, though, that a different happy ending could easily have been offered (the Molière model) of a marriage between the two young people, Eliza and Freddy. When the authors of the musical decided to bring Higgins and Eliza closer towards the end, they were not merely accommodating the audience's wish for a happy ending but were also attentive to the emotional intensity of the relationship between Higgins and Eliza, already evident in Shaw's play.

Other changes were made in the play on its way to become a successful musical: pushing Shaw's social critique into the background and instead placing the emphasis on the evolving relationship between the two main characters. Adaptation of the play into a popular musical thus had its casualties, such as literary complexity and social critique. We should not forget, however, that there were also achievement: first and foremost, a series of enchanting songs, sung or at least hummed by millions of people.

The Complex Chain of DTs (Dialoguing Texts)

The history of *My Fair Lady*, the musical and the movie adaptation, may raise interesting questions about the dynamics of associated DTs (dialoguing texts) that can be traced back to one IT (initiating text). It shows, for example, how one DT can become an IT for another DT as Shaw's *Pygmalion* did for *My Fair Lady*, which in turn served as the IT for the movie.

How should we treat this chain of DTs from the dialogic perspective when we want to compare the genealogy of works associated with a textual lineage that can be traced back to one ancestral IT (or Urtext)? Should we treat all these DTs as dialoguing with an ancestral IT? In terms introduced in Chapter 4, should we count all DTs as arching back to the same IT in the ponytail model even when one DT starts to form its own autonomous ponytail? In other words, if a text (IT) has generated some dialogues (DT-1, DT-2, DT-3 etc.) and one of these dialoguing texts (say, DT-2) has evoked some dialogues on its own (DT-2.1, DT-2.2 etc.), should we consider DT-2.1 as a dialogue only with DT-2 or also with IT? Our decision can have important implications on the way we measure IT's greatness. If we count DT-2.1 as a dialogue with IT, not only with its immediate generating text (DT-2), the status of IT seems secure as the head of this textual lineage and a "greater" book than DT-2, because every DT that DT-2 may generate will automatically be added to the list of dialogues with IT (plus DT-2 itself).

Such a sweeping decision, however, seems wrong: to consider Lerner and Loewe's *My Fair Lady* as a dialogue with Ovid in the same sense that we consider the musical a dialogue with Shaw's *Pygmalion* would stretch the meaning of the word dialogue too far. Shaw's play served as an IT for *My Fair Lady* in ways that Ovid's text could never do, even if we were told that Lerner and Loewe knew Ovid's dactylic hexameters by heart. But it would be equally wrong to make the opposite sweeping assumption, namely that we should dismiss the possibility that a text (DT-2.1), generated by a previous text (DT-2) in a certain textual lineage does not dialogue also with the IT of DT-2. We cannot know in advance what relationship will be created between texts that can be traced to the same common textual ancestor. Instead of attempting to predict this relationship, we can make explicit the criteria guiding us when we offer specific answers to specific cases.

These criteria are of two orders. First, every dialogue is a conscious, intentional act, and it is necessary that one knows the text with which one conducts a dialogue. Thus when we read DT-2.1 as a dialogue with IT, we have to assume that its author has some acquaintance with IT the same way we assume she or he knows DT-2 and to assume further that she or he wants us to think of IT and DT-2 as DT-2.1's ITs. This is one place where the dialogic approach differs from some theories of intertextuality that do not postulate an intentional act. But how do we know that authors know a text and want us to think of that text while reading their new text? One way they can make their intentions clear is by explicitly alluding to a previous text. The most conspicuous way to do this is by giving the work a name strongly associated with a specific forerunner.[7] When Shaw named his play *Pygmalion* he made an important move, directing us how to read the play and revealing what IT is involved in the dialogue.[8] Had he named the play *Cinderella*, the dialoguing and interpretative emphasis would shift. This does not mean that we cannot see the play as having some elements taken from the Cinderella tradition, notably an upper-class male character choosing an attractive young woman and raising her from her low social status. But, all other things being equal, by naming the play *Pygmalion* Shaw encourages us to read it as, first and foremost, a dialogue with Ovid's Pygmalion; other elements, like the Cinderella story, will be regarded as playing second fiddle, as auxiliary, enriching elements in the basic Pygmalion-like structure.[9] To explicitly call attention to the IT, an author can use, beside the title, a variety of means such as Genette described under the heading of *paratext* (Genette 1997 [1982]: 3–4).[10]

Secondly, to establish that DT-2.1 does dialogue with the ancestral IT and not only with DT-2 (its immediate IT), we should be able to define what specific type of dialogue is involved: pseudo- or genuine, local or global, allusion or parody, metonym or metaphor, adaptation or appropriation, versification or condensation.[11] If we can do that, and not just point to a general shared idea or element(s), then and only then, can we treat DT-2.1 as dialoguing with both DT-2 and IT.

A rich, branching tradition of textual lineage, with several ITs and DTs, as we saw in the case of Pygmalion,[12] raises another question: when should we talk about a dialogue (either genuine or pseudo-) with a *specific text* and when is it more appropriate to speak of using a *motif* or an abstract story line or a myth? In other words, does every occurrence of a story about a man trying to mold a woman to his liking make it ipso facto a dialogue with Ovid's Metamorphoses X? Or perhaps we should only talk about using a Pygmalion-motif without necessarily evoking Ovid? The answer in specific cases depends on two complementary issues: (1) does a text recall several distinctive features of the IT or does it refer to only one conspicuous characteristic associated with an IT; the more such distinctive features, the more likely we are to be dealing with a DT; (2) once we decide to read a text *as a DT* with a specific IT, this reading yields satisfying interpretative results; it leads to certain insights that could not be gained otherwise. These two dimensions usually go together: an author would plant a few clues that the text is dialoguing with a specific IT, and once we realize the dialoguing relationship our reading of the present text, and often also of the IT, is enriched.

Sometimes, even when there is only one conspicuous clue or trigger, the present text can still yield satisfying results. Moreover, the number of elements connecting DT and IT may increase during the process of interpretation: our point of departure is one conspicuous element, but by seeing a text as a DT other connecting elements may emerge. Thus Molière's *L'Ecole des femmes* was included in this chapter not only because it tells a story about a man trying to mold a woman to his liking but also because Arnolphe was motivated by the same anxiety that caused Pygmalion to create his statue; and this combination of elements is uniquely Ovidian.

To conclude: a text may be (a) dialoguing intensely with only one IT or (b) dialoguing intensely with more than one IT; or it may be (c) dialoguing intensely with one IT and at the same time using (general) motifs related to other texts and literary traditions; or it may be (d) merely using general motifs from different literary traditions. Whereas case (d) goes beyond the scope of our study, all the first three cases are variations on IT and DT relations. In fact, many cases of genuine DTs can be described as (c): engaged in an intense dialogue with one IT but as part of their dialectical innovation they bring into play motifs associated with other textual traditions – as Shaw did in *Pygmalion*.

CHAPTER

11

More's *Utopia* and Some Variations

Utopian ideas have preoccupied humanity from a very early period. The biblical Garden of Eden and Hesiod's Golden Age are two early examples of portrayals of humanity living in harmony with nature and with itself. These imagined pre-utopian states occurred in a mythical past. Plato ventured to imagine a future state founded on tenets that would bring conflicting drives together in harmony, liquidate humanity's weaknesses (such as a drive for private property and other such despicable ambitions) and with the help of a ruling class of guardians-philosophers (and the docility of the ruled people) would enable humanity to strive to its utmost endeavors in the pursuit of happiness, justice and truth. Two millennia later, a literary work again described an imagined society governed by reason, free from human foibles. This was Thomas More's *Utopia* (1516).

Unlike Plato's proposal, More's book (and the many dialogues it generated) presented a functioning society, somewhere on this globe, not a philosophical exercise describing a desired state. More's book swiftly became the seminal work in thinking on the subject, and the title became synonymous with an imagined society where reason prevails and humanity reaches happiness, justice and reunion with nature. More portrayed Utopia as a place where the irreconcilable contradictions that have plagued humanity since the beginning of history – between culture and nature, resources and supply, pleasure and reality, individual and community – are all happily resolved. More does not describe Utopia directly in his own person but rather brings it to his readers in the words of a traveler by the name of Raphael Hythlodaeus. More thus achieves at least two goals. First, he makes the story about this remote, difficult to get at country more credible: after all, only an experienced traveler could have set foot, even by chance, on the remote, isolated island of Utopia. Secondly, and not less significantly, this traveler acts as the reader's surrogate, representing her/his generally shared set of beliefs. As the traveler comes to know the Utopians' political and economic system he is surprised and at some points shows signs of resistance and even voices his amazement, as any of us would, because their ways are so different from ours. But he learns to appreciate and accept their norms, and his embrace of these norms makes it easier for the reader to do the same.

A hallmark of the utopian society described by More (and by other authors of paradigmatic works) is that it is static and isolated, with no inner conflicts, and complete in itself: when we have a perfect society, there is no reason for discontent and no motivation for change (Hadomi 1989: 31–43). However, despite its static nature, the work is fraught with conflict, though not necessarily actual conflicts between factions, classes or parties within the utopian society. Conflict is found on another level: between the rational, enlightened and egalitarian principles governing that society and the known, prevailing norms of Western society, religion and political systems. The first half of More's *Utopia* is devoted to a critical presentation of the corrupt nature of contemporary Western societies, and only in the second half of the book are we introduced, through the mediation of Raphael's eyes, to Utopia, offering a corrective alternative to all the ailments set out in the first half. In a sense, one can describe the first part of *Utopia* as a negative-satirical discourse, the dark side of the moon, preparing for the introduction of the positive alternative, the Utopia proper of the second part.

Did Thomas More believe in all the principles governing his utopian society and its political system? There is of course no way to provide a persuasive answer to this question. The fact that Utopia is presented through the eyes of a traveler and not directly in More's name makes interpretative decisions more complex. Perhaps one could argue that More did not necessarily believe that *all* the norms and practices found in Utopia should be imported *in toto* into European societies. It is reasonable to assume, for example, that as a Christian he did not approve of all aspects of the Utopians' religion, which was based partly on pagan beliefs and partly on a deist position (More 1992: 72–73). Still, there is no reason to assume that More distances himself from Utopia and the Utopian principles or that he presents them in an ironic light. By and large, we can join Paul Turner who in the introduction to his English translation of *Utopia* says "I am simple minded enough to believe, with certain qualifications, that the book means what it says, and that it does attempt to solve the problems of human society" (More 1965: 12). This assertion becomes even more persuasive when we read other literary presentations of a supposedly desirable utopian society, such as the fourth book of *Gulliver's Travels* (see later in this chapter), where the author is clearly critical of some of its norms and practices.

Bacon's Scientific Utopia

About one hundred years after More's *Utopia* was published, English readers encountered a new version of utopian society in Bacon's *New Atlantis* (1627). As with More's narrative so with Bacon's a traveler arrives in a remote, isolated country and finds there a society governed by elevated principles, free of regular human foibles, living in prosperity and harmony. Social harmony is directly linked to private happiness, with a strong emphasis on stable families, devoid of covetousness or infidelity. Chastity, both literal and metaphorical, is the hallmark of the people of Bensalem in Bacon's New Atlantis. Their society is presented as the "virgin of the world" (Bacon 1999: 173). The emphasis on pure, natural modes of behavior, without the sins of the flesh, in what is supposed to reconstruct a pre-fallen state can already be found in *Utopia*, where the custom of choosing marriage partners is thus described:

> In choosing marriage partners, they solemnly and seriously follow a custom which seemed to us foolish and absurd in the extreme. Whether she is a widow or a virgin, the bride-to-be is shown naked to the groom by a responsible and respectable matron; and, similarly, some respectable man presents the groom naked to his future bride. (More 1992: 61)

The logic behind this apparently "absurd" custom is explained, and the reader is supposed to draw the unavoidable conclusion that absurdity lies in fact with European customs where deformities can be hidden from prospective marriage partners until it is too late. In Bacon's *New Atlantis*, a guide to the European visitors explicitly rejects this custom as it is described in *Utopia*: "I have read in a book of one of your men, of a Feigned Commonwealth, where the married couple are permitted, before they contract, to see one another naked. This they dislike; for they think it a scorn to give a refusal after so familiar knowledge" (Bacon 1999: 174). However, this rejection refers only to some outer details of the procedure, when it comes to the substantial issues involved, Bacon seems to share More's basic attitude:

> But because of many hidden defects in men and women's bodies, they have a more civil way; for they have near every town a couple of pools, (which they call "Adam and Eve's pools"), where it is permitted to one of the friends of the man, and another of the friends of the woman, to see them severally bathe naked. (Bacon 1999: 174–75)

Thus, as far as marriage customs are concerned, Bacon may be offering a small variation on More's principle. But Bacon's most conspicuous contribution to More's model and to the utopian tradition in general can be found in the importance he gives to the place of science in the ideal society. In More's *Utopia* learning and scientific inquiry are presented among other areas of society and culture and the emphasis is put on the practical uses of these activities as opposed to speculative philosophy (More 1992: 49–50; 57–59). In Bacon's *New Atlantis*, experimental enterprise, which held a relatively marginal place in *Utopia*, gains prominence. The shift reflects the emergence of modern science and more specifically Bacon's preoccupation with scientific methods and the philosophy of science. Consequently, inhabitants of New Atlantis invest many resources in cultivating and advancing scientific knowledge. A large part of Bacon's work is devoted to a detailed description of Solomon's House, where their scientific activity takes place.

The visitors' guide to New Atlantis (or the people of Bensalem as they like to call themselves), tells about the most important institution founded by their legendary king: "amongst the excellent acts of that king, one above all hath the pre-eminence. It was the erection and institution of an Order or Society, which we call Salomon's House; the noblest foundation (as we think) that ever was upon the earth; and the lanthorn of this kingdom. It is dedicated to the study of the works and creatures of God" (Bacon 1999: 167). The source of the name 'Solomon's House' probably goes back to the wise king of the ancient Hebrews (although other options have been raised) and during that first introduction great emphasis is placed on the notion that scientific research does not contradict religion but is rather instrumental to the worship of God because studying nature brings one closer to God's creation. At a later stage, the visitors are introduced to the Father of Solomon's House, who gives them a grand tour of the institution. After stating its purpose, he goes on to describe its various facilities, some of them deep underground[1]:

> The End of our Foundation is the knowledge of Causes, and secret motions of things; and the enlarging of the bounds of Human Empire, to the effecting of all things possible.
>
> The Preparations and Instruments are these. We have large and deep caves of several depths: the deepest are sunk six hundred fathom; and some of them are digged and made under great hills and mountains: so that if you reckon together the depth of the hill and the depth of the cave, they are (some of them) above three miles deep ... These caves we call the Lower Region. And we use them for all coagulations, indurations, refrigerations, and conservations of bodies. We use them likewise for the imitation of natural mines; and the producing also of new artificial metals, by compositions and materials which we use, and lay there for many years. (Bacon 1999: 177)

Other installations tower high above ground to enable experiments in meteorological processes to take place. The guiding Father continues the survey of numerous facilities and then describes some scientific experiments on animals conducted there:

> We try also all poisons and other medicines upon them, as well of chirurgery as physic. By art likewise, we make them greater or taller than their kind is; and contrariwise dwarf them, and stay their growth: we make them more fruitful and bearing than their kind is; and contrariwise barren and not generative. Also we make them differ in colour, shape, activity, many ways. We find means to make commixtures and copulations of different kinds; which have produced many new kinds, and them not barren, as the general opinion is. We make a number of kinds of serpents, worms, flies, fishes, of putrefaction; whereof some are advanced (in effect) to be perfect creatures, like beasts or birds; and have sexes, and do propagate. Neither do we this by chance, but we know beforehand of what matter and commixture what kind of those creatures will arise. (Bacon 1999: 179)

Today, these descriptions may raise critical reactions, not only from people opposing experimentation on animals but also because we are aware of the ethical problems involved in such experiments. But it is quite clear that for Bacon such scientific experiments represent the cutting edge of progress and he was not aware of their possible ill uses. The emphasis is on science and technology as instruments for improving the quality of human life. Scientists in Bacon's New Atlantis do not shun research in military technology, experimenting with "new mixtures and compositions of gun-powder, wildfires burning in water, and unquenchable. Also fire-works of all variety both for pleasure and use" (Bacon 1999: 183). After referring to experiments of "flying in the air" and of "ships and boats for going under water," the guide also mentions "houses of deceits of the senses; where we represent all manner of feats of juggling, false apparitions, impostures, and illusions; and their fallacies" (ibid.). Thus, almost four hundred years ago Bacon foresaw not only airplanes and submarines but also the effect of virtual reality.

Bacon's vision of a utopian society nurturing scientific research and bestowing honor on scientists may attract our admiration, especially if we are part of the scientific community. This admiration may be balanced by reservation, even rejection. Bacon was impervious to the suffering of animals or to the dangers of developing weapons of mass destruction or of turning scientific research to the service of questionable political ends. But even before such potential ill uses and dangers became clear, one writer at least was highly suspicious of the idea of such a utopian society.

Swift contra Utopia or Sat-opia

About a hundred years after Bacon's *New Atlantis* came out, Jonathan Swift tried to critically expose some assumptions associated with the tradition of utopian writings. Swift's satirical treatment of Bacon's idealized version of modern science is quite clear in the third book of *Gulliver's Travels* (1726). Let us look at the description of Gulliver's visit to the "Grand Academy of Lagado":

> This Academy is not an entire single Building, but a Continuation of several Houses on both Sides of a Street; which growing waste, was purchased and applied to that Use.
>
> I was received very kindly by the Warden, and went for many Days to the Academy. Every Room has in it one or more Projectors; and I believe I could not be in fewer than five Hundred Rooms.
>
> The first Man I saw was of a meagre Aspect, with sooty Hands and Face, his Hair and Beard long, ragged, and singed in several Places. His Clothes, Shirt, and Skin were all of the same Colour. He has been Eight Years upon a Project for extracting Sun-Beams out of Cucumbers, which were to be put in Vials hermetically sealed, and let out to warm the Air in raw inclement Summers. He told me, he did not doubt in Eight Years more, that he should be able to supply Governors Gardens with Sun-shine at a reasonable Rate; but he complained that his Stock was low, and intreated me to give him something as an Encouragement to Ingenuity, especially since this had been a very dear Season for Cucumbers. I

made him a small Present, for my Lord had furnished me with Money on purpose, because he knew their Practice of begging from all who go to see them. (Swift 1973: 152–53)[2]

The scientist in this first chamber, his illusionary plan of extracting heat and light from cucumbers and his habitual conduct of begging for support may raise a smile. But this is merely a prelude to the second chamber:

> I went into another Chamber, but was ready to hasten back, being almost overcome with a horrible Stink. My Conductor pressed me forward, conjuring me in a Whisper to give no Offence, which would be highly resented; and therefore I durst not so much as stop my Nose. The Projector of this Cell was the most ancient Student of the Academy. His Face and Beard were of a pale Yellow; his Hands and Clothes dawbed over with Filth. When I was presented to him, he gave me a close Embrace, (a Compliment I could well have excused). His Employment from his first coming into the Academy, was an Operation to reduce human Excrement to its original Food, by separating the several Parts, removing the Tincture which it receives from the Gall, making the Odour exhale, and scumming off the Saliva. He had a weekly Allowance from the Society, of a Vessel filled with human Ordure, about the Bigness of a *Bristol* Barrel. (153)

It seems that everything that was for Bacon a source of admiration became for Swift matter for derision: the well-developed, spacious places devoted to scientific research in the *New Atlantis* are transformed into a series of small, repulsive cells; Bacon's monk-like scientists devoting their lives to the pursuit of scientific projects become a coterie of the unsavory, detached from real life. In Swift's perspective such detachment from life and nature is modern science's greatest fault. In Bacon, the drive to conquer the limitations of nature is the laudable force behind science and human progress; this force is presented by Swift as driven by man's pride and inability to accept his limited place in the divine plan.

Swift's critique of utopian ideas goes deeper than his satirical exposure of Bacon's presentation of modern science. It seems that Swift is trying to undermine some basic assumptions of More's *Utopia* and utopian literature generally, especially the assumption that man is a perfectible creature. Swift's subversive departure from More's *Utopia* is especially interesting because satire and utopian literature would seem, superficially at least, to be closely related genres. They both reject present forms of human society and they sometimes make use of similar devices (e.g., the voyage, the stranger's eye). They would seem to differ only in emphasis. Whereas the satirist focuses on criticism, the utopian writer offers an ideal alternative. The implicit social censure embedded in utopian texts, and in a complementary way the ideals assumed by satirical ones, further underscore the similarities of the two genres. According to this argument, utopian writing entices its readers into accepting an ideal alternative on the basis of implicit, and often explicit, rejection of contemporary society through satire.[3] The satirist and his readers will have to share certain human values and general utopian ideals regarding society, so that the satirical message may be conveyed and the distorted world depicted by satire be recognized as such.

It is of course no coincidence that More's *Utopia* and Swift's *Gulliver's Travels*, perhaps the most famous and powerful examples of the two genres, share so many thematic and structural characteristics. The fact that Sir Thomas More is mentioned in Book Three of *Gulliver's Travels* as one of the six noble sages "to which all the Ages of the World cannot add a Seventh" (167) – of these More is the only modern thinker and statesman, the other five are figures from ancient history – is an illustration of the close spiritual and ideological similarities between the two works. A further example can be found in the structure of voyage, in the course of which the traveler (Raphael in More, Gulliver in Swift) visits remote utopian societies and returns to the known world. In both cases, after experiencing Utopia, the traveler's life among his fellow human beings is filled with a deep and anguished sense of alienation.[4]

However, the apparently intimate relationship between the two works is open to doubt. There may of course be interesting similarities between *Utopia* and *Gulliver's Travels*, and I would like to suggest a different interpretation of these similarities. The structural analogies do not express a shared world-view and artistic sensibility, but rather reflect a mechanism of parody and playful distortion. A careful reading of Swift's portrayal of a seemingly utopian society, notably that of the horses of Book Four, leads to the conclusion that Swift the satirist, rather than embracing utopian ideas, tends to suspect, distort, and parody them. Further, this disrespectful attitude of a satirist towards utopian thinking characterizes not only Swift but also other satirists of his time, such as Voltaire (as we shall see in the next section).[5] These two eighteenth-century satirists differ in many respects, but they seem to share a suspicious attitude towards utopian ideas.

Let us examine, for instance, Gulliver's first encounter with representatives of an ideal, utopian society, the horses.[6] As with the other creatures Gulliver meets, here too Swift dwells on the peculiar language they use: "Then the Bay tried me with a second Word, much harder to be pronounced; but reducing it to the *English Orthography*, may be spelt thus, *Houyhnhnm*. I did not succeed in this so well as the former, but after two or three farther Trials, I had better Fortune; and they both appeared amazed at my Capacity" (196). The reader cannot help but be amused by the actual sounds of neighing produced by Gulliver in this particular scene. Needless to say, this comic effect is deliberate. Swift could have simply told us that the Houyhnhnms neighed, without providing an orthographic presentation of their discourse. However, we would then have missed some of the playful aspects of the situation. Had he ignored these (and other) opportunities for humor at the expense of the horses, we might have been more inclined to consider their utopia as a serious alternative to corrupt human existence. As it stands, Swift seems to be interested in ridiculing these horses almost as much as he wishes to criticize contemporary society. The peculiar nature of the horses' language is not, of course, the only target of his comic talent. These effects go hand in hand with many harsh though implicit critical comments on these self-perceived ideal creatures.

To begin with, the Houyhnhnms are sometimes stupid. This statement may sound strange to those of us who are used to perceive the horses as representatives of Rationalism, as *ratio incarnate*. But an impartial reading of Book Four leads to the conclusion that the horses are simply unintelligent. They are unable to comprehend simple facts, for example that Gulliver is wearing clothes. The epistemological confusion and complex ideological problem that Gulliver poses (is he, or is he not, a Yahoo) is based on their misunderstanding of the nature and function of his clothes.

When they finally come to realize the true purpose of Gulliver's clothes (a discovery made by chance), their stupidity together with their cruelty become apparent. After all the pathetic efforts Gulliver has made to resemble his beloved horses, and after his self-effacement and total adoption of their ideology, point of view, diet, and language, they convene to discuss how to get rid of him. Having found out that he wears clothes, these allegedly rational creatures categorize him as a Yahoo. Precisely when Gulliver has reached a state of total identification with the creatures he most admires, the horses, they decide to include him in the category he most despises, the Yahoos. In classifying Gulliver as a Yahoo, they display a combination of cognitive and moral blindness: from a cognitive point of view, their categorizing system is highly deficient if it cannot distinguish Gulliver from the Yahoos, while from a moral viewpoint, they cruelly betray their most ardent supporter when they decide to send him (the original plan was to send him swimming!) back to human society. This decision, like all the others made by the horses' general assembly, is described by the word hnhloayn, "which signifies an *Exhortation*; as near as I can render it: For they have no Conception how a rational Creature can be *compelled*, but only advised, or *exhorted*; because no Person can disobey Reason, without giving up his Claim to be a rational Creature" (245). Note how the horses' language verges on Orwellian newspeak: the term exhortation is applied to what is in fact a mandatory decree.

To accentuate the inherent cruelty of these supposedly innocent creatures, Swift tells us that during the horses' general assembly, in which they discuss the solution to the Yahoo problem, a proposal is made to castrate the Yahoos. This idea was not originally their own. In fact, it was Gulliver who put this "modest proposal" into their heads: "I mentioned a Custom we had of *castrating Houyhnhnms* when they were young, in order to render them tame; that the Operation was easy and safe" (238). Whereas the horses are usually hostile towards any idea expressed by Gulliver, when it comes to this vicious notion, they suddenly listen and become receptive.

There can be some serious doubt as to whether Swift wants us to see the horses as ideal creatures or to view their society as a desirable utopia. A suggestion of his critical attitude can be found in the way Gulliver explains the etymology of his hosts' name: "The word *Houyhnhnm*, in their Tongue, signifies a *Horse*; and in its Etymology, *the Perfection of Nature*" (203). This haughty etymology sounds all too familiar; it is nothing but an equine version of the human claim to being the Crown of Creation. An implicit analogy exists between the horses and their self-image as "the perfection of nature" and human beings who regard themselves as nature's elevated creatures. Gulliver, having been exposed to the "light" of the horses' utopia, vehemently rejects – together with Swift – human expressions of hubris. But, by calling our attention to certain analogies between the prideful human self-image and the horses' own version of hubris, Swift also satirizes the horses. This time, Gulliver does not share Swift's criticism. In fact, Swift indirectly satirizes Gulliver, in addition to the horses, as he cannot perceive the analogy between arrogant human and equine self-perception.

Thus, in Swift's world the horses do not represent ideal creatures and their society is by no means an ideal utopia. To focus on the ridiculous and unpleasant aspects of their behavior, does not mean to deny the existence or diminish the significance of certain attractive features that these creatures possess. Rather, it means a more balanced approach in which Swift's satirical temperament receives due attention. Perhaps Swift wished to portray a utopian society in which there are no painful gaps between nature and man, thinking and action, theory and praxis; the horses represent these ideals in many respects, and their society is Paradise on earth.[7] Swift, however, is basically not a utopist, but a satirist, keenly aware of ridiculous and harmful traits in man. A true satirist is always a pessimist (or perhaps a realist) at heart. Thus, no matter how Swift planned to portray his horses, as a satirist he could not simply represent an ideal alternative society of impeccable creatures. These creatures may possess certain lovable characteristics (perhaps as a result of a momentary Swiftian utopist impulse), but Swift cannot resist the frequent temptation to deflate this utopian image that he himself has created. Driven by his satirical temperament, he adds many funny and ridiculous aspects to his depiction of the horses, as well as giving them some serious moral faults in the form of cruelty and hubris. In the final analysis, it is the playful, critical, and satirical manipulations that express Swift's innermost artistic inclinations.

One major reason for Swift's negative attitude to utopian ideals was a deep suspicion that elevated talk merely veils evil intentions; that utopian aspirations ignore the basic *condition humaine* with its inherent shortsightedness and imperfections. The utopian attempt to ignore human beings' nature and to assign to them a quasi-angelic status in a heavenly society is portrayed by the satirist as but another symptom of human shortsightedness. In addition to the playful ironies that ensue from this situation (the attempt to transcend human imperfections is a manifestation of these imperfections) there are some serious moral issues at stake. These utopian ideals may give birth to previously unknown barbarities and atrocities. Utopian ideals, on their way to heaven, can increase the amount of stupidity and cruelty on earth. Thus, a major cause of Swift's suspicion and hostility towards utopian notions can be attributed to moral or ethical objections. Utopian ideals portraying people as perfectible creatures, capable of achieving complete moral integrity and social harmony, are exposed by the satirist as part of human vanity and pride and as inherently chimerical and harmful delusions.

Voltaire's Short Comical Version

In addition to the moral issue, yet another factor can be identified in a satirist's aversion to utopian ideas. To illustrate this point let us turn to Voltaire's description of El Dorado in *Candide*.[8] As in More's classical *Utopia*, here too gold serves as a central symbol; it emphasizes the contrast between utopia and everyday, Western, society. The inhabitants of More's Utopia and the people of El Dorado in *Candide* both treat gold as just another basic mineral, as opposed to Western, corrupted societies (and, of course, the grotesque Yahoos in *Gulliver's Travels*), which adore and cherish it.

However, Voltaire is writing a satire, not merely another version of utopia. To begin with, he enjoys exploring some of the ludicrous aspects of life in his version of utopia. An example is the El Doradoans' use of sheep as a means of transport: "Candide and Cacambo climbed into the carriage; the six sheep flew, and in less than four hours they arrived at the palace of the king" (Voltaire 1963: 155).[9] There is nothing intrinsically bad, of course, in being drawn by sheep, it is just a bit ridiculous and Voltaire does not want us to unduly admire this special and essentially good place. In addition to these playful aspects, Voltaire reveals his true satirical attitude towards utopia when his two hero-travelers, Candide and Cacambo, decide to leave Eldorado. It is interesting to see how Voltaire explains their reasons for abandoning a place which is, by their own admission, a heaven on earth:

> They spent a month in this refuge. Candide never stopped saying to Cacambo: "It is true, my friend, once again, that the country house where I was born can't be compared to the country where we are; but after all Mademoiselle Cunégonde is not here, and doubtless you have a mistress in Europe. If we stay here, we will only be like the others; whereas, if we return to our world merely with twelve sheep laden with pebbles of El Dorado, we shall be richer than all the kings put together; we'll no longer have Inquisitors to fear, and we'll easily be able to recover Mademoiselle Cunégonde."
>
> This observation pleased Cacambo; people so much enjoy running about, showing off before one's own friends, making a parade of what one has seen on one's travels, that the two happy men resolved not to be so any longer, and to ask His Majesty's permission to go. (159)

So why are they leaving El Dorado, after Candide admits that it is indeed a far better place than the country house he was born in? The passage does not provide a single answer alone to this question. Rather, we encounter a conglomeration of possible answers: they are leaving because Mademoiselle Cunégonde is not there; because Cacambo probably has a mistress too; because if they stay they will lose their individuality; because they can become the richest men in the world; because they will be able to free Mlle Cunégonde; because they will enjoy telling their adventures. The longer the list becomes, the more we begin to suspect that perhaps these many reasons, each of which is sufficient in and of itself, only conceal a more fundamental reason – Voltaire's reason.

The true reason lies in the fact that our two travelers, as well as Voltaire, are simply bored to death in El Dorado. They are eager to get back to their adventures, and Voltaire, of course, is eager to comply. He wants to put them into new situations that will enable him to explore additional human follies and vices. In El Dorado there simply are none. He wants to describe more extraordinary, deviant, and perverse kinds of human behavior and in El Dorado there are none. He wants to go on depicting the bizarre panorama of inhumanities that humans are capable of. El Dorado, with its utopian way of life, is characterized by high moral standards and is static in nature. It provides a poor target for a satirist's pen. In comparison with the interesting and colorful possibilities available to the depiction of a sinful society, the satirist finds utopia a dull and unattractive prospect for artistic development.

Every satirist could thus rephrase Tolstoy's opening lines in *Anna Karenina*: "All utopias are happy in the same way, but all existing societies are unhappy in many different ways." It is in the diversity of unhappiness, and in the variety of vices and follies that produce this unhappiness, that the satirist is best able to articulate his innermost artistic talent and aesthetic inclination.

Different Stances and Structural Variations

Utopia and satire express two extremely different types of moral stance and artistic sensibility despite their apparent similarities. The former is an optimistic vision of what humanity could achieve as opposed to the latter, which is a pessimistic view of humanity's inherent shortcomings and self-delusions. Utopian writing communicates a fascination with describing the harmonious nature of life in a utopia, while satire deals with the seductive force of diverse and colorful portrayals of sinful societies.

One possible implication of the above description is that the satirical treatment of utopian ideas can be distinguished not only from utopian writings but also from what is known as anti-utopia, or dystopia.[10] Whereas the former ridicules utopian ideas in a playful, parodic, or even sarcastic, manner, and shares the anti-utopian pessimistic view of human nature, the latter usually portrays a frightful reverse mirror-like image of utopia (e.g., Orwell's *1984*). We are dealing with a fundamentally different artistic sensibility. Utopias and dystopias (or anti-utopias) differ in their moral assessment of mankind. As far as artistic sensibilities and aesthetic inclinations are concerned, utopias and dystopias are very much alike in their serious portrayal of a static and isolated society, and both differ from the ironic, playful, parodic inventions of the satopia, the satirical treatment of utopian ideas whether in literature or in philosophy.

In terms of authors' attitudes towards utopia, both More and Bacon seem to share Wilde's often quoted words reflecting a belief in progress: "A map of the world that does not include Utopia is not worth even glancing at, for it leaves out the one country at which Humanity is always landing. And when Humanity lands there, it looks out, and, seeing a better country, sets sail. Progress is the realisation of Utopias." (Wilde 1968: 269–70) While Voltaire may join forces with these predecessors in advocating human progress, he seems also to be keenly aware of ingrained human habits (e.g. avarice, pride, the need for excitement and for being individual). Such habits die hard. They may also have endearing qualities that make human beings what they are: Cunégonde may not be the most beautiful woman on earth (in fact, towards the end she becomes truly ugly), nor is she very innocent (Voltaire makes that clear). There is nothing neither ideal or rational about Candide's love for her, but for this love he is willing to leave utopian El Dorado, because it makes his life meaningful. Swift, however, does not seem to share Wilde's sentiments; conservative to his bones, both Utopia and Progress are ideas that make him deeply suspicious. According to Swift, humanity is often tempted to set sail for an imagined better country, only to find that our deepest nightmares, and not necessarily our beautified dreams, are realized there.

Thus, dialogues with More's *Utopia* may express different approaches towards the notion of an ideal society, moving from asserting the notion and giving it a specific elaboration (Bacon) to a satirical, harsh exposure (Swift) or an amused parody (Voltaire). From the structural point of view, it is clear that of these four More's work plays the role of the IT (initiating text) – not only because chronologically he was the first but also because his work became a focal point for future references. As we have seen, however, part of Swift's critical exposure, that focusing on modern scientific research, is a dialogue with Bacon's description of Solomon's House in *New Atlantis* more than with any particular scene from More's *Utopia*. When Voltaire mocks utopian society in his portrayal of El Dorado, he is evoking an image which is not necessarily associated with More's work but that rather evokes some general utopian qualities (perhaps with the exception of the special attention given to the insignificance of gold). More created a systematic representation of a utopian society somewhere on this globe, and at some point the image of a utopian society became part of the cultural baggage of educated people, free from the specifics of More's work. Thus, when an author alludes to the image of a utopian society, either favorably or critically, this does not necessarily mean that she or he wishes to evoke the specific portrayal found in More's *Utopia*.

Here lies one of the deepest characteristics of dialogues with great books, something we can also see in other cases discussed in this book: when a work generates many and diverse dialogues, part of these dialogues pertain to the pyramid's base described in Chapter 4, namely references to some general images associated with the IT (initiating text) or with some catch phrases associated with it. In other words, the references to a great book that circulate en masse in culture, are those that do not necessarily evoke the specifics of the work evoked. When a work has gained the status of greatness, readers can make sense of a reference to an IT, but chances are that they have never actually read it. Thus, in some deep sense, the greatest triumph of a book is also its greatest defeat: by generating many diverse dialogues, it is denied its specificity. People can talk about it, evoke it, embrace it or mock it – but without actually having read it – as they often do with *Utopia*.[11]

CHAPTER

12

Robinson Crusoe – The Variety Principle Revisited

Even the most eagle-eyed of readers would not have been able to find Defoe's name on the front page of *Robinson Crusoe* on its first appearance almost three hundred years ago (1719). When contemporary literary rumors cast doubt on the veracity of the story and the existence of its alleged writer,

> THE
>
> # LIFE
>
> AND
>
> STRANGE SURPRIZING
>
> ## ADVENTURES
>
> OF
>
> *ROBINSON CRUSOE,*
> Of *YORK*, MARINER:
>
> Who lived Eight and Twenty Years,
> all alone in an un-inhabited Island on the
> Coast of AMERICA, near the Mouth of
> the Great River of OROONOQUE;
>
> Having been cast on Shore by Shipwreck, where-
> in all the Men perished but himself.
>
> WITH
> An Account how he was at last as strangely deli-
> ver'd by PYRATES.
>
> *Written by Himself.*
>
> *LONDON:*
> Printed for W. TAYLOR at the *Ship* in *Pater-Noster-
> Row.* MDCCXIX.

"Robinson Crusoe, of York, mariner," Defoe hastened to rebut these allegations in the introduction to the second sequel he wrote to *Robinson Crusoe*, entitled *Serious Reflections during the Life and Surprising Adventures of Robinson Crusoe* (published in 1720):

> I have heard, that the envious and ill-disposed Part of the World have rais'd some Objections against the two first Volumes, on Pretence, *for want of a better Reason*; That (*as they say*) the Story is feign'd, that the Names are borrow'd, and that it is all a Romance; that there never were any such Man or Place, or Circumstances in any Mans Life; that it is all form'd and embellish'd by Invention to impose upon the World.
>
> I *Robinson Crusoe* being at this Time in perfect and sound Mind and Memory, Thanks be to God therefore; do hereby declare, their Objection is an Invention scandalous in Design, and false in Fact; and do affirm, that the Story, though Allegorical, is also Historical; and that it is the beautiful Representation of a Life of unexampled Misfortunes, and of a Variety not to be met with in the World. (Defoe 1994: 240)

My guess is that Defoe was smiling to himself while writing these paragraphs. Regardless of his personal mood, it is clear that by hiding behind the invented character-narrator-alleged-writer, protesting (as Crusoe) the accusation that he was a fictional invention – Defoe, sometimes called the father of the English novel, was following the example set by Cervantes, the "grandfather" of the European novel. But unlike *Don Quixote*, where the manipulations of invented identities occupy an important part of the work's playful self-reflexive meta-fiction (Alter 1975; Waugh 1984), in *Robinson Crusoe* the author's concealment behind Crusoe is, first and foremost, in the service of the work's serious, truth-like and realistic effect. Aside from using a similar literary device (albeit towards different goals), *Robinson Crusoe* and *Don Quixote* share another feature: the two works have created – alongside a handful of other literary inventions of the past millennium (e.g., Hamlet, Don Juan) – what can be described as modern myths: figures who touch deep cultural nerves, who have evoked innumerable (pseudo- and genuine) dialogues since their conception, and who are better known through their widespread cultural echoes than through a first-hand acquaintance with the literary works where they made their debut.

Robinson Crusoe and the Dialogic Approach

Today, *Robinson Crusoe*'s status as a great book and the position of its main character as a modern myth seem unshakable. This, however, was not always the case. Precisely because the book's rise to greatness was not always obvious and because it is a relative newcomer into the hall of literary fame, it provides an interesting test case for the dialogic approach to great books. Unlike previous chapters of Part II, where a few dialogues produced in response to a great book were discussed, here a brief (and necessarily somewhat superficial) survey of different types of dialogues generated by *Robinson Crusoe* will be offered. This survey will offer an opportunity – before concluding this study – to revisit the hypothesis introduced in the first part of the book, associating a work's greatness with the number and *diversity* of dialogues it arouses and to re-examine the positions of the two prevailing parties in the debate on canon formation.

If one examines the reactions to *Robinson Crusoe* when it was first published or looks at Defoe's literary reputation in his lifetime, it would be difficult to predict the work's bright future. To say that Defoe did not enjoy the support of the contemporary literary elite is a mild understatement. In fact, Defoe never belonged to those circles and his works were habitually not even considered as serious literary achievements (that is, when they were acknowledged to be Defoe's). To his contemporaries Defoe's reputation was first and foremost that of a political pamphleteer, and he was more than once criticized and ridiculed (Rogers 1972: 9–14). Pope's satirical reference to Defoe in *The Dunciad* (II, 145–48), lumped together with other unworthy writers, is symptomatic of the attitude of highly educated literary circles to Defoe's oeuvre:

> Instructive work! whose wry-mouthed portraiture
> Displayed the fates her confessors endure.
> Earless on high, stood unabashed Defoe,
> And Tutchin flagrant from the scourge below.
> (Pope 1963: 383–84)[1]

The first conclusion one can draw from this is that a marginal position in the literary system does not thwart a writer from achieving fame and glory. The second is that advocates of the power party are in trouble, at least as long as they emphasize top-down processes in explaining a work's way to fame. Note, however, that simply replacing a top-down with a bottom-up explanation (the *vox populi* factor) will prove equally misleading. A bestseller's success has some impact, but if it is not accompanied by many and diverse dialogues, the work will prove ephemeral.

The difficulties experienced by advocates of the power party in explaining *Robinson Crusoe*'s rise to greatness may add wind to the sails of advocates of the beauty party. But their joy is premature. As long as their arguments rely on traditional aesthetic qualities, they face difficulties of their own. *Robinson Crusoe* did not become a classic thanks to stylistic beauty and sophisticated composition. Defoe was a natural story teller, gifted with an inventive imagination, an eye for detail and, above all, a master at artfully entwining history and fiction. As a story teller, he is able to create and sustain complex narrative effects like curiosity, suspense and surprise (Fishelov 2004–5). All this, however, does not make *Robinson Crusoe* an exquisitely, well-formed aesthetic object. Compared to other authors of narrative fiction in the eighteenth century – Fielding comes naturally to mind in this context – Defoe's narrative art seems quite crude.

The fact that *Robinson Crusoe* was not sanctioned by the contemporary literary elite and the fact that it has no memorable aesthetic qualities pose serious difficulties to advocates of both prevailing parties. One important advantage of the dialogic approach is that it does not stipulate top-down processes nor does it demand conspicuous aesthetic qualities. Instead, it directs our attention to the number and diversity of dialogues a work elicits. And on that front, *Robinson Crusoe* has an abundance of supporting evidence. Whereas some of these dialogues may seem strange and others surprising, their multitude and heterogeneity is precisely what explains the work's reputation.

Some Versions of Pseudo-Dialogues

First, we should note that within four months of the book's publication in April 1719, *Robinson Crusoe* had six printings. Perhaps, with an estimated sale of not much more than 5000 (Rogers 1972: 7), the book was not a true bestseller, but these repeated printings are undoubtedly an indication of readers' interest. This initial success was followed by numerous editions and printings during the next three centuries. The Library of Congress, for example, holds 352 different copy-editions of the book (compared to only 92 of Fielding's *Tom Jones* and 101 of Richardson's *Pamela*).[2] As suggested in Chapter 2, from a dialogical perspective the act of reading can be described as the most passive form of echo-dialogue, like the act of nodding in a real-life conversation. Furthermore, the fact that *Robinson Crusoe* has become a true modern myth and an inevitable part of our cultural baggage, means that most of those who know of the book and its story have never read it in its original, unabridged form.[3]

Still, even if only a small fraction of those who know of the book have actually read it, we would still have a huge number of young and adult readers. Alongside wide and diversified readership – the most passive form of echo-dialogue – one can find numerous examples of active forms of echo-dialogue. We can start by recalling that to capitalize on *Robinson Crusoe*'s success, Defoe wrote, in the same year of its publication, *The Farther Adventures of Robinson Crusoe*, and in the following year he recycled some essays as *Serious Reflections of Robinson Crusoe*. Perhaps sequels are not typical cases of echo-dialogues because they express a wish for a story never to end as opposed to the wish to re-tell or re-hear the same story in adaptations, abridgements and translations. Still, in addition to being an important indication of a work's impact and success among readers, sequels also signal readers' wish for repeating a story.[4] Success can breed sequels but also envy and disapproval. One important form of a critical echo-dialogue is parody: in the same year that the book was published, Charles Gildon, a minor playwright and political pamphleteer, wrote a parody entitled "The Life and Strange Surprising Adventures of Mr. D_____ De F_____ " in which he satirizes Defoe's style and character (Rogers 1972: 41–47). Literary history has its own sense of irony: parody, instead of ruining a work's reputation and assigning it to oblivion, can sometimes enhance its visibility and fame.[5]

Because of its commercial success, *Robinson Crusoe* was pirated, abridged, imitated, translated and adapted for the stage as pantomime and as drama – and all these are typical forms of echo-dialogue. By the end of the nineteenth century, 196 editions of *Robinson Crusoe* had been published, 114 revisions, 277 imitations, and 110 translations, including languages such as Hebrew, Armenian, Bengali, Persian, and even Eskimo-Aleut.[6] The enormous body of translations indicates, among other things, the book's ability to transcend its specific time and place. While being deeply rooted in England of its time, it evokes perennial dreams, nightmares and questions that haunt human beings: what is a person apart from society; what is the right path to choose in life; where can one find strength and solace; what makes man-in-culture different from man-in-nature; how should we relate to "the other"?

In our discussion of translation as a form of echo-dialogue in Chapter 2, it was emphasized that every translator has to accommodate two conflicting demands: faithfully replication of the source text, thus bending the target language and culture towards the foreign, and at the same time domestication of the source text to the target system. Every achieved translation presents a specific compromise between the two tacit demands. While some contemporary theories of literary translation emphasize the target system's ideology in determining the outcome of the translation process (Lefevere 1992), we should not forget that the process always involves a crucial dialogic dimension, creating a "middle zone" between the two languages/cultures (Robinson 1991). As far as the translations of *Robinson Crusoe* are concerned, it is especially important to take note not only of the quantity but also of the diversity: in addition to being translated into European languages, the book reaches out to cultures like the Chinese and Japanese, resonating with some unexpected local issues and dilemmas (Liu 2000 and Zwicker 2000).

Robinson Crusoe has also been widely and continuously illustrated and sometimes even packaged as a picture book with little or no text. David Blewett's exemplary study of two centuries of the book's illustrations traces the changing ways the original text has been perceived, understood and pictorially represented at different periods and by different artistic schools and sensibilities (Blewett 1995). *Robinson Crusoe*'s long and diversified history of illustration is closely related to the fact that the book was widely read and perceived as a children's book. For most people (unless they are majoring in English Literature), the only encounter with *Robinson Crusoe* is in the form of an abridged-adaptation for children. Abridgements and adaptations for children are typical cases of echo-dialogue where the original text is transformed according to some fixed rules: focusing on the major part of the story, namely Crusoe on the desert island and his encounter with Friday. What preceded and what followed are trimmed away, to make what Genette calls the "twice-amputated" model (Genette 1997 [1982]: 230), and the complex theological and moral reflections that pervade the book are skimmed over. The huge body of translations and adaptations offers some odd cases, like the German translation by Joachim Campe titled *Robinson der Jüngere* (1779–80). This manipulated the work to suit Romantic notions emanating from Rousseau and was in turn translated back into English.[7]

As long as adaptations follow a relatively predictable set of rules (trimming, simplifying, bypassing complicated issues), they exemplify the category of echo-dialogue. When an adaptation opts for a more inventive and unpredictable angle it moves towards the category of genuine dialogue. Thus, the category of adaptation (and perhaps to a lesser degree also that of translation) oscillates between the categories of pseudo- and genuine dialogue, depending on the author's inventions and originality and the predictability of the outcome (see Table 2.1 in Chapter 2).

So far, some versions of echo-dialogue inspired by *Robinson Crusoe* were touched on: parodies, abridgements, illustrations, translations and adaptations (provided they do not involve too much inventiveness). Can we also find cases of the other version of pseudo-dialogue, namely dialogue-of-the-deaf in which a text evokes another text but without attaining – or attempting – a true give-and-take dialogue? Such cases exist, though they are far less common. The case of *The Swiss Family Robinson* (the original German title is *Der Schweizerische Robinson*) might perhaps illustrate this category. By naming the book and its chief characters "Robinson" and telling a story of survivors of a shipwreck on an uninhabited island, the author, Johann David Wyss, was clearly evoking Defoe's famous work when he published his novel in 1812. One can identify specific changes in the story of *The Swiss Family Robinson* as compared to Defoe's, as Green does in his informative discussion of the transformations of the Robinson story (Green 1990: 67–71). Going beyond a list of specific traits that were preserved as opposed to those that were altered or added, it is highly questionable whether the novel (which gained its own popularity, sequel and adaptations) conducted a true, dialectical dialogue with *Robinson Crusoe*. The constant tension between a moralistic tone (advocating moderation) and the love for rebellious adventure – central to Defoe – has disappeared from the moralistic *The Swiss Family Robinson*; whereas Defoe examines in depth the question "What is man without society?" (suggesting that society dwells within man), the Swiss novel brings an entire family to the island, thus bypassing the question altogether; and while Crusoe's encounter with Friday holds an extremely important place in Defoe's work, Wyss does not seem to be interested in an encounter between Europeans and "the other."

Moving from the realm of fiction to critical discourse, at least one influential philosophical discussion of Defoe's work, Rousseau's *Emile*, can be described as a typical dialogue-of-the-deaf. According to Rousseau, Crusoe (the character) should serve as a model for young people and the reading of

Robinson Crusoe (the book) is deemed more important in educating young souls than the reading of great philosophers (Rousseau 1972). In these comments, Rousseau seems to use *Robinson Crusoe* to promote his own ideas without paying much real attention to Defoe's work. True, Crusoe "lives in nature" but he survives thanks to many technological tools and cultural modes of thinking (which Rousseau, actually, detests). Defoe's book is more a eulogy of Western civilization and the ethics of a developing capitalist society (hard work, investment, profits and luxuries) than it is a tribute to the idea of "man living-in-nature." Rousseau was not the only thinker who exploited Defoe's book without truly paying attention to it as a complex artistic creation. Karl Marx's comments on *Robinson Crusoe* in *Das Capital* (Marx 1972) launched a rich series of discussions centering on Crusoe as *homo economicus*. These comments had some importance for economics theory, but it is difficult to see them as genuine dialogue with Defoe's work.

Versions of Genuine Dialogues

Unlike the numerous cases of echo-dialogue, which try to reproduce *Robinson Crusoe* according to a relatively fixed set of rules (e.g., simple, predictable translations and adaptations) and unlike some cases of dialogue-of-the-deaf, where a text evokes Defoe's work without engaging in a true dialogue (e.g., Wyss's *The Swiss Family Robinson*, Rousseau's *Emile*), *Robinson Crusoe* has also inspired writers, artists and critics to a multi-dimensional, dialectical process of give-and-take, hence to engage in genuine dialogues.

Historically, genuine dialogues with *Robinson Crusoe* emerged – alongside a continuous flourishing of echo-dialogues – primarily during the second half of the twentieth century. The emergence of this new form of dialogue is related to changing expectations concerning the role of the artist and art in post-Romanticism and Modernism. The source text is not perceived as a revered object and an artist is expected to exercise poetic license and to assert her/his individual perspective on the initial text. What Michel Tournier did in *Vendredi* and what J. M. Coetzee did in *Foe* with regard to *Robinson Crusoe* is similar to what Joyce did in *Ulysses* with regard to the *Odyssey* (albeit on a much smaller scale): creating a multi-dimensional, unpredictable genuine dialogue with a classic.

Coetzee's *Foe* (1987) can illustrate some important characteristics of genuine dialogues: it keeps intact a few important features of Defoe's plot and characters (a shipwreck, life on a desert island, an encounter between Crusoe and Friday) but at the same time it alters significant details and adds others: the major character-narrator is no longer Crusoe but Suzan Barton, a woman who finds herself on Crusoe's island after she has survived a shipwreck of her own; another unexpected "new" character is Defoe-the-writer, to whom Suzan tries to sell her (and/or Crusoe's?) story. Some central themes of Defoe's work receive a new twist: Defoe's Friday becomes an enigmatic character whose tongue has been literally cut out. Such changes not only resonate with contemporary, post-colonial sensibilities but also suggest that Defoe was (metaphorically) "silencing" the non-European Friday in his classic, reinforcing the colonial ethos and attitudes (Sanders 2006: 106–12). A closer look at *Robinson Crusoe* shows that Defoe exposes Robinson's condescending attitude towards Friday in a sharply ironic light (Fishelov 2004–5), but no matter what our conclusion is, Coetzee's novel compels us to re-read and re-interpret the classic. On another front, reading Coetzee's *Foe* makes us think about various issues involved in the art of writing: whereas in Defoe the questions of storytelling (and writing) are part of the technical level of the book – Crusoe as a narrator, Crusoe as a writer of a diary – in *Foe* Coetzee explores the complex, perplexing relationship between fiction and reality, rhetoric and truthfulness, constantly frustrating the reader's attempts to determine what really happened. Suzan Barton and Defoe (the character in Coetzee's book) are presented as unreliable narrators and, by implication, every storyteller becomes suspect. While reading Coetzee, the reader is invited to continually compare the two works and to decipher what has been changed and for what reasons. Such complex, attentive, comparative reading is the hallmark of a genuine dialogue.

Genuine dialogues with literary works are not confined to literature. *Robinson Crusoe*'s popularity has drawn some film-makers to produce cinematic adaptations. Some of these simply tailor the original story to the new medium, and thus can be labeled echo-dialogues. Others add some personal, unexpected touch – like the version of the Surrealist director Luis Buñuel who added some of his own idiosyncratic preoccupations (e.g. insects) to the classic adventure story (Buñuel 1954 [1952]). And others still have made films, characterized by a strong tension between repetition and invention, hence genuine dialogues.

As suggested in Chapter 2, the answer to the question "What makes a specific work (written, visual or interpretative) an echo-dialogue and what makes another a genuine dialogue?" lies in the concept of predictability. If after being told that a novel has been adapted (for children or for a film scenario), we can foresee the result, at least in broad outline, we are in the territory of echo-dialogues. If, on the other hand, it is difficult to predict the outcome, we are in the realm of genuine dialogue. Rod Hardy and George Miller's *Robinson Crusoe* (1997), starring Pierce Brosnan, adds some elements to Defoe's story, notably framing it in a love story between Robinson and a lovely young woman, and elaborating on a friendship between Crusoe and Friday. Despite these new aspects, the movie does not seem to constitute a genuine dialogue with Defoe's work. True, based on Defoe alone, the addition of a love story is unpredictable; one of *Robinson Crusoe*'s marked characteristics is the absence of women and romance. But, with the tacit rules of a Hollywood production in mind, the addition of a sentimental love story and of politically correct attitude towards "the other" becomes quite predictable.

Robert Zemeckis's *Cast Away* (2000), starring Tom Hanks, on the other hand, can be described as a genuine dialogue with *Robinson Crusoe*, despite the fact that it did not even present itself as an adaptation of Defoe's work. Like many genuine dialogues, the reader-spectator constantly oscillates between the two works with the question "What has been retained from the original story, what has been changed, and why?" The film attempts to re-tell a *Robinson Crusoe*-like story situated in the USA of today. This very decision opens up new avenues for the imagination: what would today's Crusoe look like; what would be his occupation; how could he find himself on a desert island in today's developed world? The fact that all these questions can be answered in many different ways makes the outcome less predictable than any simple adaptation. The idea to portray "today's Crusoe" in the character of Chuck Noland, an efficient FedEx executive, suggests an interesting analogy between eighteenth-century English capitalist ethics of work-hard-save-and-prosper (embedded in Defoe's book) and the contemporary American capitalist ethos of time-is-money.

Other details make the comparison of the two works rewarding: the idea of making a volleyball ("Wilson") Chuck's human-like companion is an unexpected recreation of Crusoe's communication with the parrot and of course of his relationship with Friday, reminding us of *Robinson Crusoe*'s theme of human beings' desperate need for companionship. On a different level, the barely hidden reference to Chuck's attempted suicide can be seen as an intensified version of Crusoe's despair in Defoe's book. Zemeckis's film also frames the original story in an added love story. But unlike the version of Hardy and Miller, *Cast Away* sticks to a realistic, non-sentimentalist tone: there is no happy reunion of the two lovers, only a painful recognition that life's demands and obligations prevail.[8] In that respect, the film can be seen as a tribute to Defoe's spirit rather than a predictable response to movie-goers' expectations. To call attention to the unexpected mixture of recognizable and novel elements does not amount, of course, to offering an interpretation of *Cast Away*, but only to justify the claim that this film can be described as a genuine dialogue with Defoe's classic.

As far as criticism and scholarly works are concerned, we should note the steady and fast-growing stream of discussions of *Robinson Crusoe* during the past two and a half centuries. The MLA International Bibliography lists 66 entries for the years 1926–1975, compared with 443 from 1976 to 2007. This impressive number over the past three decades may reflect, among other things, the renewed interest of various contemporary schools of criticism in Defoe's classic, and especially post-colonial preoccupations with the role of Friday, "the other."[9] In addition to some simple explications and commentaries (e.g., *Cliff's Notes*) – typical critical versions of echo-dialogue that work according to some set formulae – and some notable dialogues-of-the-deaf mentioned earlier, there remains a large body of critical work engaged in different kinds of genuine dialogues. Here, an important role was assumed not only by critics, biographers and scholars but also by some prominent writers like Samuel Taylor Coleridge, James Joyce and Virginia Woolf, or perceptive critics like Ian Watt who wrote illuminating essays on Defoe's classic, thus making a major contribution to the work's reputation as a great book (Rogers 1972: 142–43, 146–47; Ellis 1969: 19–24; 39–54; Watt 1963: 66–103).

A Concluding Image

The rich and heterogeneous body of dialogues inspired by *Robinson Crusoe* seems to provide ample support for the hypothesis that this is in fact the source of its consensual greatness – neither top-down institutionalized processes nor conspicuous aesthetic qualities. And since this chapter opened with the image of the front page of the first edition, it might be appropriate to conclude with another image, taken from an extremely rich history of illustration. In a sense, the illustration of *Robinson Crusoe* is both a metonymy (part of) and a metaphor (analogous to) the book's history of reception. The illustration reproduced was made by Grandville (Jean Ignace Isidore Gérard), a French artist and caricaturist (1803–1847), whose illustrated edition of *Robinson Crusoe* came out in both France and England in 1840. The frontispiece of that edition (see p. 182) depicts a gigantic Crusoe seated on a pedestal (decorated with the head of Friday ...), and accompanied by his parrot, dog and rifle.

The fathers and mothers below the pedestal, pointing out the magnificent figure of Crusoe to their children, represent the readers of the work. Despite the ironic intention, the illustration clearly reflects, in David Blewett's words, "the monumental status that Crusoe now enjoys" (Blewett 1995: 79). One hundred and twenty years after the book was first published – Robinson Crusoe had already turned into a true modern myth.

Concluding Remarks

To conclude, it is worthwhile to call special attention to a few points that arose in the discussions of both parts of the book and suggest some matters that need to be addressed in future studies of dialogues and canon formation.

Points Deserving Special Attention

- Chapter 4 argued for the dialogic approach to great books and tried to respond to some expected challenges. One serious challenge was that dialogues generated by a work are merely "symptoms" that still need to be explained, preferably by intrinsic aesthetic qualities. Some cases discussed in the second part (e.g., the biblical story of Samson, Defoe's *Robinson Crusoe*) show that it is quite difficult to explain these dialogue by aesthetic qualities as such. What seem to generate dialogues with these stories have little to do with the traditional set of aesthetic qualities and much more with certain representative human traits of the major character and his actions. Readers, writers, artists and critics can easily relate to perennial human dilemmas and archetypal meanings embodied in character and story. Thus, the "symptoms" (the produced dialogues) are as close as one can get to "the real thing" (the potential for generating dialogues with fellow human beings at a different time and place).
- The three chapters devoted to dialogues with the Bible show the predominant tendency of modern artists to approach the sacred text with a critical eye. This tendency results in a wide range of parodies, funny and iconoclastic (Levin in the sacrifice scene, Monty Python with respect to Christ's life on earth) but also in some versions of serious, critical re-writing (e.g. Saramago's treatment of the New Testament). In cases where some of the satire is directed not at the biblical text itself but at the religious establishment that canonized it (e.g. Monty Python), it may still reflect on the Bible and its followers. Moreover, even in a case where a biblical character is adopted as a national hero, as in Jabotinsky's *Samson*, the author still undermines religious beliefs and critically exposes established religion. And even where the Bible was looked at with reverence, Kierkegaard's *Fear and Trembling*, the

established Christian religion is satirically exposed. Still, alongside these examples (and many others like them), there are cases such as DeMille's *Samson and Delilah* that take the Bible as a source of spiritual inspiration. We should thus be careful not to formulate a rule, but we can still say with relative confidence that the dominant tendency in modern genuine dialogues with the Bible is to adopt a critical stand.

- The case of biblical Samson in Jabotinsky's novel and DeMille's film, the case of Horace's *Dulce et decorum est pro patria mori* in Owen's poem and in Spektor's song, the case of Ovid's Pygmalion in Shaw and Lerner and Loewe – all show us how a DT (dialoguing text) can become itself an IT (initiating text) for other DTs. When a modern author evokes a classical text as it is already mediated (or filtered) through another post-classical text, both of these preceding texts can take credit. In the case of DeMille, it is clear that despite some elements borrowed from Jabotinsky's novel, DeMille's major relevant IT is still the Bible. The explicit reference to an IT (or to ITs) is an important indication, but it is not the only factor that determine the actual role played by an IT within the DT. The fact that DeMille explicitly mentions Jabotinsky's novel in the opening titles of the film means first and foremost that he was legally bound to do so by copyright law, not necessarily that he was interested in conducting a dialogue with it. The more a text already has an established canonical status, as the Bible in this case, the greater are the chances that a DT will be considered as primarily conducting a dialogue with this text rather than with a less known one. There are other cases, however, where a specific DT overshadows the original IT to the point where it is not clear whether the modern artist is even aware of the IT from which an expression or a motif originated. Thus, when we detect a chain of DTs we should be careful to examine which text serves as the dominant IT with regard to a specific DT and which plays only a secondary, auxiliary role.
- When we detect many and diverse chains of DTs there is a good chance that the IT has become, through a process of abstraction, part of our extended linguistic and cultural vocabulary. Hence, when we encounter an expression taken from the IT, it has in fact lost its function of a pointer to the specific IT. For example, Juvenal's *mens sana in corpore sano* no longer functions as a pointer to his Satire 10 but has become a general maxim about the connection between body and mind; the name Pygmalion does not necessarily evoke Ovid's *Metamorphoses* (or for that matter Shaw's play) but simply designates a man trying to mold a woman to his liking; and "to be or not to be" is used to evoke an ambivalent attitude, not the specific monologue from *Hamlet*. We should be cautious and attentive in examining if and when these expressions and motifs have become part of the extended cultural vocabulary, and whether and how they are still used as genuine literary allusions. Such cases illustrate the situation where an author's ultimate dream

coincides with her/his biggest nightmare: that the work will become so great, so well-known, that people will no longer bother to read it.
- There is something inherently ambivalent about the role played by genuine dialogues in establishing the perceived greatness of a book. On one level, a genuine DT attests by its very existence to the IT's importance: after all, the author of the DT has invested time, talent and energy in dealing with the IT. At the same time, however, the author of almost every genuine DT aspires that her/his work would become an IT in its own right. In other words, whereas the raison d'être of echo-dialogues is subordinated first and foremost to promote the dissemination of the IT, genuine dialogues have their own agenda. Thus, genuine dialogues simultaneously perform a double function: they pay homage to and re-affirm the reputation of the IT, but at the same time they draw attention to their own qualities as independent works of art, pulling attention away from the IT, creating an alternative to it. As with the situation mentioned in the previous point – a work becomes so well-known to the point where people no longer bother to read it – here too we witness an ambivalent situation, perhaps even more acute: authors wish that the best artists would engage themselves in dialoguing with their work, but they also know that this involves the risk of being overshadowed by the new, genuine DT. This ambivalence may be the source of frequently found tensions between novelists whose work is adapted to the screen and the artists involved in the process, especially when a highly creative script writer or director is involved. Note, however, that whereas simple, echo-type adaptations usually better serve an author's immediate narcissistic needs, genuine dialogues do play an important role in keeping the IT alive in the long run.

Points Deserving Further Research

The perspective offered by the dialogic approach to great books opens new paths for research and sheds fresh light on some known data. Nevertheless, certain methodological, conceptual and empirical issues should be more intensively treated in order to further corroborate present and future results. The first two points listed below address the applicability of the dialogic approach to cultural fields other than literature. The remaining two points raise questions primarily specific to literary dialogues.

- This study focuses on literary works, but its principles can easily be extended to other art forms. The analogy with processes that take place in the plastic arts is almost unavoidable (the term 'masterpiece' was, after all, originally coined in discussions of plastic art; Cahn 1979). When McMullen (1976) and Bohn-Duchen (2001: 44–67), for example, describe the way of the *Mona Lisa* to its almost mythical status, a great part of their discussion is unsurprisingly devoted to the dialogues the work has generated throughout the ages. When one follows the trail of these dialogues, it becomes clear that the dialogic approach, with its emphasis on quantity and diversity, is the best way for answering "the million dollar question" of how does one account for the *Mona Lisa*'s celebrated reputation (Bohn-Duchen 2001: 67). The *Mona Lisa* undoubtedly owes its perceived greatness to the innumerable dialogues it spawned from the very start, including contemporary nude versions, artistic, psychoanalytic, and ideological interpretations (Gautier, Houssaye, Taine, Freud, Dali, Clark, Paglia), parodies (Duchamp, Leger), different versions of homage and parodic homage (Warhol), as well as its omnipresence in popular culture (postcards, souvenirs). Thus, the way of a work of the plastic arts to greatness seems quite similar to that of a literary work. While acknowledging this basic similarity, we should also be aware of one interesting difference: despite of the developing techniques of mass reproduction, the original in the plastic arts, notably painting, still enjoys a unique status and possesses an "aura" (Benjamin 2008 [1936]) that the original script of a literary piece does not have. This aspect is evident not only when we compare the market value of a book's first edition, however rare, to that of a Van Gogh but also has important implications with regard to the role played by museums in the process of canon formation. The dramas and melodramas associated with a painting's display (purchasing, moving or, even better, stealing) contribute in their turn to the work's perceived greatness. Thus, future research should outline, alongside the dialogical principles operative in all artistic fields, the specific characteristic of the respective sub-fields.

- Can we apply the dialogic approach to cultural fields other than art such as science? Whereas the dual principle of quantity and diversity seems to be operative also in non-artistic domains, its formulation should be modified. In order to understand and appreciate a scientific work, one needs training much more specific than is required in experiencing a literary or an artistic work. This difference can account for the fact that there is sometimes a discrepancy between the greatness attributed to scientists by the general public and their established reputation among peers. Such a discrepancy is most noticeable when we leave the very top of a list representing the "canon" in a specific scientific field. Whereas Einstein's reputation seems secure among scientists and the general public alike (T-shirts carrying the formula $E=MC^2$), this is definitely not the case with some others. The general public considers Richard Hawking, for example, to be one of the greatest physicists of all times, but according to the consensual opinion of experts, he has not made his way into the list of the "top twenty" in the field of physics (Murray 2003: 126). In a complementary manner, very few people have even heard of Ernest Rutherford, whose accomplishments in physics are rated by experts second only to that of Newton and Einstein (Murray 2003: 126). Consequently, if we want to detect the greatest scientific works, we should look first and foremost for many and diverse (period, school) dialogues generated within the pertinent scientific community. Perhaps the names of those representing the very top achievements in a scientific field would also loom in a database such as Google-Images (Newton's apple tree; Einstein sticking out his tongue) but we should be careful not to use the results obtained from such databases the way we can use them with regard to literature and art, namely as dialogues indicative of and contributing to a work's reputation. Unlike scientific works, great works of art resonate in a wide range of cultural fields because they evoke archetypal stories that appeal to almost anyone and because they usually do not presuppose a specific background knowledge or training.

- When applied to literature and other forms of art, the dialogic approach should outline more specifically the kinds of dialogue associated with different genres. Thus, for example, a prominent kind of dialogue with a play would be to produce it in the theatre: the more productions a play receives, and the more these productions offer different interpretations (and are not merely more of the same), the greater the play's claim to fame (see the discussion of Shakespeare's plays in Chapter 4). This kind of dialogue is of course irrelevant, say, to a novel. A novel can of course be adapted to the stage and as a play can get many and different productions, but as a novel it aims at other kinds of dialogues, such as readership, reviews, interpretations and, in today's culture, film adaptations. Lyrical poetry, unlike both plays and novels, strives towards slightly different kinds of dialogue: whereas readership always plays an important role for literary texts, this has a different meaning when it comes to poetry, which, since the epic age, does not usually address a mass audience. Poetry might be directed to educated, artistically oriented people (from my personal experience I know that readers of poetry are usually also museum goers). As for poetry's circulation and dissemination, an important part is played by anthologies where a poem is reprinted in different formats and under diverse headings (*Poems of the Renaissance*; *Love Poems*; *Poetry of First World War*; *Anti-War Poetry* etc.), an option which is hardly relevant, for example, for novels. Songs composed to a poem (e.g. the tradition of the German *Lied*) is another conduit open almost exclusively to poetry's dissemination.
- Finally, the question of the relationship between the quantitative requirement (that an IT should generate many DTs) and the principle of diversity (that these DTs will be of different kinds) should be addressed in more concrete terms: do these two requirements have the same weight? In all genres? Can the principle of diversity also be quantified?

188 | Dialogues with/and Great Books

Is it the case that the more kinds of dialogue are involved the better an IT's chances to be included in the great books club? Another way to treat this series of questions is through the pyramid model presented at the end of Chapter 4: can we detect a specific ratio between different levels of that pyramid? Perhaps it is impossible to offer such a specific formula, but it is evident that the principle of a gradated pyramid holds: the number of passive echo-dialogues (e.g. readers) is always much higher than the number of certain forms of genuine dialogue (e.g. re-writings) or some types of echo-dialogue (e.g. film adaptations). Another question: does a large number on the base level guarantee a relatively great number on the upper levels or does each level or kind of dialogue have its own autonomy? The phenomenon of bestsellers indicates that a wide base does not guarantee great numbers on the upper levels and some classical poems, which have generated literary allusions (in the pyramid's upper level), do not necessarily draw wide readership. Nevertheless, when it comes to consensually perceived great books, the different levels of the pyramid seem to be mutually supporting.

If the above series of questions can be satisfactorily examined, the dialogic approach to great books has a bright future and might propagate and generate a few dialogues of its own.

Notes

Chapter 1   Real Life Dialogues

1. In addition to 'literary masterpiece,' connoting (male) master-servant relationships, there is also the term 'classic,' evoking a Euro-centric perspective. For the latter, see Sainte-Beuve's Romantic-flavored "Qu'est-ce qu'un classique?" (Sainte-Beuve 1926–28), Eliot's re-interpretation of the term a century later, with the central role assigned to Virgil (Eliot 1946), and the instructive survey of the historical contexts of its use by Kermode (Kermode 1983). In this study I chose to use 'great books' because it is relatively free from some undesirable evaluative presuppositions associated with the other two terms, although it carries its own unwelcome connotations, favoring large volumes over short literary pieces (e.g. lyric poems). I am grateful to Moshe Ron for calling my attention to this last terminological problem, but in the way I use the term it can be also applied to short literary works.
2. I do not introduce Genette's terms para-text and archi-text because they are only indirectly relevant to the phenomena I discuss here.
3. When there are more than two participants, the dialogue may turn into a multi-participant conversation or a series of inter-connected dialogues. The main principles discussed here could also be applied to situations that include more participants than the duo of a dialogic "kernel."
4. For a survey of the different layers involved in every-day dialogues, promoting dialogism (as against monologism) in language study, see Linell 1998.
5. For a thorough discussion of these pairs, see Lyons 1968: 53ff; 1970: 12ff.
6. In many everyday situations we are capable of identifying a speaker, especially when we personally know her/him and have heard her/his voices many times. As the speech sample that we hear is shorter or when various distortions occur, the accuracy of identification falls (Knapp and Hall 2006: 375–77).
7. The term 'dialogue' is sometimes contrasted with 'debate': whereas the former requires a well-disposed attitude shared by interlocutors, the latter implies a more antagonistic attitude. The term 'genuine dialogue' as used here covers both. For a useful presentation of different terms used in French to cover the field of verbal interactions (conversation, dialogue, discussion, débat, etc) and the shades of meanings associated with each term, see Kerbrat-Orecchioni 1990: 113–123.
8. Dialogues-of-the-deaf can be found not only in social conversations but also in literary criticism; for describing a famous debate in the history in the interpretation of *Hamlet* as *dialogue de sourds*, see Bayard 2002.
9. The English Translation is Wood's and Coward (Molière 2000: 208).

10 It is not surprising that when the King and Queen address Rosencrantz and Guildenstern, they too seem to be echoing each other:

> King: Thanks, Rosencrantz and gentle Guildenstern.
> Queen: Thanks Guildenstern and gentle Rosencrantz. (2.2.33–34)

These examples of verbal repetition, taken from a play, are representative of a pervasive phenomena in everyday conversations. For a presentation of patterns and functions of verbal repetition in day-to-day conversation, see Tannen 1989: 36–97.

11 Note, however, that Searle himself argues (Searle 1992) that Speech Acts Theory as such cannot explain the dynamics of actual conversations.

12 For the role of conversational demand in shaping the dynamics of ongoing conversation, see Dascal 1992.

13 See, for example, Bakhtin 1981, Holquist 1990, Todorov 1984, and Morson 1986. For the central role of dialogue in human communication and cognition, and the need to develop a comprehensive theory that would account for its multi-facetedness, see also the works of linguists and philosophers of language such as Dascal 1985 and Weigand 1995.

Chapter 2 Literary Dialogues

1 The French term is used here in the sense it has in the theatre: "En termes de Théâtre, il désigne Ce qu'un acteur a à dire au moment où un autre finit de parler. *Manquer la réplique. Donner la réplique. Être attentif à la réplique*" (*Dictionnaire de L'Académie française*, 8th edition, 1932–5).

2 We can of course postulate that in every dialogue the first, initiating speaker is able to respond to the reaction she/he gets, a requirement evident in real-life conversations but not in literary communication. Such a restrictive understanding of a dialogue would lead to adopt a different terminology for literary phenomena discussed in this study. While acknowledging that such a tacit requirement is present in genuine real-life dialogues, the term dialogue still seems appropriate for describing literary phenomena because it calls attention to certain aspects present in the heterogeneous field of human communication, literary and non-literary alike.

3 For the widespread of Petrarchan poetry in Europe and England, see Guss 1966, 21–45.

4 I emphasize lines where the sonnet goes beyond simple parody, because, as will become clear in this chapter, simple parodies can exemplify the category of echo literary dialogue, whereas Shakespeare's parody has elements that put it in the category of genuine literary dialogue.

5 The literal translation is by Anat Schultz; for the original Russian, see Esenin 1955, vol. 1: 321.

6 The literal translation is by Anat Schultz; for the original Russian, see Mayakovsky 1955–1956, vol. 7: 104.

7 I put "passively" in quotation marks because the act of reading involves many complex cognitive and emotive processes. For the complexities of the reading process, including gap filling, anticipations, frustrations, retroactive corrections and the like, see Iser 1978, Perry 1979 and Sternberg 1978.

8   For a study introducing the concept of dialogue (not necessarily echo-dialogue) into translation theory, see Robinson 1991.
9   These compromises are not necessarily harmonious and some of them may sometimes produce the effect of unconscious parody (Brower 1974: 4–6).
10 In fact, the term originally used to designate the translator's activity was 'to interpret.' OED Online notes, in the first listing of the verb 'interpret': "Formerly, also, to translate (now only contextually, as included in the general sense)."
11 All quotations from the English translation of Ovid's *Metamorphoses* are taken from Ovid 2000, translated by A. S. Kline.
12 Hebrew poets in Medieval Spain used, as part of their declared poetics, verses and expressions from the Hebrew Bible, but without necessarily producing a meaningful relation between the alluding and alluded texts. See Pagis 1976, 71–72.
13 In other respects, however, Bloom's description of "strong poets" (1973, 1975) fits what I call here genuine dialogue.
14 The psychological and textual relationship between influencing and influenced authors is further complicated because they are also related to "the chain of previous influences" or to "the universe of the encyclopaedia" (Eco 2004).
15 For discussions of the different layers involved in the literary communicative situation see Leech 1969, 187–88; for the different voices in literature and in poetry, see Eliot 1954 and Brower 1962.

Chapter 3   The Battle of the (Great) Books

1   For the Greco and Christian roots of the concept of the canon, and its changes in modern times, see Gorak 1991: 9–43. For the cultural processes that led to changes in the Western Canon, especially in North America, its opening to marginal voices and becoming more fluid, see, for example, the Introduction in Palumbo-Liu 1995. These processes are closely related to a loss of totalizing principles in literary (and cultural) history and historiography (Gumbrecht 1985). The fluidity of the emerging canon is associated with a call to acknowledge personal, subjective and emotional response (love) of readers as a base for establishing the new canon or "paracanon" (Stimpson 1990).
2   The following description of the two "parties" is partly based on Adams 1988.
3   The *OED* quotes a usage of the word from 1832: "Beautiful and ugly depend on principles of taste, which it would be very convenient to designate by an adjective ... Some English writers have adopted the term *esthetical*. This has not however yet become an established English word."
4   Bloom's polemical introduction of *The Western Canon* echoes Robert M. Hutchins's defense of liberal arts education in the United States, advocating the teaching of books that constitute "The Great Conversation" of Western culture (Hutchins 1952). Bloom's argument is also on a par with Kenneth Clark's defense of the concept of artistic masterpiece, associated with specific aesthetic qualities (e.g. density, unity, originality) and a profound assertion of human values (Clark 1979). For the debate following Clark's book, see Berman 1980.
5   For a criticism of Bloom's "quasi-religious worship" of certain canonical authors, see Milner 1996: 19–26. Milner, building on Williams's version of Neo-Marxist thinking (Williams 1961), argues convincingly against Bloom's contention that cultural studies necessarily poses a threat to the very notion of literature.
6   Not all defenders of the beauty party adhere to the belief that the aesthetic quali-

ties have an objective status. Still, because some criticism of the beauty party make that assumption and in order to make the opposition between the two parties sharper, I have added this dimension.

7   For a lucid survey of the issues involved in interpreting the different relationship between 'base' and 'superstructure', see Haslett 2000, 17–24.
8   For different versions of Marxist and Neo-Marxist approaches, see Eagleton and Milne 1996.
9   An interesting exception to this generalization can be found in Alick West, a British Neo-Marxist thinker, defending the notion of the value of a literary work, linked to "the value we give our lives" (West 1996 [1937]: 105), transcending its mutable popularity with certain social classes.
10 The distinction presented in this section was suggested by Meir Sternberg as part of a discussion following the presentation of my paper on Dialogues with/and Great Books at Tel Aviv University in 2006.
11 Note, however, that even if we decide to side with the beauty party, we would need to revise our understanding of the term aesthetic qualities so that it include meanings that are not part of a traditional set of such qualities (for further discussion of this point, see Chapter 5, Chapter 6 and the Concluding Remarks).
12 For a persuasive presentation of the ideologically charged debate on the Western Canon, especially in North America, and its shortcomings as a basis for research, see Sela-Sheffy 2002.

Chapter 4   The Dialogic Approach to Great Books

1   Adams 1988, who outlined some important characteristics of the two "parties," attempted to propose a new way to bypass the prevailing views, but a closer look shows that his proposal is in fact a version of a humanistic, aesthetic-oriented approach.
2   In his introduction to a special issue of *Critical Inquiry* on canon formation, Von Hallberg delineates three perspectives on the issue: "how artists determine canons by selecting certain styles and masters to emulate; how poet-critics and academic critics, through the institutions of literary study, construct canons; and how institutionalized canons effectively govern literary study and instruction" (Von Hallberg 1983: iii–iv). He adds that most essays in the volume are concerned with the second and third perspectives. My aim in this study is among other things to remind us of the central role played by the first issue.
3   For important studies of the relationship of history of reading, literary history and dissemination of literary forms, especially the novel, see Moretti 1998: 141–97 and Moretti 2005, especially 3–33.
4   For some instructive warnings against a mechanical application of biological principles to the literary and cultural field, see Todorov 1975 and Schaeffer 1989. In their comprehensive study, Jablonka and Lamb (2006) present a multi-layered model for understanding evolution in both nature and culture. By systematically mapping similar and dissimilar aspects of evolution in nature and culture, the authors not only challenge simplistic perceptions of the nature–culture divide but also convincingly argue against reducing cultural phenomena to randon, mechanistic processes associated primarily with genetic evolution. Still, by calling attention to some analogies between biological and cultural processes (Moretti 1988: 262–78, Gould 1991: 57–75, Sperber 1996: 98–118) one can gain insights

into the dynamics of literary endurance (Smith 1988: 47–53), dissemination of literary forms (Moretti 2005), "speciation" and periodization of literary genres (Fishelov 1994), and heterogeneous forms and functions of adaptation (Bortolotti and Hutcheon 2007).
5 There are of course other thinkers to which the present dialogical perspective is indebted. A special tribute is due to Lefevere (1992) who presented an explicit and systematic argument about the close ties between different forms of re-writings and the process of canon formation. The connection between the principle of dialogue and great books was already suggested by Hutchins in his defense of liberal arts education in the United States. Hutchins, however, does not discuss the role played by dialogues in establishing a book's perceived greatness but rather focuses on the dialogue among the great books themselves, which represents for him a fundamental characteristic of Western culture: "No other civilization can claim that its defining characteristic is a dialogue of this sort" (Hutchins 1952: 48).
6 The usefulness of Jauss's approach is evident, for example, in Martindale and Thomas 2006, presenting different aspects of reception of the classics.
7 Art may sometimes serve less noble, even anti-emancipatory functions, as unfortunately it did in some totalitarian regimes.
8 Many companies are eager to decipher Google's formula for scoring sites, in order to enhance their chance to appear as high as possible on the list of results. The present study, however, is not interested in the internal hierarchies of sites, only in the number of occurrences of a specific work within sites, representing a work's dissemination on the cyberspace and indirectly in culture.
9 The use of the University of Columbia's Library catalogue reflects a clear focus on Anglo-American databases. Still, searches done on La Bibliotèque Nationale de France, for example, show similar tendencies, especially when we take into account that French works would have there more occurrences (e.g. Molière *Tartuffe* has 157 occurrences in Clio as opposed to 587 in the Bibliotèque). The similar tendencies become clear once we translate the specific number of occurrences to a digit-number (e.g. Homer's *Odyssey* has 785 and Virgil's *Aeneas* 409 items in Clio and 744 and 159 respectively in the Bibliotèque – all three-digit number). Thus, searches on Clio seem to represent, *grosso modo*, important Western libraries.
10 This pattern is a rough approximation, representing most of the results.
11 Unfortunately, I could not find a reliable data base that would enable us to compare the number of translations of the examined works. The Unesco database, Index Translationum (http://databases.unesco.org), gives only "The top ten" authors translated from a given language (or country). It is symptomatic, though, that within the top ten in English Shakespeare has acquired more translations than Danielle Steel, the author of successful Romantic novels (3,590 against 2,858). This is another indication that when it comes to the truly great works, the conventional opposition of classical and popular literature collapses.
12 Some references on this search were related to cinematic versions of Purcell's tragic opera *Dido and Aeneas*.
13 This number is a rough approximation. There are a few films that have "Don Quixote" in the title but they are adaptations of works that were themselves inspired by Cervantes's classic.
14 Here the phrase "Gargantua and Rabelais" was used in the searches.

15 The phrase "Gulliver and Swift" was used in the Google searches.
16 The phrase "Oedipus and Sophocles" was used in the Google searches, assuming that most references are to "Oedipus Rex". I decided for this short version also because the play is sometimes translated as "Oedipus Tyrannus" and "Oedipus King."
17 Here the title "Prometheus" was used.
18 These were the results of a search for '"Abe Lincoln in Illinois"' and Sherwood." Results for just "Abe Lincoln in Illinois" were 90. The reason is simple: most references in the all-inclusive Google belong to a film based on Sherwood's play, not to the play itself.
19 Such lists participate in creating, according to Guillory, an "imaginary totality," a "*tradition*" (Guillory 1993, especially 28–33). One may wonder, however, whether tradition is in fact a totally fictional construct with no psychological and cultural ground, as Neo-Marxists like to argue.
20 Another instructive example of the process by which certain authors change their relative canonical status due to patterns of dissemination can be found in the case of two Modern Hebrew poets: the fact that Haim Nachman Bialik's canonical status has surpassed that of Saul Tchernichovsky during the past decades can be explained by the great number of echoes generated by Bialik's poetry, notably by his poems that became popular songs (the data supporting this argument was presented at the 23rd conference of Hebrew Literature Studies at Bar-Ilan University, June 8–9, 2009).
21 The principle that initial success in distribution is responsible for future greater success (regardless of the quality of the product) – the principle of increasing returns – was described as a marginal phenomenon in classical economic thinking, but became central in complexity theory. See Waldrop 1992: 17–18, 34–38, 44–46. For calling attention to the operation of this principle in the dispersion of certain form of the novel, see Moretti 1998: 191–195.
22 Stage productions may of course be labeled "interpretations" in a sense close to playing a piece of music in a certain way. Such "interpretations" are distinguished from verbal statements that purport to convey the "meaning" of a work of art. The distinction was made by Beardsley 1958: 9–10.
23 The list of plays in The Designing Shakespeare Collections of the AHDS includes works that were staged (*Edward IV*, *The Two Noble Kinsmen* and *Venus and Adonis*) but are not considered part of the Shakespearean canon of plays. Consequently, I omitted them from Table 4.5 and 4.6.
24 http://www.ahds.ac.uk/performingarts/collections/designing-shakespeare.htm. This databases draws on already existing archives (e.g., the Royal Shakespeare Company, the National Theatre).
25 Note also that these three plays gained the longest discussions in *The Oxford Companion to Shakespeare* (Dobson and Wells 2001): *Hamlet* 4.5 pages, *Macbeth* 4.5 pages and *Romeo and Juliet* 4.37 pages (the mean length of discussions devoted to a play is around 3.5 pages).
26 From the present perspective, emphasizing the vital role played by different kinds of dialogue in a work's enduring survival, it is easy to accept the important role of the once dismissed Restoration and eighteenth-century adaptations of Shakespeare's plays (Dobson 1992; Dobson and Wells 2001: 375–77). Furthermore, when Dobson argues that "adaptation and canonization, so far from being contradictory processes, were often mutually reinforcing ones"

27 Searches for Shakespeare's plays were conducted during October 2008. In Google, Google-Image and Clio I used the play's title and Shakespeare. In IMDb I used only the title.
28 In searching a play's title under Keywords, IMDb gives results for "Shakespeare's-[the play's name]" and in most cases I used the numbers given under this heading.
29 Because I conducted the search in December 2008 and wished to have a ten years span, I stopped the searches on 1998.
30 These searches did not include of course the book's title, because the prize is awarded to "the very best *book of the year.*"
31 There were joint winners in 1974 and in 1992.
32 The writing of scholarly articles is not detached from the political echoes that followed the publication of Rushdie's *The Satanic Verses* (1988) and the *fatwa* pronounced in 1989. The decade of 1988–1998 produced 453 references to the author's name on MLA.
33 Searches used author and title (both between quotation marks, to ensure accuracy) and were conducted in November 2008.
34 The results of Google and Google-Image are quite unusual, probably because of the relatively common name of the author and the extremely short title of the book. Thus, there is good reason to believe that many of the results are not relevant and consequently were not marked in bold.
35 In Google, Google-Image and IMDb I used "Possession" as the title.
36 The tendency of convergence in literary prizes was observed by English (English 2005: 334–45).
37 See also Hornstein's (et al.) *The Reader's Companion to World Literature* (2002), where Johnson is mentioned only in the context of Boswell's *The Life of Samuel Johnson*. And even Bloom's discussion of Johnson in his list of the one hundred exemplary creative minds does not focus on *Rasselas* (Bloom 2002: 155–73).
38 To explain *Candide*'s strong position as resulting from continuous promotion by institutional hegemonies would be quite difficult, because from the time of publication until quite recently the book met powerful institutionalized opposition; even French schools began to teach it as a prescribed text only after 1968 (Mason 1992: 15).
39 For *Rasselas*'s initial mixed critical reception, see Boulton 1971: 5, 141–47.
40 To witness the intricate relationships between scandals and literary fame, we can go back to ancient Greece (e.g. the reactions to some of Aristophanes' plays).
41 The QWERTY case and its implications have also been adopted by advocates of complexity theory, attempting to connect economics with other scientific disciplines (Waldrop 1992).
42 This point may be re-enforced from an additional angle: ancient texts, especially Greco-Roman ones, have generated echoes and dialogues throughout the ages partly because they were the only ones that (physically) survived, not necessarily because they were the best contemporary artistic texts. Some of them may of course deserve this label, but it is reasonable to assume that some texts that were randomly destroyed in the Library of Alexandria (either by Julius' fire or by continuing acts of destruction) were aesthetically superior to some of those that still circulate.

(Dobson 1992: 5), he calls attention not only to eighteenth-century processes responsible for begetting Bardolatry (the subject matter of his thorough study), but also to a principle underlying the making of any "great author" or "great book."

43 The case of *Moby Dick* can illustrate such a postponed wave. The book elicited only a small number of critical responses when it was first published in 1851 (Melville: http://www.melville.org/hmmoby.htm) and had to wait until after World War I for a significant re-appraisal. Whereas there were important ideological factors contributing to this development (Spanos 1995: 12–36), from the dialogic perspective it is significant that this revival consisted of a big and *heterogeneous* wave of echoes and dialogues (including two movie adaptations, in 1926 and 1930). I would like to thank Ilana Pardes for calling my attention to the interesting case of *Moby Dick*'s history of reception.

44 We might also add the popular You Tube, where one can find (in April 2009) 133 references to *Candide* and none to *Rasselas*.

45 The Playwrights Database, Doollee.com, the free online guide to modern playwrights and theater plays written or translated into English since the production of *Look Back in Anger* in 1956.

46 I advocated a similar perspective in my discussion of literary genres; not as static forms, but as generating principles, "giving birth" to new works. See Fishelov 1993a, 19–52, and Fishelov 1999.

47 The results for *Harry Potter* were over ten million occurrences, as opposed to less than three million for the *Odyssey* (searches done in July 2006).

48 The MLA International Bibliography, for example, shows a continuing growth in items devoted to the *Harry Potter* series. I would like to thank Eyal Segal for calling my attention to these data.

49 We can remember in this context Bourdieu's emphasis on the autonomy of the literary field in generating its own hierarchies (Bourdieu 1993: 37–39).

50 I used the tree model and the next ponytail model in my discussion of the transformations of biblical Samson in literature and art (Fishelov 2000: 201–2). The usefulness of a tree model for literary history has been convincingly demonstrated by Franco Moretti (2005: 67–92).

51 The phrase "cross-fertilisation of the packaged textual material," introduced by Worton and Still to describe intertextuality in general, seems particularly appropriate to the bi-directional dialogical relationship (Worton and Still 1990: 1).

Chapter 5 The Sacrifice Scene – Kierkegaard and Levin

1 For an analogy between the Hebraic biblical canon and the modern canon as "a grand cultural narrative," see Gorak 1991: 259.

2 Searches in Google, Google-Image and were for Bible and Judith (or Bible and Nahum). These results were obtained in August 2008.

3 To effectively pinpoint results, I conducted searches in Clio using call numbers: BS1734 and BS1735 text and commentary devoted to the Book of Judith and BS1625 for the Book of Nahum. Note that four out of the fourteen references to the Book of Nahum include discussions of Habakkuk and Zephaniah.

4 I suggested these three factors in trying to decipher the attractiveness of the biblical Samson (Fishelov 2000: 16–17).

5 Since I do not read Danish, I used the English translation of Hannay. To minimize possible mistakes I checked this translation against Hebrew (1997) and French (1935) translations, and was helped by a literal translation of this passage, prepared by Nan Jacques Zilberdik.

6 Some Midrashic texts suggest that on the way to Mount Moriah Abraham was

accosted by Satan who meticulously examined his conviction that he had indeed heard God's voice (Ginzberg 1968: 276–78).
7   See, for example, in Ginzberg 1968, volume 1: 271–86 and volume 5: 248–55.
8   Perhaps Levin was influenced by some elements in Isaac's speech in this legend. But there is no reason to assume that Isaac is speaking ironically in this legend as he is in Levin's sketch.

Chapter 6   Samson – Jabotinsky, DeMille and Milton

1   Searches in Google, Google-Image and in Clio (in the Keyword section) were under Bible and Samson (or Bible and Gideon); in IMDb I browsed through titles (or parts of titles) containing the names Samson and Gideon respectively. These results were obtained on August 2008.
2   This number is a crude approximation since some titles at IMDb do not contain satisfactory information to help in determining if the film is about the biblical Samson or if it conducts a meaningful dialogue with the biblical story.
3   True, unlike Christian monasticism, the laws of the Torah (Numbers 6) do not order a Hebrew *Nazir* (or monk, the term means literally one who abstains) to withdraw from women. Still, Samson's whole conduct does not seem typical of the solemn, other-worldly conduct associated with a *Nazir*, and in some respects he either violates or comes close to violating the explicit strictures imposed on a *Nazir* – with respect to drinking wine (he attends a feast), to touch a dead body (the lion's carcass) and of course not to cut his hair.
4   For an overview of this diversity and the changing aesthetic and ideological agenda it served through the ages, see my book (Fishelov 2000).
5   His translations of Edgar Allen Poe's "The Raven" into Hebrew and Russian are still considered masterpieces. A Russian literary critic even lamented Jabotinsky's defection from Russian literature to the politics of the Zionist movement (see Katz 1996: 80–81 and Katz 1993: 59–60).
6   After citations from this translation (Jabotinsky 1986 [1928]) I will indicate the page number.
7   DeMille's decision to redeem Delilah is related to a "need for film heroines to be saved from their wicked ways" (Forshey 1992: 62).
8   This is one important aspect of Milton's Dalila. For the rich net of meanings, including classical allusions, associated with her character see, for example, Kilgour 2008 and the works she cites in her essay.
9   For the novel's impact on modern Hebrew culture and literature, see my book (Fishelov 2000), especially pp. 47–60.

Chapter 7   Jesus Christ – Monty Python and Saramago

1   This scene starts the actual story-line of the film; before the titles are presented, we have a short parody of the Nativity scene with the three magi.
2   Interestingly enough, the film's screening is still banned in some places, including the Welsh town of Aberystwyth, whose mayor, Sue Jones-Davies, played Judith, Brian's lover in the film (Sky News 2008).
3   The woodcut, whose origin is not specified in the book, is Dürer's "The Crucifixion" taken from the series The Large Passion (1498). Dürer's woodcut is,

needless to say, part of a rich history of pictorial representations of Jesus Christ (more than thirteen million in Google-Image). In fact, it would be quite difficult to imagine how to account for the New Testament's cetral place in Western culture without taking into accout the innumerable pictorial dialogues the story and its main character have inspired throughout the ages.

4   In the following paragraphs, I follow the opening description which stretches over pages 1–6 of Saramago's book (1993 [1991]). I give the page number in the English translation after each quotation. As with Kierkegaard in Chapter 5, I allowed myself to discuss a text in translation since my analysis treats thematic and rhetorical, not linguistic or stylistic issues.

5   For a reading of the novel that connects the author's complex handling of the novel's major characters, especially Jesus, with the question of freedom of choice and political issues in Modern Portugal see Frier 2005.

6   Sometimes, the parodied text maintains its status as the high measuring rod against which the low, ridiculous parodying text and reality are compared, as evident in the tradition of mock-epic or mock-heroic (Jump 1972: 37–51). While this form draws on the prestige of the epic, it also "surrounds epic forms in destabilising laughter" (Dentith 2000: 102).

Chapter 8   Horace in Pushkin, Owen and Diderot

1   Highet's impressive survey of Greek and Roman influences on Western Literature concludes with an argument against those who underestimate the vitality of Classical tradition (Highet 1950: 544–46). He is right in pointing out that unlike physical death, ancient languages and literatures do not die as long as they are read. His advocacy of a humanistic culture that keeps embracing the rich classical tradition seems somewhat anachronistic in today's culture of mass communication and sound bites.

2   Searches were made in October 2008. The first number in Google and Google-Image represents results for the Latin phrase, the second for the phrase and Horace.

3   One result was obtained for the expression *Pro Patria Mori*; none for the complete Latin expression.

4   Note, however, that searches in Clio for an English equivalent ("The Sweet and the Useful") produced 16 results. Since I decided to stick to the Latin expressions in these searches, I marked the result here as zero.

5   Shakespeare's Sonnets 18 and 55 contain similar ideas, though here the promise of everlasting life is transferred to the subject of the poem, who will live through the immortality of the poet's lines.

6   The literal translation is by Anat Schultz. For the original text, see Pushkin 1938, vol. 2: 261–62.

7   Owen's anti-Horatian poem was an exception amidst Edwardian and Georgian poetic enlistment of Horace in British imperial ideology (Harrison 2007: 339–40).

8   This issue is discussed from a different angle also in Chapter 10, tracing some transformations of the Pygmalion story.

9   Vertumnus was a god of the changing year, assuming different shapes. Quotations of the English translation of Horace's Satire 2.7 are taken from Horace 2004.

10 Quotations from Diderot indicate the page number of the Tancock translation (Diderot 1966).

Chapter 9 Juvenal's Satire 10 – Johnson and Swift

1. Searches in this table were conducted in September 2008. In the first three searches I used the authors' names and satires.
2. The results of searches done in September 2008: in the first three searches I used Horace and satires: Google – 1,010,000; Google-Images – 23,300; Clio – 160; IMDb – 0.
3. Search results for Virgil, conducted on September 2008: I checked Virgil, Horace, Juvenal and Persius using and Rome in the first three searches (results in the IMDb refer to Virgil as the author of the Dido and Aeneas story).

Results of searches of Four Roman Authors

	Google	Google-Image	Clio	IMDb
Juvenal	214,000	8,860	47	1
Persius	49,000	2,230	28	0
Horace	1,910,000	75,400	193	0
Virgil	1,610,000	65,700	276	6

4. Searches were conducted on October 2008. In Google and Google-Image the first number represents results obtained for the saying itself; the second, search results for the expression and the author's name.
5. One TV series with the English title "Healthy Body, Healthy Mind" was retrieved. There were no results for the Latin expression.
6. We know very little of his life, let alone the dates of his birth or death – see Braund's introduction in Juvenal 2004: 18–20.
7. In the citations that follow I will indicate the page and line numbers (of the Latin text) of the Ramsay edition (1940). As in other case, I use prose translation because Juvenal's effects often depend on specific wording and images. In reading the description of the fate of Sejanus, the prefect who ran the Roman Empire for Tiberius, one can think of some recent events such as the toppling of Saddam Hussein's statue in Baghdad and of memorials to Stalin in some parts of the former Soviet Union.
8. For the analogy between the individuals who try to find some hope and solace in conventional prayers (on the fictional level of the fictional world of the poem) and the reader who tries, disenchanted, to reach for the next prayer as a source of unshakeable comfort, see my article (Fishelov 1990).
9. In the citations that follow I will indicate the page and line numbers of the Smith and McAdam edition (1974).
10. See here also the discussion of translation and adaptation as versions of echo-dialogue in Chapter 4.
11. For Johnson's use of the phrase "China to Peru" to represent mankind, see Jain 1993.
12. And the organ is, of course, with "enlarged vein" (Braund 2004: 383).
13. Boswell: "when I once regretted to him that he had not given us more of Juvenal's

Satires, he said he probably should give more, for he had them all in his head... some of them, however, he observed were too gross for imitation" (Boswell 1952: 138).

14 Johnson is not alone in shunning Juvenal's explicit sexual references; one can find this tendency as late as the beginning of the twentieth century, in Ramsay's translation of Satire 10, where three dots replaced lines 204–209 (see Juvenal 1940: 209). This omission was rectified in the Loeb Classical Library edition in 2004, with Braund's translation.
15 For more characteristics of Johnson's imitation of Juvenal, notably the tendency to heighten the original text, see Selden 1970, comparing Johnson's version with other English translations and imitations of the Roman satirist.
16 After citations from this edition (Swift 1973) I will indicate the page number.
17 Eliot, however, also said more complimentary things about Johnson the satirist. For the complexity of Eliot's critical assessment, see O'Flaherty 1967: 80–81.

Chapter 10   Ovid's Pygmalion in Shaw & *My Fair Lady* via Molère

1 Quotations are from Ovid's prose translation by A. S. Kline (Ovid 2000).
2 Quotations from *L'Ecole des femmes* are indicated by act and scene, followed by the page number in the translation I use here by John Wood and David Coward (Molière 2000).
3 But what if Shaw had not called his play Pygmalion? How would this affect our reading of the play as a dialogue with Ovid's story? For some comments on the way we identify a dialoguing text, see the last section of this chapter.
4 After quotations from the Penguin edition of Shaw's play (Shaw 1941), I will indicate the page number. The peculiar spellings (e.g. youre) here and elsewhere are Shaw's.
5 Galatea as the name of the statue-come-to-life does not appear in Ovid's version and is, in fact, quite a modern addition, showing up first in a relatively obscure version of the story by Rousseau, *Pygmalion, scène lyrique*, composed in 1762 and published in 1771 (see Law 1932 and Rubin 1985).
6 After quotations from the Penguin edition of *My Fair Lady* (Lerner 1956), I will give the page number.
7 The name of a work strongly suggests but cannot guarantee that we have a dialoguing text. Theoretically, an author may want to play with readers' expectations, but it is difficult to find a case where a name evoking a previous text was chosen merely to frustrate the reader.
8 In this context it is interesting to speculate how we would read and interpret Joyce's *Ulysses* had he not used that name. For aspects related to the book's title and the headings of the chapters from the perspective of intertextual relations, see Genette 1997 [1982], especially 3–5, 307–11.
9 The relationship between dialoguing with a specific IT and evoking some general motifs associated with other textual traditions can change: the movie *Pretty Woman* (1990), starring Richard Gere and Julia Roberts, can be described as a contemporary adaptation (of the genuine type) of the classical Cinderella story which also uses motifs from the Pygmalion story.
10 I believe though there is a difference in order and not only in degree between giving a work its name and using some of the other textual means listed by

Genette in this context of the *paratext*: "prefaces, postfaces, notices, forewords ... marginal, intrapaginal, terminal notes; epigraphs" (Genette 1997: 3).
11 Some of these terms are taken from Ben-Porat 1985, Genette 1997 [1982], Sanders 2006.
12 For the diversity of this textual and artistic tradition, see Aurnhammer and Martin's anthology of the Pygmalion story from Ovid to John Updike (2003).

Chapter 11   More's *Utopia* – Bacon, Swift and Voltaire

1 It seems that the idea to conduct scientific experiments deep underground was envisioned by Bacon long before CERN.
2 Here and elsewhere, quotations from *Gulliver's Travels* are followed by the page number in Swift 1973.
3 This approach may overemphasize the satirical dimension of classical utopias at the expense of their positive utopian aspect (see, e.g. Ravins 1973). For the close links between satire and utopia, see Kantra 1984, especially 75–92.
4 Accounts of the similarities between More's *Utopia* and Swift's *Gulliver's Travels* can be found in articles by Traugott (1964, 1984) and by Vickers 1968.
5 This tendency perhaps characterizes the satirical temperament in general; see Fishelov 1993c.
6 Swift's irony takes us far beyond the supposition that the horses are not an ideal we should, in actuality, strive to attain. See also Ehrenpreis's and Mack's articles in Tuveson 1964.
7 Anderson (1984) points out the interesting biblical allusions to Eden in the description of the Houyhnhnms' utopian society. At the same time, he is keenly aware of the mechanism of parody these allusions undergo.
8 Curiously enough, this typical utopia is not analyzed or even mentioned in most of the critical discussions of the relation between utopia and satire. Even Krishan Kumar's comprehensive account of anti-utopias (Kumar 1987) refers to Voltaire's ironical comments on Rousseau's utopian thinking, but neglects his experiment in *Candide*.
9 Here and elsewhere, I quote from Gay's translation (Voltaire 1963), with the page number following the quotations.
10 Most critical treatments of the subject do not make this distinction and lump together satirical treatments of utopias with anti-utopias. See, for example, Hadomi 1989, especially 44–91, and Kumar 1987, especially pp. 99–131. Northrop Frye's distinction between two kinds of satirical utopias (Frye 1973) also neglects the exuberance and the playful aspects that dominate satirical and parodic treatments of utopian ideas.
11 For an account of how we talk about books we have not read, see Bayard 2007. Note that there is a direct correlation between a book's "greatness" and our ability to talk about it without reading it.

Chapter 12   *Robinson Crusoe* – The Variety Principle Revisited

1 Pope adds a note on Tutchin: "*John Tutchin*, author of some vile verses, and of a weekly papwr call'd the *Observator*: He was sentenc'd to be whipp'd thro' several towns in the west of *England*, upon which he petition'd King *James* II to be

hanged. When that Prince died in exile, he wrote an invective against his memory, occasioned by some humane Elegies on his death. He liv'd to the time of Queen Anne." John Butt, the editor of the Methuen edition, explains: "Tutchin, a stubborn Whig, died in 1707, after being attacked in the street by ruffians. He published in 1685 *Poems on several Occasions* (the 'vile verses'), and [in] 1701 the invective to which Pope alludes: *The British Muse: or Tyranny exposed. A Satire; occasioned by all the fulsome and lying Poems and Elegies that have been written on the Death of the late King James*" (384). For other derogatory reactions of the Scriblerus circle, see Rogers 1972: 38–40.

2 These numbers were retrieved from the Library of Congress On-Line catalogue on March 2008. Since then, some specific numbers have naturally changed, but the overall picture remains basically the same.
3 See the introductory chapters in Seidel 1991 and Spaas and Stimpson 1996.
4 See Castle 1986: 134, Garber 2003: 73–81 and Hutcheon 2006: 9.
5 In his perceptive analysis of parody's role in the mechanism of literary history, Tynianov emphasizes its function as a liberating power, helping writers to undermine the poetics of parental figures and establishing their own poetic identity (Tynianov 1975 [1921]), but he does not pay enough attention to parody's unintentional effect of sometimes strengthening the status of the parental, parodied figure.
6 These numbers are offered in: http://academic.brooklyn.cuny.edu/english/melani/novel_18c/defoe/
7 For an interesting discussion of this case as representing the norms operative in children's literature and in translation, see Shavit 1986: 126–27.
8 A lighter, sentimental and optimistic note is nonetheless introduced in the final scene, suggesting a new love story. It is, after all, a Hollywood production.
9 These results were obtained in searching for Defoe and Robinson Crusoe during August 2008 in MLA International Bibliography.

Bibliography

Adams, Hazard. 1988. Canons: Literary Criteria/Power Criteria. *Critical Inquiry* 14: 748–64.
Allen, Graham. 2000. *Intertextuality*. London and New York: Routledge.
Alter, Robert. 1975. *Partial Magic: The Novel as a Self-Conscious Genre*. Berkeley: University of California Press.
——. 2000. *Canon and Creativity: Modern Writing and the Authority of Scripture*. New Haven: Yale University Press.
Altieri, Charles. 1983. An Idea and Ideal of a Literary Canon. *Critical Inquiry* 10: 37–60.
Anderson, William S. 1982. *Essays on Roman Satire*. Princeton, NJ: Princeton University Press.
——. 1984. Paradise Gained by Horace, Lost by Gulliver. In Rawson 1984, 151–66.
Aristotle. 1895. *Poetics*, trans. Samuel H. Butcher. London: Macmillan.
Auerbach, Eric. 1953. *Mimesis: The Representation of Reality in Western Literature*. Princeton, NJ: Princeton University Press.
Auracher, Jan and Willie Van Peer, eds. 2008. *New Beginnings in Literary Studies*. Newcastle: Cambridge Scholars Publishing.
Aurnhammer, Achim und Dieter Martin. 2003. *Mythos Pygmalion: Texte von Ovid bis John Updike*. Leipzig: Reclam.
Austin, J. L. 1971 [1955]. *How to do Things with Words*. London: Oxford University Press.
Bacon, Francis. 1999. *New Atlantis*. In Bruce 1999.
Bakhtin, Mikhail M. 1981. *The Dialogic Imagination*, trans. Caryl Emerson and Michael Holquist. Austin: University of Texas Press.
Barton, John. 1988. *People of the Book? The Authority of the Bible in Christianity*. Louisville: Westminster John Knox.
Bayard, Pierre. 2002. *Enquete sur Hamlet: le dialogue de sourds*. Paris: Editions de Minuit.
——. 2007. *How to Talk about Books You Haven't Read*, trans. Jeffrey Mehlman. New York: Bloomsbury.
Beardsley, Monroe C. 1958. *Aesthetics: Problems in the Philosophy of Criticism*. New York: Harcourt and Brace.
Benjamin, Walter. 2008 [1936]. *The Work of Art in the Age of Its Reproducibility and Other Writings on Media*, ed. Michael W. Jennings, Brigid Doherty, and Thomas Y. Levin, trans. by Edmund Jephcott et al. Cambridge, Mass.: Harvard University Press, 19–55.
Ben-Porat, Ziva. 1978. The Poetics of Literary Allusion. *PTL* 1: 105–128.
——. 1979. Method in Madness: Notes on the Structure of Parody, based on Mad's T.V. Satires, *Poetics Today* 1: 245–72.

———. 1985. Intertextuality. *Hasifrut/Literature* 34: 170–78. (In Hebrew)
———. 2003. Saramago's Gospel and the Poetics of Prototypical Rewriting. *Journal of Romance Studies* 3: 93–105.
Berman, Avis. 1980. What Makes a Masterpiece? *Art News* (March): 128–32.
Blewett, David. 1995. *The Illustration of "Robinson Crusoe" 1719–1920*. Gerrards Cross, UK: Colin Smythe.
Bloom, Harold. 1973. *The Anxiety of Influence*. New York: Oxford University Press.
———. 1975. *A Map of Misreading*. New York: Oxford University Press.
———. 1994. *The Western Canon*. New York: Riverhead Books.
———. 2001. The One with the Beard Is God, the Other Is the Devil. *Portuguese Literary and Cultural Studies* 6: 155–66.
———. 2002. *Genius: A Mosaic of One Hundred Exemplary Creative Minds*. New York: Warner Books.
Bohn-Duchen, Monica. 2001. *The Private Life of a Masterpiece*. Berkeley: University of California Press.
Bortolotti, Gary and Linda Hutcheon. 2007. On the Origin of Adaptation – Rethinking Fidelity Discourse and "Success" – Biologically. *New Literary History* 38: 443–58.
Boswell, James. 1952. *Boswell's Life of Johnson*. London: Oxford University Press.
Boulton, James T. 1971. *Johnson: The Critical Heritage*. London: Routledge & Kegan Paul.
Bourdieu, Pierre. 1993. *The Field of Cultural Production: Essays on Art and Literature*, ed. Randal Johnson. Cambridge: Polity Press.
Brooks, Cleanth. 1949. The Language of Paradox. In Stallman 1949: 66–79.
Brower, Reuben A. 1962. *The Fields of Light: An Experiment in Critical Reading*. New York: Oxford University Press.
———. 1974. *Mirror on Mirror: Translation, Imitation, Parody*. Cambridge, Mass.: Harvard University Press.
Bruce, Susan, ed., 1999. *Thomas More: Utopia, Francis Bacon: New Atlantis, Henry Neville: The Isle of Pines*. Oxford: Oxford University Press.
Buber, Martin. 1970. *I and Thou*, trans. Walter Kaufmann. Edinburgh: T & T Clark.
Buñuel, Luis, director. 1954 [1952]. *The Adventures of Robinson Crusoe*. Oscar Dancigers Production (a film).
Burt, Daniel S. 2001. *The Literary 100: A Ranking of the Most Influential Novelists, Playwrights, and Poets of All Time*. New York: Checkmark Books.
Cahn, Walter. 1979. *Masterpiece, Chapters on the History of an Idea*. Princeton, NJ: Princeton University Press.
Calvino, Italo. 1999. *Why Read the Classics?* trans. Martin McLaughlin. New York: Pantheon.
Castle, Terry. 1986. *Masquerade and Civilization*. Stanford: Stanford University Press.
Clark, Kenneth. 1979. *What Is a Masterpiece?* London: Thames and Hudson.
Clayton, Jay and Eric Rothstein, eds. 1991. *Influence and Intertextuality in Literary History*. Madison: University of Wisconsin Press.
Coetzee. J. M. 1987. *Foe*. London: Penguin.
Curtius, Ernest Robert. 1953. *European Literature and the Latin Middle Ages*. New York: Pantheon Books.
Damrosch, David. 2006. World Literature in a Postcanonical, Hypercanonical Age. In *Comparative Literature in an Age of Globalization*, ed. Haun Saussy. Baltimore: The Johns Hopkins University Press, 43–53.

Dascal, Marcelo, ed. 1985. *Dialogue: An Interdisciplinary Approach*. Amsterdam: John Benjamins Publishing Company.
——. 1992. On the Pragmatic Structure of Conversation. In Searle 1992, 35–56.
David, Paul A. 1985. Clio and the Economics of QWERTY. *American Economic Review Papers and Proceedings* 75: 332–337.
Defoe, Daniel. 1994. *Robinson Crusoe: An Authoritative Text, Contexts, Criticism*, ed. Michael Shinagel. New York: W.W. Norton & Company.
DeMille, Cecil B., director. 1949. *Samson and Delilah*. Paramount Pictures (a film).
——. 1959. *The Autobiography of Cecel B DeMille*, ed. Donald Hayne. New Jersey: Prentice-Hall.
Denby, David. 1996. *Great Books*. New York: Simon & Schuster.
Dentith, Simon. 2000. *Parody*. London: Routledge.
Diderot, Denis. 1966. *Rameau's Nephew and D'Alembert's Dream*, trans. Leonard Tancock. Harmondsworth: Penguin.
Dieckmann, Herbert. 1952. The Relationship between Diderot's Satire I and Satire II. *Romanic Review* 43: 12–26.
Dobson, Michael. 1992. *The Making of the National Poet: Shakespeare, Adaptation and Authorship, 1660–1769*. Oxford: Clarendon Press.
Dobson, Michael and Stanley Wells, eds. 2001. *The Oxford Companion to Shakespeare*. Oxford: Oxford University Press.
Duarte, Ferreira João. What is it that Saramago is doing in *The Gospel according to Jesus Christ*? Rewriting the Gospels into Genre. In: http://www.docstoc.com/docs
Eco, Umberto. 2004. Borges and My Anxiety of Influence. In *On Literature*, trans. Martin McLaughlin. Orlando: Harcourt.
Eagleton, Terry and Drew Milne, eds. 1996. *Marxist Literary Theory*. Oxford: B. Blackwell.
Edwards, Philip, ed. 2003. *Hamlet, Prince of Denmark*. Cambridge: Cambridge University Press.
Ehrenpreis, Irvin. 1964. The Meaning of Gulliver's Last Voyage. In Tuveson 1964, 123–42.
Eliot, T. S. 1946. *What Is a Classic?* London: Faber & Faber.
——. 1954. *The Three Voices of Poetry*. London: Cambridge University Press.
——. 1957. *On Poetry and Poets*. London: Faber and Faber.
Elizur, Shulamit. 1998. Isaac's Akedah: In Weeping or in Joy? *Et Hada'at* 1: 15–36. (In Hebrew)
Elliott, Robert C. 1960. *The Power of Satire: Magic, Ritual, Art*. Princeton, NJ: Princeton University Press.
Ellis, Frank H., ed. 1969. *Twentieth Century Interpretations of Robinson Crusoe*. Englewood Cliffs, NJ: Prentice-Hall.
Empson, William. 1947 [1930]. *Seven Types of Ambiguity*. New York: New Directions.
English, James F. 2002. Winning the Culture Game: Prizes, Awards, and the Rules of Art. *New Literary History* 33: 109–35.
——. 2005. *The Economy of Prestige: Prizes, Awards, and the Circulation of Cultural Value*. Cambridge, Mass.: Harvard University Press.
Erlich, Victor. 1955. *Russian Formalism: Doctrine and History*. The Hague: Mouton.
——. ed., 1975. *Twentieth-Century Russian Literary Criticism*. New Haven: Yale University Press.

Escarpit, Robert. 1971. *Sociology of Literature*, trans. Ernest Pick. London: Frank Cass.
Esenin, Sergei. 1955. *Sochineniia / Sergei Esenin*. Moskva: Gosudarstvennoe izd-vo khudozhestvennoi literatury.
Even-Zohar, Itamar. 1978. *Papers in Historical Poetics*. Tel Aviv: The Porter Institute for Poetics and Semiotics.
Fish, Stanley. 1980. *Is There a Text in this Class?* Cambridge, Mass.: Harvard University Press.
Fishelov, David. 1990. The Vanity of the Reader's Wishes: Rereading Juvenal's Satire 10, *American Journal of Philology* 111: 370–82.
———. 1993a. *Metaphors of Genres*. University Park: Penn State University Press.
———. 1993b. Interpretation and Historicism, *Iyuun* 42: 19–27.
———. 1993c. *Satura Contra Utopiam*: Satirical Distortions of Utopian Ideas. *Revue de littérature comparée* 268: 463–461.
———. 1994. The Strange Life and Adventures of Biological Concepts in Genre Periodization. *Canadian Review of Comparative Literature* 21: 613–26.
———. 1999. The Birth of a Genre. *European Journal of English Studies* 3: 51–63.
———. 2000. *Samson's Locks: The Transformations of Biblical Samson*. Tel Aviv and Haifa: Haifa University Press. (In Hebrew)
———. 2004–5. Robinson Crusoe, "The Other," and the Poetics of Surprise. *Connotations: A Journal for Critical Debate* 14: 1–18.
———. 2008a. Dialogues with/and Great Books: With Some Serious Reflections on *Robinson Crusoe*. *New Literary History* 39: 335–353.
———. 2008b. What Is, Empirically, A Great Book? In Auracher and Van Peer 2008, 423–45.
Fokkema, Douwe. 1999. The Art of Rewriting the Gospel. *Revista Colóquio/Letras* 151/152: 395–402.
Forshey, Gerald E. 1992. *American Religious and Biblical Spectaculars*. Westport, Conn: Praeger.
Foucault, Michel. 1984. *The Foucault Reader*, ed. Paul Rabinow. New York: Pantheon.
Frier, David. 2005. Jose Saramago's O Evangelho Jesus Cristo: Outline of a New Testament. *The Modern Language Review* 100: 367–82.
Frye, Northrop. 1973. Varieties of Literary Utopias. In *Utopias and Utopian Thought*, ed. Frank Manuel. London: Souvenir Press, 25–49.
Garber, Marjorie. 2003. *Quotation Marks*. London: Routledge.
Genette, Gerard. 1997 [1982]. *Palimpsests: Literature in the Second Degree*, trans. Channa Newman and Claude Doubinsky. Lincoln and London: University of Nebraska Press.
Ginzberg, Louis. 1968. *Legends of the Jews*, trans. Henrietta Szold. Philadelphia: Jewish Publication Society of America.
Goldmann, Lucien. 1996 [1963]. Sociology of the Novel. In Eagleton and Milne 1996, 204–20.
Gorak, Jan. 1991. *The Making of the Modern Canon*. London: Athlone.
Gould, Stephen Jay. 1991. *Bully for Brontosaurus: Further Reflections in Natural History*. New York: W. W. Norton.
Green, Martin B. 1990. *The Robinson Crusoe Story*. University Park: Penn State University Press.
Grice, Paul H. 1975. Logic and Conversation. In *Syntax and Semantics*, vol. 3, *Speech Acts*, ed. P. Cole and J. Morgan. New York: Academic Press, 41–58.

Guillory, John. 1993. *Cultural Capital: The Problem of Literary Canon Formation.* Chicago: Chicago University Press.
Gumbrecht, Ulrich. 1985. History of Literature – Fragment of a Vanished Totality? *New Literary History* 8: 467–79.
Guss, Donald L. 1966. *John Donne, Petrarchist.* Detroit: Wayne State University Press.
Hadomi, Lea. 1989. *Between Hope and Doubt: The Story of Utopia.* Tel Aviv: Hakibutz Hameuchad Publishers. (In Hebrew)
Hardy, Rod and George Miller, directors. 1997. *Robinson Crusoe.* Miramax Films (a film).
Harrison, Stephen, ed. 2007. *The Cambridge Companion to Horace.* Cambridge: Cambridge University Press.
Haslett, Moyra. 2000. *Marxist Literary and Cultural Theories.* New York: St. Martin's Press.
Highet, Gilbert. 1950. *The Classical Tradition: Greek and Roman Influences on Western Literature.* New York: Oxford University Press.
——. 1961. *Juvenal the Satirist.* Oxford: The Clarendon Press.
Holquist, Michael. 1990. *Dialogism: Bakhtin and his World.* London: Routledge.
Horace. 2004. *The Works of Horace*, trans. literally into English Prose by C. Smart. http://www.gutenberg.org [Release Date: November 11, 2004]
Hornstein, Lillian Herlands and G. D. Percy et al., eds. 2002. *The Reader's Companion to World Literature.* New York: Signet Classic.
Hundsnurscher, Franz and Edda Weigand, eds. 1995. *Future Perspectives of Dialogue Analysis.* Tübingen: Max Niemeyer Verlag.
Hunter, R. L. 1985. *The New Comedy of Greece and Rome.* Cambridge: Cambridge University Press.
Hutcheon, Linda. 2000 [1985]. *A Theory of Parody.* Urbana: University of Illinois Press.
——. 2006. *A Theory of Adaptation.* New York: Routledge.
Hutchins, Robert M. 1952. *The Great Conversation: The Substance of a Liberal Education.* Chicago: Encyclopedia Britannica.
Iser, Wolfgang. 1978. *The Act of Reading: A Theory of Aesthetic Response.* London: Routledge and Kegan Paul.
Jablonka, Eva and Marion J. Lamb. 2006. *Evolution in Four Dimensions: Genetic, Epigenetic, Behavioral, and Symbolic Variation in the History of Life.* Cambridge, Mass.: MIT Press.
Jabotinsky, Zeev (Vladimir). 1986 [1927]. *Samson*, trans. Cyrus Brooks. New York: Judea Publishing Company.
Jacobson, David C. 1987. *Modern Midrash: The Retelling of Traditional Jewish Narratives by Twentieth-Century Hebrew Writers.* Albany: State University of New York Press.
Jain, Nalini. 1993. Samuel Johnson's "China to Peru" and Joseph Glanvill. *A Quarterly of Short Articles, Notes and Reviews (ANQ)* 6 (4): 207–08.
Jakobson, Roman. 1960. Closing Statement: Linguistics and Poetics. In *Style in Language*, ed. Thomas A. Sebeok. Cambridge, Mass.: MIT Press, 350–77.
Jauss, Hans Robert. 1982. *Toward an Aesthetic of Reception*, trans. by Timothy Bahti with an Introduction by Paul de Man. Minneapolis: University of Minnesota Press.
Johnson, Samuel. 1974. *The Poems of Samuel Johnson*, ed. David Nichol Smith and Edward L. McAdam, second edition. Oxford: The Clarendon Press.

———. 1990. *Rasselas and Other Tales*, ed. Gwin J. Kolb. New Haven: Yale University Press.
Jump, John D. 1972. *Burlesque*. London: Methuen & Co Ltd.
Juvenal. 1940. *Juvenal and Persius*, trans. G.G. Ramsey. Cambridge, Mass.: Harvard University Press.
Kantra, Robert A. 1984. *All Things Vain: Religious Satirists and Their Art*. University Park: Penn State University Press.
Kartun-Blum, Ruth. 1999. *Profane Scriptures: Reflections on the Dialogue with the Bible in Modern Hebrew Poetry*. Cincinnati: Hebrew Union College Press.
Katz, Shmuel. 1993. *Z'abo: biyografyah shel Ze'ev Z'aboṭinski [A Biography of Ze'ev Jabotinsky]*. Tel Aviv: Devir. (In Hebrew)
———. 1996. *Lone Wolf: A Biography of Vladimir (Zeev) Jabotinsky*. New York: Barricade Books.
Kerbrat-Orecchioni, Catherine. 1990. *Les Interactions verbales*. Paris: Armand Colin.
Kermode, Frank. 1983. *The Classic: Literary Images of Permanence and Change*. Cambridge, Mass.: Harvard University Press.
Kierkegaard, Søren. 1985 [1843]. *Fear and Trembling: Dialectical Lyric by Johannes de silentio*, trans. Alastair Hannay. Harmondsworth: Penguin.
———. 1997. *Khil u-re'ada [Frygt Og Baeven]*, trans. Eyal Levin. Jerusalem: The Magnes Press. (In Hebrew)
———. 1935. *Crainte et Tremblement*, traduit par M.-H. Tisseau. Paris: Fernand Aubier.
Kilgour, Maggie. 2008. Heroic Contradictions: Samson and the Death of Turnus. *Texas Studies in Literature and Language* 50: 201–34.
Knapp, Mark L. and Judith A. Hall. 2006. *Nonverbal Communication in Human Interaction*. Belmont CA: Thomson/Wadsworth.
Kristeva, Julia. 1980. *Desire in Language: A Semiotic Approach to Literature and Art*. Ed. Leon S. Roudiez. Trans. Thomas Gora, Alice Jardine, and Leon S. Roudiez. New York: Columbia University Press.
Krouse, Michael. 1949. *Milton's Samson and the Christian Tradition*. Princeton, NJ: Princeton University Press.
Kumar, Krishan. 1987. *Utopia and Anti-Utopia in Modern Times*. Oxford: Basil Blackwell.
Law, Helen H. 1932. The Name Galatea in the Pygmalion Myth. *The Classical Journal* 27 (5): 337–42.
Leech, Geoffrey. 1969. *A Linguistic Guide to English Poetry*. London: Longman.
Lefevere, André. 1992. *Translation, Rewriting, and the Manipulation of Literary Fame*. London: Routledge.
Lerner, Alan Jay. 1956. *My Fair Lady*. Harmondsworth: Penguin.
Levin, Hanoch. 1987 [1970]. *What Does The Bird Care: Songs, Sketches and Satires*. Tel Aviv: Sifrei Siman-Kri'a/Hakkibutz Hameuchad Publishers. (In Hebrew)
Linell, Per. 1998. *Approaching Dialogue: Talk, Interaction and Contexts in Dialogical Perspectives*. Amsterdam: John Benjamins Publishing Company.
Liu, Lydia He. 2000. Robinson Crusoe and His Adventures in China: A Cross-Cultural Perspective on the Problem of Realism and Science Fiction. *Abstracts of the 2000 AAS Annual Meeting*. San Diego, CA. In: http://www.aasianst.org/absts/2000abst/Inter/i-toc.htm.
Longinus. 1967. On the Sublime, trans. Rhys Roberts. In *The Great Critics*, eds. James H. Smith and Edd W. Parks. New York: Norton, 65–111.

Lyons, John. 1968. *Introduction to Theoretical Linguistics*. Cambridge: Cambridge University Press.
———. 1970. *New Horizons in Linguistics*. Harmondsworth: Penguin.
Mack, Maynard. 1964. Gulliver's Travels. In Tuveson 1964, 111–14.
———. ed. 1997. *The Norton Anthology of World Masterpieces*. New York: Norton.
Magill, Frank N. 1952. *Masterpieces of World Literature*. New York: HarperCollins.
Martindale, Charles and Richard F. Thomas, eds. 2006. *Classics and the Uses of Reception*. Oxford: Balckwell Publishing.
Marx, Karl. 1972. Karl Marx on *Robinson Crusoe*. In Rogers 1972, 166–68.
Mason, Haydn Trevor. 1992. *Candide: Optimism Demolished*. New York: Twayne's Publishers.
Mayakovsky, Vladimir. 1955–1956. *Polnoe sobranie sochinenii / Vladimir Maiakovskii*. Moskva: Gosudarstvennoe izd-vo khudozhestvennoi literatury.
McDonald, Lee Martin. 2007. *The Biblical Canon: Its Origin, Transmission, and Authority*. Peabody, MA: Hendrickson Publishers.
McMullen, Roy. 1976. *The Mona Lisa: The Picture and the Myth*. London: Macmillan.
Melville. Moby Dick; or the Whale, Publishing History: http://www.melville.org/hmmoby.htm
Metzger, Bruce M. 1987. *The Canon of the New Testament*. Oxford: Clarendon Press.
Milner, Andrew. 1996. *Literature, Culture and Society*. London: UCL Press.
Milton, John. 1937. *Paradise Regained, the Minor Poems and Samson Agonistes*, ed. Herritt Y. Hughes. Indianapolis: The Odyssey Press.
Molière. 2000. *The Miser and Other Plays*, trans. John Wood and David Coward. Harmondsworth: Penguin.
Monty Python. 1979. *The Life of Brian*. Warner Bros. and Orion Pictures (a film).
More, Thomas. 1965. *Utopia*, trans. Paul Turner. Harmondsworth: Penguin.
———. 1992. *Utopia*, trans. and ed. Robert Adams. New York: W. W. Norton & Company.
Moretti, Franco. 1988. *Sings Taken For Wonders: Essays in the Sociology of Literary Forms*. London: Verso.
———. 1998. *Atlas of the European Novel, 1800–1900*. London: Verso.
———. 2005. *Graphs, Maps, Trees: Abstract Models for a Literary History*. London: Verso.
Morson, Gary Saul. 1986. Dialogue, Monologue, and the Social: A Reply to Hen Hirschkop. In *Bakhtin: Essays and Dialogues on His Work*, ed. Gary Saul Morson. Chicago: University of Chicago Press, 81–88.
Mukarovsky, Jan. 1976. *On Poetic Language*, trans. John Burbank and Peter Steiner. Lisse, Belgium: Peter de Ridder Press.
Murray, Charles. 2003. *Human Accomplishment: The Pursuit of Excellence in the Arts and Sciences, 800 BC to 1950*. New York: HarperCollins.
O'Flaherty, Patrick. 1967. Johnson as Satirist: A New Look at The Vanity of Human Wishes. *English Literary History* 34: 78–91.
Ohmann, Richard. 1983. The Shaping of a Canon: U.S. Fiction, 1960–1975. *Critical Inquiry* 10: 199–219.
Orr, Mary. 2003. *Intertextuality: Debates and Contexts*. Cambridge: Polity Press.
Ovid. 2000. *Metamorphoses*, trans. by A. S. Kline. http://www.poetryintranslation.com

Owen, Wilfred. 1973. *War Poems and Others*, ed. Dominic Hibberd. London: Chatto and Windus.
Oz, Amos. 1972 [1968]. *My Michael*, trans. Nicholas de Lange. London: Chatto & Windus.
Pagis, Dan. 1976. *Innovation and Tradition in Medieval Hebrew Secular Poetry.* Jerusalem: Keter (In Hebrew).
Palumbo-Liu, David, ed. 1995. *The Ethnic Canon: Histories, Institutions, and Interventions.* Minneapolis: University of Minnesota Press.
Perry, Menakhem. 1979. Literary Dynamics: How the Order of a Text Creates Its Meanings, *Poetics Today* 1: 35–64, 311–61.
Plautus, Titus Maccius. 1995 [1924]. *Plautus*, trans. Paul Nixon. Cambridge, Mass.: Harvard University Press.
Pope, Alexander. 1963. *The Poems of Alexander Pope*, ed. John Butt. New York: Methuen.
Pushkin, Aleksandr Sergevitch. 1938. *Stikhotvoreniia / Pushkin.* Moskva: Gosudarstvennoe izd-vo khudozhestvennoi literatury.
Ravins, Burton. 1973. *More's Utopia - A Satiric Dystopia?* MA Thesis, Jerusalem: The Hebrew University of Jerusalem.
Rawson, Claude, ed. 1984. *English Satire and the Satiric Tradition.* Oxford: B. Blackwell.
Robinson, Douglas. 1991. *The Translator's Turn.* Baltimore: Johns Hopkins University Press.
Rogers, Pat. 1972. *Defoe: The Critical Heritage.* London: Routledge and Kegan Paul.
Rousseau, Jean-Jacques. 1972. Rousseau on *Robinson Crusoe*. In Rogers 1972, 52–53.
Rubin, James H. 1985. 'Pygmalion and Galatea': Girodet and Rousseau. *The Burlington Magazine* 127 (989): 517–20.
Rudd, Niall. 1982. *The Satires of Horace.* Berkeley: University of California Press.
Sainte-Beuve, Charles Augustin. 1926–28. Qu'est-ce qu'un classique? In: *Causeries du lundi* III. Paris: Librairie Garnier, 38–55.
Sanders, Julie. 2006. *Adaptation and Appropriation.* New York: Routledge.
Saramago, José. 1993 [1991]. *The Gospel According to Jesus Christ*, trans. Giovanni Pontiero. London: The Harvill Press.
Schaeffer, Jean-Marie. 1989. *Qu'est-ce qu'un genre littéraire?* Paris: Seuil.
Searle, John. 1969. *Speech Acts: An Essay in the Philosophy of Language.* Cambridge: Cambridge University Press.
———. 1992. Conversation and Conversation Reconsidered. In Searle et al. 1992, 7–29, 137–47.
——— et al. 1992. *(On) Searle on Conversation.* Amsterdam: John Benjamins Publishing Company.
Seidel, Michael. 1991. *Robinson Crusoe: Island Myths and the Novel.* Boston: Twayne Publishers.
Sela-Sheffy, Rakefet. 2002. Canon Formation Revisited: Canon and Cultural Production. *Neohelicon* 29: 141–159.
Selden, Raman. 1970. Dr. Johnson and Juvenal: A Problem in Critical Method. *Comparative Literature* 4: 289–302.
Shavit, Zohar. 1986. *Poetics of Children's Literature.* Athens, GA: University of Georgia Press.
Shaw, Bernard. 1941. *Pygmalion: A Romance in Five Acts.* Harmondsworth: Penguin.

Shklovsky, Victor. 1965. Art as Technique. In *Russian Formalist Criticism*, trans. and eds. Lee T. Lemon and Marion J. Reis. Lincoln: University of Nebraska Press, 3–24.
Sibley, Frank. 1987. Aesthetic Concepts. In *Philosophy Looks at the Arts*, ed. Joseph Margolis. Philadelphia: Temple University Press, 29–52.
Sky News. 2008. Bid to Overturn *Life of Brian* Ban (3:27 a.m. UK, Sunday July 20, 2008).
Smith, Barbara Herrnstein. 1978. *On the Margins of Discourse*. Chicago: University of Chicago Press.
——. 1988. *Contingencies of Value: Alternative Perspectives for Critical Theory*. Cambridge, Mass.: Harvard University Press.
Spaas, Lieve and Brian Stimpson. 1996. *Robinson Crusoe: Myth and Metamorphoses*. London: Macmillan Press.
Spanos, William V. 1995. *The Errant Art of Moby-Dick: The Canon, The Cold War, and The Struggle for American Studies*. Durham: Duke University Press.
Spektor, Regina. Dulce et Decorum Est pro Patria Mori. http://www.lyricstime.com/regina-spektor-dulce-et-decorum-est-pro-patria-mori-lyrics.html
Sperber, Dan. 1996. *Explaining Culture: A Naturalistic Approach*. Oxford: Blackwell Publishers.
Spitzer, Leo. 1948. The Style of Diderot. In his *Linguistics and Literary History: Essyas in Stylistics*, Princeton, NJ: Princeton University Press.
Stallman, Robert W., ed., 1949. *Critiques and Essays in Criticism, 1920–1948*. New York: Ronald Press.
Stanford, William B. 1954. *The Ulysses Theme: A Study in the Adaptability of a Traditional Hero*. Oxford: Basil Blackwell.
Sternberg, Meir. 1978. *Expositional Modes and Temporal Ordering in Fiction*. Baltimore: Johns Hopkins University Press.
Stimpson, Catherine R. 1990. Reading for Love: Canons, Paracanons, and Whistling Jo March. *New Literary History* 21: 957–76.
Swift, Jonathan. 1973. *The Writings of Jonathan Swift*, ed. Robert A. Greenberg and William Bowman Piper. New York: W.W. Norton & Company.
Tannen, Deborah. 1989. *Talking Voices*. Cambridge: Cambridge University Press.
Tate, Allen. 1949. Tension in Poetry. In Stallman 1949, 55–65.
Thacker, Christopher. 1967. Sons of Candide. *Studies in Voltaire and the Eighteenth Century* 58: 1515–31.
Tillotson, Geoffrey et al. 1969. *Eighteenth-Century English Literature*. New York: Harcourt Brace Jovanovich.
Todorov, Tzvetan. 1975. *The Fantastic: A Structural Approach to a Literary Genre*, trans. Richard Howard. Ithaca: Cornell University Press.
——. 1984. *Mikhail Bakhtin: The Dialogical Principle*. Minneapolis: University of Minnesota Press.
Toury, Gideon. 1995. *Descriptive Translation Studies and beyond*. Amsterdam: John Benjamins.
Traugott, John. 1964. A Voyage to Nowhere with Thomas More and Jonathan Swift: Utopia and the Voyage to the Houynhnms. In Tuveson 1964, 143–69.
——. 1984. The Yahoo in the Doll's House: "Gulliver's Travels" the Children's Classic. In Rawson 1984, 127–50.
Trotsky, Leo. 1996 [1923]. The Formalist School of Poetry and Marxism. In Eagleton and Milne 1996, 46–59.

Tuveson, Ernest, ed. 1964. *Swift: A Collection of Critical Essays*. Englewood Cliffs, N.J., Prentice-Hall.
Tynianov, Jurij. 1975 [1921]. Dostoevsky and Gogol: Theory of Parody. In Erlich 1975, 102–16.
Van Rees, C. J. 1983. How a Literary Work Becomes a Masterpiece: On the Threefold Selection Practised by Literary Criticism. *Poetics* 12: 397–417.
Verboord, Marc. 2003. Classification of Authors by Literary Prestige. *Poetics* 31: 259–81.
Vickers, Brian. 1968. The Satiric Structure of Gulliver's Travels and More's Utopia. In *The World of Jonathan Swift*, ed. Brian Vickers. Cambridge, Mass.: Harvard University Press, 233–57.
Voltaire. 1957. *Candide ou L'optimisme*, édition critique avec une introduction et un commentaire par André Morize. Paris: Librairie Marcel Didier.
———. 1958. *Romans et contes*, texte établit et annoté par René Groos. Paris: Gallimard.
———. 1963. *Voltaire's Candide: A Bilingual Edition*, trans. Peter Gay. New York: St. Martin's Press.
———. 1966. *Candide ou l'optimism*, avec une introduction et un commentaire par René Pomeau. Paris: A. G. Nizet.
Von Hallberg, Robert. 1983. Editor's Introduction. *Critical Inquiry* 10: iii–vi.
Waldrop, Mitchell M. 1992. *Complexity: The Emerging Science at the Edge of Order and Chaos*. New York: Simon & Schuster.
Watt, Ian. 1963. *The Rise of the Novel: Studies in Defoe, Richardson and Fielding*. Harmondsworth: Penguin.
Waugh, Patricia. 1984. *Metafiction: The Theory and Practice of Self-Conscious Fiction*. London: Methuen.
Weigand, Edda. 1995. *Looking for the Point of the Dialogic Turn*. In Hundsnurscher and Weigand 1995, 95-120.
West, Alick. 1996 [1937]. The Relativity of Literary Value. In Eagleton and Milne 1996: 103–6.
Wilde, Oscar. 1968 [1891]. The Soul of Man under Socialism. In *The Artist as Critic, Critical Writings of Oscar Wilde*, ed. Richard Ellmann. New York: Random House, 255–89.
Williams, Raymond. 1961. *The Long Revolution*. London: Chatto & Windus.
Wilson, Arthur M. 1972. *Diderot*. New York: Oxford University Press.
Worton, Michael and Judith Still, eds. 1990. *Intertextuality: Theories and Practice*. Manchester: Manchester University Press.
Wyss, Johann David. 2007 [1816]. *The Swiss Family Robinson*. London: Penguin.
Zemach, Eddy M. 1997. *Real Beauty*. University Park: Penn State University Press.
Zemeckis, Robert, director. 2000. *Cast Away*. DreamWorks SKG [A Film]
Zwicker, Jonathan. 2000. Robinson Crusoe Stories: Translation, the Novel, and the Literary Market in Nineteenth-Century Japan, *Abstracts of the 2000 AAS Annual Meeting*, San Diego, CA. (http://www.aasianst.org/absts/2000abst/Inter/i-toc.htm).

Index

Adams, Hazard, 191n.2, 192n.1
adaptation, 19, 21, 22–29 passim, 34, 41, 46–56 passim, 61, 66, 73, 74, 87, 90, 135, 138, 146, 155–58 passim, 175–80 passim, 185, 187, 188, 193n.4, 193n.13, 194n.26, 196n.43, 199n.10, 200n.9. *See also* appropriation; parody; re-writing; translation
Aeschylus, *Prometheus Bound*, 52
aesthetic qualities (aesthetic value), ix, 30–36, 42–45 passim, 63–67 passim, 79, 90, 174, 175, 182, 183, 191n.4, 192n.11. *See also* beauty party
Agamemnon (and Iphigenia), 82
Allen, Graham, 3
allusion, 25, 26, 28, 29, 46, 47, 68–69, 71–74 passim, 116, 117, 121, 123, 135, 158, 184, 188, 197n.8, 201n.7. *See also* adaptation; epigraph; parody; re-writing; translation
Alter, Robert, 77–78, 173
Altieri, Charles, 42–43
Amis, Kingsley, *The Old Devils*, 59, 61
Anderson, William S., 126–27, 201n.7
appropriation, 22–23, 158. *See also* adaptation
archetype (archetypal), 183, 187
Aristophanes, 135, 195n.40
Aristotle, 31, 33
Auerbach, Eric, 80
Augustine, Saint, 77
Aurnhammer, Achim, 201n.12
Austin, J. L., 9, 12

Bacon, Francis, *New Atlantis*, 160–64, 170, 201n.1
Bakhtin, Mikhail M., 1, 12, 190n.13
Balibar, Étienne, 37
Barker, Pat, *The Ghost Road*, 59, 61
Barrie, J. M., *Dear Brutus*, 53
Barton, John, 77
Battle of the Books (Quarrel of the Ancients and the Moderns), 30. *See also* canon
Bayard, Pierre, 18, 189n.8, 201n.11 (ch. 11)
Beardsley, Monroe C, 33, 194n.22

beauty party, 30–36, 39, 40, 42, 44–45, 79, 174, 192n.6, 192n.11. *See also* aesthetic qualities; power party
Benjamin, Walter, 186
Ben-Porat, Ziva, 3, 71, 108, 115, 117, 201n.11 (ch. 10)
Berger, John, G., 59, 60
Berman, Avis, 191n.4
Bible:
  Abraham and Chedorlaomer (Gen. 14), 78
  Abraham and Isaac, The Sacrifice (Gen. 22), 80–89, 196n.6
  Beatitudes, 106
  Book of Judith (Apocrypha), 79
  Book of Nahum, 79
  canonization of, 26–27, 67, 77–79
  Christian Bible, 77–79, 191n.1
  Garden of Eden, 159, 201n.7
  Gideon (Judges 6–8), 90–91
  Hebrew (Jewish) Bible, 77–79, 191n.12, 196n.1
  Jephthah (Judges 11–12), 82
  Jesus, 98–99, 104–115, 197–98n.3
  Samson (Judges 13–16), 90–103, 183, 184, 196n.50, 196n.4, 197n.3
  See also canon; DeMille, Kierkegaard; Jabotinsky, Levin, Milton, Monty Python; Saramago
Bialik, H. N., 93, 194n.20
Blewett, David, 176, 181
Bloom, Harold, 27, 35, 39, 114, 191n.13, 191n.4, 191n.5, 195n.37
Bohn-Duchen, Monica, 185–86
Booker Prize, 56–62, 66
  as metaphor of canon formation, 57–58
Bortolotti, Gary, 193n.4
Boswell, James, *The Life of Samuel Johnson*, 63, 195n.37, 199–200n.13
Boulton, James T., 195n.37
Bourdieu, Pierre, 39–40, 41, 42, 49, 196n.49
Brookner, Anita, *Hotel du Lac*, 59, 61
Brooks, Cleanth, 32, 42
Brower, Reuben A., 19, 191n.9, 191n.15
Buber, Martin, 1, 7

Buñuel, Luis, *The Adventures of Robinson Crusoe*, 179
Burt, Daniel S., 62
Byatt, A. S., *Possession: A Romance*, 59, 61

Cahn, Walter, 3, 185
Calvino, Italo, 75
Campe, Joachim, *Robinson der Jüngere*, 177
canon:
  and adaptation, 194–95n.26
  and countercanon, 49
  and hypercanon, 49
  and paracanon, 191n.1
  and shadow canon, 49
  canonical authors, 49, 191n.5
  canonical status, 48–53 passim, 58, 65, 77, 79, 90, 184, 194n.20
  canonical (canonized) text, 26, 77–79, 183
  formation of, ix–x, 35, 39, 41, 42, 43, 49, 57, 58, 67, 77, 174, 183, 186, 192n.2, 193n.5
  "hard core," 51–53, 67, 134
  literary canon, ix–x, 30, 35, 39–45 passim, 49, 58, 65, 77–78, 79, 186, 192n.2
  Shakespearean, 194n.23
  Western Canon, 35, 42, 43, 191n.1, 191n.4, 192n.12
  See also adaptation; Bible; Booker Prize; dialogic approach to great books; parody; power party; re-writing
Carey, Peter, *Oscar and Lucinda*, 59, 61
Castle, Terry, 202n.4
Cervantes, *Don Quixote*, 52, 72, 117, 173, 193n.13
Cinderela (story), 157, 200n.9
Clark, Kenneth, 39, 186, 191n.4
Clayton, Jay, 3, 27
Coetzee. J. M., 59, 60, 178–79
  Foe, 178–79
  Life & Times of Michael K, 59, 60
Coleridge, Samuel Taylor, 181
conversation. *See* real-life dialogue
Curtius, Ernest Robert, 122–23
Cukor, George, *My Fair Lady*, 156
Czech Structuralism (Prague Structuralist Circle), 34. *See also* Russian Formalism

Dali, Salvador, 186
Damrosch, David, 49
Dante, Alighieri, *Divine Comedy*, 52
Dascal, Marcelo, 190n.12, 190n.13
David, Paul A., 64–65
Defoe, Daniel, 36, 68, 73, 172–82, 183, 202n.9
  The Farther Adventures of Robinson Crusoe, 175
  The Life and Surprising Adventures of Robinson Crusoe, 36, 68, 73, 172–82, 183
  Serious Reflections during the Life and Surprising Adventures of Robinson Crusoe, 173, 175
de Man, Paul, 39
DeMille, Cecil B., *Samson and Delilah*, 91, 96–100, 101, 102, 103, 184, 197n.7
Denby, David, 50, 51, 53, 62
Dentith, Simon, 198n.6
dialogic approach to arts, 185–86
dialogic approach to great books, ix–x, 46–74 passim, 116, 118, 135, 157, 173, 175, 183–88 passim
dialogic approach to science, 186–87
dialogue. *See* literary dialogue; monologue; model, ponytail; real-life dialogue
Diderot, Denis, *Le Neveu de Rameau*, 121–23, 127–33
Dieckmann, Herbert, 123
dissemination, xi, 22, 48, 51, 53, 56, 60, 61–62, 66, 72–74, 78, 94, 116, 134–35, 185, 187, 192n.3, 193n.4, 193n.8, 194n.20. *See also* endurance; model, pyramid; procreation; survival
Dobson, Michael, 194n.25, 194–95n.26
Don Juan, 173
Doyle, Roddy, *Paddy Clarke Ha Ha Ha*, 59, 61
Duarte, Ferreira João, 114
Duchamp, Marcel, 186

Eagleton, Terry, 37, 192n.8
Eco, Umberto, 191n.14
Edwards, Philip, 54–55
Ehrenpreis, Irvin, 201n.6
Einstein, Albert, 186–87
Eliot, T. S., 39, 77, 144, 189n.1, 191n.15, 200n.17
Elizur, Shulamit, 88
Elliott, Robert C., 23
Ellis, Frank H., 181
Empson, William, 32
endurance, 48, 63, 65, 193n.4. *See also* procreation; survival
English, James F., 56, 57, 64, 195n.36
epigraph, 26, 28, 29, 46, 121–22, 132, 201n.10
Erlich, Victor, 34
Escarpit, Robert, 65
Esenin, Sergei, "Goodbye, my friend," 16–17
Euripides, *Medea*, 52
Even-Zohar, Itamar, 23
evolution (biological and cultural), 65, 69, 192n.4
  multi-layered model, 192n.4
  See also adaptation; dissemination; endurance; survival

Farrell, J. G., *The Siege of Krishnapur*, 59, 60
Fénelon, François, *Télémaque*, 71

Fielding, Henry, *Tom Jones*, 175
Fish, Stanley, 36
Fishelov, David, 44, 47, 99, 138, 193n.4, 196n.46, 196n.50, 196n.4, 197n.4, 197n.7, 201n.5
Fitzgerald, Penelope, *Offshore*, 59, 60
Fokkema, Douwe, 114
Forshey, Gerald E., 197n.7
Foucault, Michel, 35, 38–39, 40, 42
Freud, Sigmund, 27, 71, 186
Frier, David, 198n.5
Frye, Northrop, 201n.10

Gadamer, Hans Georg, 43
Garber, Marjorie, 202n.4
Gautier, Théophile, 186
generative potential, 78–80, 90, 91, 105, 183
Genette, Gerard, 3, 157, 177, 200n.8, 200–1n.10, 201n.11
Gildon, Charles, *The Life and Strange Surprising Adventures of Mr. D—— De F——*, 175–76
Ginzberg, Louis, 87, 196–97n.6, 197n.7
Girard, René, 38
Goethe, Johann, *Faust*, 52
Golding, William, 58, 59, 60
   Rites of Passage, 59, 60
Goldmann, Lucien, 37–38, 42
Gorak, Jan, 191n.1, 196n.1
Gordimer, Nadine, *The Conservationist*, 59, 60
Gould, Stephen Jay, 65, 192n.4
Grandville (Jean Ignace Isidore Gérard), 181–82
Green, Martin B., 177
Grice, Paul H., 11–12
Guillory, John, 41–42, 194n.19
Gumbrecht, Ulrich, 191n.1
Guss, Donald L., 190n.3

Hadomi, Lea, 160, 201n.10
Hall, Judith A., 10, 189n.6
Hamlet (character), 7, 8, 50, 54, 72, 173. *See also* Shakespeare (*Hamlet*)
Hardy, Rod, *Robinson Crusoe*, 179, 180
Harrison, Stephen, 117, 198n.7
Harry Potter (J. K. Rowling), 67–68, 196n.47, 196.n.48
Haslett, Moyra, 192n.7
Hawking, Richard, 186
hegemony, ix, 36, 39, 41, 42, 45, 63, 67, 77, 195n.38. *See also* power party
Hesiod, 159
Highet, Gilbert, 136, 198n.1
Holquist, Michael, 190n.13
Homer, 20, 41, 45, 47, 52, 67, 68, 69, 71, 73, 193n.9
   Iliad, 52
   Odyssey, 47, 52, 68, 71, 73, 178, 193n.9

Horace, 116–33, 135, 184, 198n.7, 199n.2, 199n.3
   Ode 3.2 (*Dulce et decorum est*), 119–21, 184, 198n.7
   Ode 3.30 (*Exegi monumentum*), 118–19
   Satire 2, 7, 121–27, 132–33
   See also Diderot; Owen; Pushkin; Spektor
Hornstein, Lillian Herlands, 195n.37
Houssaye, Henry, 186
Hulme, Keri, *The Bone People*, 59, 61
Hunter, R. L., 21
Hutcheon, Linda, 22, 115, 193n.4, 202n.4
Hutchins, Robert M., 191n.4, 193n.5

imitation, 15, 20–21, 64, 114, 115, 116, 138–39, 144, 145, 176, 199n.13, 200n.15. *See also* adaptation; parody; re-writing; translation
intertextuality, x, 3, 157, 196n.51. *See also* adaptation; allusion; imitation; literary dialogue; parody; re-writing
Iser, Wolfgang, 18, 190n.7
Ishiguro, Kazuo, *The Remains of the Day*, 59, 61

Jablonka, Eva, 192n.4
Jabotinsky, Zeev (Vladimir), *Samson*, 91–96, 97–103 passim, 183, 184, 197n.5
Jacobson, David C., 87
Jain, Nalini, 199n.11
Jakobson, Roman, 10, 12
Jameson, Fredric, 37
Jauss, Hans Robert, 39, 48, 193n.6
Jhabvala, Ruth Prawer, *Heat and Dust*, 59, 60
Johnson, Samuel, 20, 54, 62–66, 138–41, 144–45, 195n.37, 199n.11, 200n.14, 200n.15, 200n.17
   Rasselas, 54, 62–66, 195n.37
   The Vanity of Human Wishes, 20, 138–41, 144–45, 199n.11, 200n.14, 200n.15
Joyce, James, 51, 71, 178, 181, 200n.8
   Ulysses, 71, 178, 200n.8
Jump, John D., 198n.6
Juvenal, 20, 184, 117, 134–45, 184, 199n.3, 199n.6, 196n.7, 199n.13, 200n.14, 200n.15
   Satire 10, 20, 136–45, 184, 196n.7, 200n.14, 200n.15
   See also Johnson, Swift

Kantra, Robert A., 201n.3
Kartun-Blum, Ruth, 85, 87, 88
Katz, Shmuel, 92, 93, 197n.5
Kelman, James, *How Late It Was, How Late*, 59, 61
Keneally, Thomas, *Schindler's Ark*, 59, 60
Kerbrat-Orecchioni, Catherine, 189n.7
Kermode, Frank, 189n.1

Kierkegaard, Søren, *Fear and Trembling*, 3, 80–84, 88–89, 105, 183–84
Kilgour, Maggie, 197n.8
Knapp, Mark L., 10, 189n.6
Kristeva, Julia, 3
Krouse, Michael, 99
Kumar, Krishan, 201n.8, 201n.10

Lamb, Marion J., 192n.4
Law, Helen H., 200n.5
Leech, Geoffrey, 191n.15
Lefevere, André, 19, 176, 193n.5
Leger, Fernand, 186
Lerner, Alan Jay, *My Fair Lady*, 146, 154–58, 184
Levin, Hanoch, *The Queen of the Bathtub*, 84–89, 105, 183, 197n.8
Lied (German), 187
Linell, Per, 189n.4
literary dialogue, 3, 14–29, 30, 46, 69–74, 117, 145, 147, 185–88, 191n.4
　active, 18–19, 67, 73, 74, 102, 175
　dialoguing text (DT), 70–71, 101–3, 121, 133, 146, 156–58, 184–85, 187, 200n.3, 200n.7
　echo, 18–25, 27–29, 46–50, 53–56, 58, 63–68, 70–74, 78–79, 103, 105, 121, 134, 141, 145, 173, 175–80, 185, 188, 190n.4, 191n.8, 194n.20, 195n.32, 195n.42, 196n.43
　genuine, 15, 17, 18, 20–29, 43, 46, 55, 68, 71–74, 75–80 passim, 84, 88, 89, 103, 115, 117, 132–33, 134, 145, 147, 158, 173, 177–81, 184, 185, 188, 189n.7, 190n.2, 190n.4, 191n.13, 200n.9
　initiating text (IT), 70–71, 101–3, 116–17, 119, 121, 132–33, 146, 156–58, 170–71, 184–85, 187–88, 200n.9
　non-declared (implicit), 145, 147, 148–50, 180
　of-the-deaf, 18, 20, 23, 25–29, 55, 74, 103, 177–78, 180
　passive, 18–19, 28, 47, 72, 73, 74, 116, 134, 175, 188, 190n.7
　pseudo, 28–29, 46, 73, 158, 173, 175–78
　See also adaptation; allusion; generative potential; imitation; parody; predictability; quantity of dialogues; translation; real-life dialogue; variety (diversity) of dialogues
Liu, Lydia He, 176
Lively, Penelope, *Moon Tiger*, 59, 61
Longinus, 75
Loewe, Frederick, *My Fair Lady*, 146, 154–58, 184
Lukács, György, 37, 38
Lyons, John, 189n.5

Macherey, Pierre, 37

Mack, Maynard, 50, 53, 201n.6
Magill, Frank N., 50, 53, 62
Mann, Thomas, 49
Marquez, Garcia, 23–24
Martin, Dieter, 201n.12
Martindale, Charles, 193n.6
Marx, Karl, 35, 40, 178
　Das Capital (on *Robinson Crusoe*), 178
Marxism, 36, 37, 38, 192n.8. *See also* Neo-Marxism
Mason, Haydn Trevor, 195n.38
Matthew effect, 54
Mayakovsky, Vladimir, "To Sergei Esenin," 16–17
McDonald, Lee Martin, 77
McEwan, Ian, 58, 59, 61
　Amsterdam, 59, 61
McMullen, Roy, 185–86
Melville, Herman, *Moby Dick*, 196n.43
Merton, S. K., 54
Metzger, Bruce M., 77
Middleton, Stanley, *Holiday*, 59, 60
Miller, George, *Robinson Crusoe*, 179, 180
Milne, Drew, 192n.8
Milner, Andrew, 191n.5
Milton, John, 52, 69, 91, 101–3, 197n.8
　Paradise Lost, 52, 69
　Samson Agonistes, 91, 101–3, 197n.8
model:
　Neo-Marxist (base and super-structure), 41–42
　Freudian, 27
　of biblical canonization, 77–78
　dialectical (Hegelian), 7
　ladder, 69
　ponytail, 69–71, 100–2, 156–58
　pyramid, 72–74, 116–17, 188
　tree, 69–71, 196n.50
Molière, 7–8, 52, 146–50, 151–58 passim, 193n.9
　L'Avare, 7–8
　L'Ecole de femmes, 146, 147, 148–50, 151–58 passim
　Tartuffe, 51, 52, 193n.9
Mona Lisa (Leonardo da Vinci), 185–86
monologue, 6–7, 9–10, 11, 12, 27, 28, 184
　and passive dialogue, 9–10
　genuine, 6, 7
　Hamlet's (soliloquy), 184
　pseudo, 6, 7
　See also dialogue
Monty Python, 105–8, 114–15, 183
　The Flying Circus, 105
　The Holy Grail, 105
　The Life of Brian, 105–8, 114–15, 183
More, Thomas, *Utopia*, 3, 159–60, 161, 164, 165, 168, 170, 201n.4. *See also* Bacon; Swift; Voltaire

Moretti, Franco, 192n.3, 193n.4, 194n.21, 196n.50
Morson, Gary Saul, 190n.13
Mukarovsky, Jan, 34–35
Murdoch, Iris, 58, 59, 60
  The Sea, the Sea, 59, 60
Murray, Charles, 49, 54, 186–87

Nabokov, Vladimir, *Lolita*, 64
Naipaul, V. S., *In a Free State*, 59, 60
Neo-Marxism, 37, 41–42, 191n.5, 192n.8, 192n.9, 194n.19. See also Marxism
Newby, P. H., *Something to Answer For*, 59, 60
New Criticism (New Critics), 32–34
Newton, Isaac, 187

O'Flaherty, Patrick, 200n.17
Ohmann, Richard, 41
Okri, Ben, *The Famished Road*, 59, 61
Ondaatje, Michael, *The English Patient*, 59, 60, 61
Orr, Mary, 3
Orwell, George, *1984*, 166, 169
Ovid, 24–25, 146–47, 149–58 passim, 184, 200n.3, 200n.5, 201n.12
  Metamorphoses 3.339–510 (Echo and Narcissus), 24–25
  Metamorphoses 10.243–97 (Pygmalion), 146–47, 149–58 passim, 184, 200n.3, 200n.5, 201n.12
  See also Lerner; Loewe; Molière; Shaw
Owen, Wilfred, "Dulce et decorum est pro patria mori," 119–21, 132–33, 184, 198n.7
Oz, Amos, *My Michael*, 92

Pagis, Dan, 191n.12
Paglia, Camille, 186
Palumbo-Liu, David, 191n.1
parody, 15–16, 17, 29, 46, 48, 63, 158. See also adaptation; allusion; predictability; re-writing; translation
Pascal, Blaise, 37
Perry, Menakhem, 190n.7
Plato (Platonic), 143, 159
Plautus, Titus Maccius, *Milies Gloriossus*, 21
Pope, Alexander, 20, 141, 174, 201–2n.1
  The Dunciad, 174, 201–2n.1
power party, 30, 35–45, 48, 77–79, 174–75. See also beauty party; hegemony
Prague Structuralist Circle (Czech Structuralism), 34. See also Russian Formalism
predictability (unpredictability), 18, 20, 21, 22, 23, 28, 29, 74, 55, 80, 102–3, 133, 145, 177–80
Pretty Woman, 200n.9
procreation (of great books), 24, 25, 48, 62, 71, 78, 79, 80. See also dissemination; endurance; survival
Pushkin, Aleksandr Sergevitch, "Exegi monumentum," 118–19, 132

quantity of dialogues, 46–49, 56, 62–67 passim, 72–74, 79, 103, 105, 116, 135, 159, 170–71, 174, 176, 184, 186–88, 196n.43. See also variety (diversity) of dialogues
Quarrel of the Ancients and the Moderns (The Battle of the Books), 30
QWERTY, 64–66, 195n.41

Rabelais, François, *Gargantua and Pantagruel*, 52
Racine, Jean, 37, 129
Ravins, Burton, 201n.3
reading. See literary dialogue, passive
real-life dialogue, x, 3–15, 18, 19, 22, 27–28, 30, 175, 189n.3, 189n.7, 189n.8, 190n.10, 190n.11, 190n.12, 190n.2
  active, 9–12, 18–19, 27
  behaviorist model, 12–13
  echo, 6, 8–12, 27, 190n.10
  genuine, 4, 6, 7–13, 27
  inner and outer level, 5–6, 12
  multi-dimensional model, 4, 12, 30, 190n.13
  of-the-deaf, 7–9, 11, 12, 18, 20, 45, 88, 189n.8
  passive, 9–12, 18, 175
  pseudo, 6–9, 11–13, 15
  forms and functions, 4–5
  See also voice
reception:
  theory, x, 39, 48, 193n.6
  and classical literature, 193n.6
  of *Candide* (Voltaire), 62–65
  of *Moby Dick* (Melville), 196n.43
  of *The Queen of the Bathtub* (Levin), 84–85
  of *Robinson Crusoe* (Defoe), 172–75, 182
  of *Rasselas* (Johnson), 62–65, 195n.39
  See also dialogic approach to great books
Reduced Shakespeare Company, 23
Rembrandt van Rijn, 80
re-writing, 28, 29, 73, 74, 93, 102–3, 115, 116, 117, 183, 188, 193n.5. See also adaptation; allusion; parody; translation
Richardson, Samuel, *Pamela*, 175
Robinson, Douglas, 19, 176, 191n.8
Robinson Crusoe as a model for youth, 177–78
Rogers, Pat, 174, 175, 176, 181, 202n.1
Roth, Philip, 49
Rothstein, Eric, 3, 27
Rousseau, Jean-Jacques, 177–78, 200n.5, 201n.8

Rousseau, Jean-Jacques *(continued)*
  Emile, 177–78
  Pygmalion, scène lyrique, 200n.5
Roy, Arundhati, *The God of Small Things*, 58, 59, 61
Rubens, Bernice, *The Elected Member*, 59, 60
Rubin, James H., 200n.5
Rudd, Niall, 121–22, 126
Rushdie, Salman, 58, 59, 60, 64, 195n.32
  Midnight's Children, 58, 59, 60
  Satanic Verses, 64, 195n.32
Russian Formalism, 33–34. *See also* Czech Structuralism (Prague Structuralist Circle)
Russell, William Clark, *Wreck of the Grosvenor*, 53
Rutherford, Ernest, 186–87

Sainte-Beuve, Charles Augustin, 189n.1
Sanders, Julie, 22–23, 179, 201n.11
Sappho, 43
Saramago, José, *The Gospel According to Jesus Christ*, 105, 108–14, 115, 183
Schaeffer, Jean-Marie, 192n.4
Scott, Paul, *Staying On*, 59, 60
Searle, John, 9, 12, 190n.11
Seidel, Michael, 202n.3
Sela-Sheffy, Rakefet, 192n.12
Selden, Raman, 200n.15
Shakespeare, William, 3, 15–17, 22, 23, 41, 45, 52, 54, 55–57, 61, 68, 116, 187, 190n.4, 193n.11, 194n.23, 194n.25, 194n.26, 198n.5
  Works:
  A Midsummer Night's Dream, 55, 57
  All's Well That Ends Well, 55, 57
  Antony and Cleopatra, 55, 57
  As You Like It, 55, 57
  Comedy of Errors, 55, 57
  Coriolanus, 55, 57
  Cymbeline, 55, 57
  Hamlet, 3, 8, 22, 43, 52, 54–57 passim, 68, 184, 189n.8, 194n.25
  Henry IV, parts 1 and 2, 55, 57
  Henry V, 55, 57
  Henry VI, parts 1, 2 and 3, 55, 57
  Henry VIII, 55, 57
  Julius Caesar, 55, 57
  King John, 55, 57
  King Lear, 55, 57
  Love's Labour's Lost, 55, 57
  Macbeth, 55, 56, 57, 194n.25
  Measure for Measure, 55, 57
  The Merchant of Venice, 55, 57
  The Merry Wives of Windsor, 55, 57
  Much Ado About Nothing, 55, 57
  Othello, 55, 57
  Pericles, 55, 57
  Richard II, 55, 57
  Richard III, 55, 57, 117
  Romeo and Juliet, 55, 56, 57, 194n.25
  The Taming of the Shrew, 55, 57
  The Tempest, 55, 57
  Timon of Athens, 55, 57
  Titus Andronicus, 55, 57
  Troilus and Cressida, 55, 57
  Twelfth Night, 55, 57
  Two Gentlemen of Verona, 55, 57
  The Winter's Tale, 55, 57
Shavit, Zohar, 202n.7
Shaw, Bernard, *Pygmalion*, 146, 150–58, 184, 200n.3
Sherwood, Robert E., *Abe Lincoln in Illinois*, 53, 194n.18
Shklovsky, Victor, 33–34, 37
Sibley, Frank, 35
Smith, Barbara Herrnstein, 14, 48, 65, 193n.4
Sophocles, 52, 53
  Ajax, 53
  Antigone, 52
  Oedipus at Colonus, 53–54
  Oedipus Rex, 52, 53, 71
  Philoctetes, 53
Spaas, Lieve, 202n.3
Spanos, William V., 196n.43
Spektor, Regina, 121, 184
Sperber, Dan, 192n.4
Spitzer, Leo, 128–29, 131
Stanford, William B., 71, 87, 93
Sternberg, Meir, 190n.7, 192n.10
Still, Judith, 3, 196n.51
Stimpson, Brian, 202n.3
Stimpson, Catherine R., 191n.1
Stoppard, Tom, *Rosencrantz and Guildenstern Are Dead*, 3
Storey, David, *Saville*, 59, 60
survival, 25, 41, 47–48, 54, 194n.26. *See also* endurance; procreation
Swift, Graham, 58, 59, 61
  Last Orders, 59, 61
Swift, Jonathan, 3, 52, 68, 135, 141–45, 163–68, 170, 201n.4, 201n.6
  Gulliver's Travels, 3, 52, 68, 141–45, 163–68, 170, 201n.4, 201n.6
Swinnerton, Frank Arthur, *Nocturne*, 53

Taine, Hippolyte, 186
Tannen, Deborah, 190n.10
Tate, Allen, 32–33
Tchernichovsky, Saul, 194n.20
Thacker, Christopher, 64
Thomas, Richard F., 193n.6
Tillotson, Geoffrey, 64
Todorov, Tzvetan, 190n.13, 192n.4
Tolstoy, Leo, 49, 51, 72, 169

Anna Karenina, 72, 169
Tournier, Michel, *Vendredi*, 178
Toury, Gideon, 19
translation, 19–25, 27, 28, 29, 46, 47, 63, 64, 73, 74, 78, 116, 117, 135, 138, 139, 175–77, 178, 191n.8, 193n.11, 202n.7. *See also* adaptation; literary dialogue, echo; imitation; parody; re-writing
Traugott, John, 201n.4
Trotsky, Leo, 36–37, 42
Turner, Paul, 160
Tutchin, John, 174, 201n.1
Tuveson, Ernest, 201n.6
Tynianov, Jurij, 202n.5

Unsworth, Barry, *Sacred Hunger*, 59, 60, 61
utopia, 159–71

Van Gogh, Vincent, 186
Van Rees, C. J., 40–41, 49
variety (diversity) of dialogues, ix, 23, 24, 46–56 passim, 62, 64–68 passim, 79, 91, 112, 116, 145, 170–71, 172–82 passim, 184, 186–88, 197n.4, 201n.12. *See also* quantity of dialogues
variety within unity (aesthetic principle), 31
Verboord, Marc, 49, 57
Vickers, Brian, 201n.4
Virgil, 52, 69, 135, 189n.1, 193n.9, 199n.3

Aeneid, 52, 69, 135, 193n.9
voice, 4, 6–8, 28, 87–88, 191n.15
  outer, 6–8, 28, 87–88, 189n.6
  inner, 6–8, 18, 28, 87–88
  See also real-life dialogue; literary dialogue; monologue
Voltaire, 52, 54, 62–66, 135, 165, 168–70, 201n.8
  Candide, 52, 54, 62–66, 168–70, 201n.8
Von Hallberg, Robert, 192n.2

Waldrop, Mitchell M., 194n.21, 195n.41
Warhol, Andy, 186
Watt, Ian, 181
Waugh, Patricia, 173
Weigand, Edda, 190n.13
Wells, Stanley, 194n.25, 194n.26
West, Alick, 192n.9
Wilde, Oscar, 170
Williams, Raymond, 37, 191n.5
Wilson, Arthur M., 131
Winfrey, Oprah (book club), 44
Woolf, Virginia, 181
Worton, Michael, 3, 196n.51
Wyss, Johann David, *The Swiss Family Robinson*, 177, 178

Zemach, Eddy M., 35
Zemeckis, Robert, *Cast Away*, 180
Zwicker, Jonathan, 176

PN 81 .F575 2010

Fishelov, David.

Dialogues with/and great books

GAYLORD